Never Better!

Michigan Studies in Comparative Jewish Cultures emphasizes the dynamic interplay of Jews as historical subjects, Judaism as faith and practice, and Jewishness as a repertoire of cultural practices with other peoples and cultures. It addresses a wide range of cultural forms, including art and theater, music and film, in relation to literature and history.

Series Editors:
Jonathan Freedman, University of Michigan
Anita Norich, University of Michigan
Scott Spector, University of Michigan

Nothing Happened: Charlotte Salomon and an Archive of Suicide
Darcy C. Buerkle

Languages of Modern Jewish Cultures: Comparative Perspectives
Joshua Miller and Anita Norich, editors

Never Better! The Modern Jewish Picaresque
Miriam Udel

Franz Kafka: Subversive Dreamer
Michael Löwy, translated by Inez Hodges

Never Better!

THE MODERN
JEWISH PICARESQUE

Miriam Udel

UNIVERSITY OF MICHIGAN PRESS
ANN ARBOR

Published in the United States of America by the
University of Michigan Press
Printed and bound by CPI Group (UK) Ltd, Croydon, CR0 4YY

2019   2018   2017   2016   4   3   2   1

A CIP catalog record for this book is available from the British Library.

Library of Congress Cataloging-in-Publication Data

Names: Udel, Miriam, author.
Title: Never better! : the modern Jewish picaresque / Miriam Udel.
Description: Ann Arbor : University of Michigan Press, [2016] | ©2016 | Series: Michigan
    studies in comparative Jewish cultures | Includes bibliographical references and index.
Identifiers: LCCN 2015046488 | ISBN 9780472073054 (hardcover : alk. paper) | ISBN
    9780472053056 (pbk. : alk. paper)
Subjects: LCSH: Marginality, Social, in literature. | Yiddish literature—History and
    criticism. | Jews in literature. | Outsiders in literature. | Picaresque literature—Themes,
    motives.
Classification: LCC PN56.M27 U34   2016 | DDC 839/.13087709—dc23
LC record available at http://lccn.loc.gov/2015046488

The University of Michigan Press and Miriam Udel gratefully acknowledge the generous
support of the William Landau Lecture and Publication Fund at the Center for Jewish
Studies, Harvard University, as well as the Harvard Studies in Comparative Literature Publication Subsidy, the Tam Institute for Jewish Studies at Emory University, and the Memorial
Foundation for Jewish Culture.

Dedicated, with boundless love, to Adam Zachary Newton—
whose hard-won joys exemplify the bending of the
picaresque toward Bildung

ACKNOWLEDGMENTS

The time and freedom to write this book came from a series of fellowships and leaves that my departmental chairs graciously allowed me to accept. The idea for the book germinated during a Harry Starr Fellowship at the Harvard Center for Jewish Studies (CJS), where it was refined by the presence of the other fellows, faculty, and graduate students. Further progress was enabled by the Memorial Foundation for Jewish Culture, as well as a year-long research leave from the Emory University Research Committee. Its publication was aided by subventions from the Harvard Department of Comparative Literature, the Harvard CJS, and Emory's Tam Institute for Jewish Studies.

My gratitude to individuals begins with the Spanish teachers who came in pairs, the Señoras (some of whom, unbeknownst to me at the time, were really Doctoras): Julia Rodriguez and Freya Rosales, whose efforts in turn prepared me to reap the riches on offer from María Elena Villalba and Marta Loyola. My start in Spanish gave me the confidence to tackle Hebrew, and without Hebrew, Ruth Wisse would not have tapped me as a natural for Yiddish. My excellent language teachers, who also include Rina Winkelman, Irit Aharony, Sheva Zucker, Kalman Weiser, and the incomparable Dovid Braun, have imparted to me the pleasure of the unmediated text, which compensates abundantly for the constant frustrations of roaming among languages and literatures far beyond my native tongue.

I owe an enormous debt to those who taught me to read, in the deepest senses. Philip Fisher demonstrated week after week and book after book the enchantment of a fine and subtle reading. Bernard Septimus taught me the satisfaction of precise textual mastery and the wisdom of representative texts, as well as establishing the realistic expectation that the only value in reading a text the first time is to set up the possibility of review. Over the past fifteen years, Ruth Wisse has imparted too many lessons to summarize in this space about how to conduct oneself as a scholar and a human being. Above all, I cherish one of her lessons taught outside the seminar room, her insistence that *s'iz do a lang lebn af tsu redn yidish* (there's a long life for speaking Yiddish). So may it be for all of us! With their overlapping curiosities and competencies, Professors Wisse and Septimus made of Jewish literature one capacious garment, mine to don as best I might.

I was inordinately fortunate to be offered a position at Emory. I am grateful to the many colleagues at Emory in German Studies, the Tam Institute, Russian and East Asian Literatures and Cultures, and History who encouraged me, made suggestions for improvement, and provided me with valuable references. I offer special thanks to Elena Glazov-Corrigan, Hazel Gold, Eric Goldstein, Peter Höyng, Melvin Konner, Deborah Lipstadt, Hiram Maxim, Caroline Schaumann, and Ofra Yeglin.

Deepest thanks go to colleagues beyond Emory, who engaged my ideas at their various stages of germination and flourishing: Robert Alter, Justin Cammy, Marc Caplan, Jeremy Dauber, Mikhail Krutikov, Olga Litvak, Dan Miron, and David G. Roskies. I am grateful for their intertwining of rigor and joy. I owe special thanks to David Roskies for reading with a notebook, literally and figuratively, and teaching me to do the same.

This book took its own picaresque journey to publication, and it required some angels and special advocates along the way, especially Steven Zipperstein, Anita Norich, and David Biale. I am also grateful to the anonymous reviewers.

The manuscript has been greatly enriched by the careful eye of Aaron McCullough at the University of Michigan Press, who blends sharp discernment with a gentle editorial touch. It has been a pleasure to work with the editorial staff at Michigan, including especially Kevin Rennells, Allison Peters, and Scott Ham. Likewise, I am grateful to the editors of this series for taking a chance on the work of a first-time author. I thank Heather Dubnick for her swift and professional work on the index.

Next, I thank a group of friends who have assisted materially with the thought process and spiritually with maintaining the author's morale: Wendy Amsellem, Michal and Elitzur Bar-Asher Segal, Adina Gerver, Chavi Karkowsky, Rashmi Murthy, Vivek Murthy, and Annie Washburn. Life in Atlanta has been sweetened over the years by the friendship and support of many. I am so appreciative of this tribe.

A special kind of gratitude is owed to my sons' caregivers and teachers. Confidence that they were being well cared for and well educated has enabled me to work each day with a sense of peace and contentment.

I thank my parents, whose disparate approaches to life and parenting ended up providing a curiously effective balance. I am grateful to my mother, Ann Robbins-udel, who pushed me toward excellence and striving, and to my father, Edward Udel, who has always been exquisitely proud of me just as I am. I also wish to thank my stepmother, Lisa Fletcher-Udel, and Aaron and Ariel Udel for their solicitude and encouragement.

I am grateful both *for* and *to* my older sons, Yitz and Kobi, whose conception of my abilities is very motivating, if somewhat exaggerated. Yitz did great wonders for the manuscript by caring greatly about its progress, and Kobi did equally great things by caring about it not at all. So that we always remember it, I would like to mention here a remarkable streak over the course of Yitz's third-grade spring: we would check in with each other each afternoon ("How was your writing day, Imma?" "How was yours, Yitz?") only to discover an uncanny daily match. Kobi has kept existential ennui and even garden variety boredom far from our abode: I never know what kind of animal will arrive next in his imaginary packages from the pet store.

Finally, to my dearest and most wanted man, Adam Zachary Newton. There is no one with whom I would rather be writing, thinking, dreaming, dancing, walking, waking, and now, caring for our Emmanuel Hasdai. You know better than most that every word is half another's. My best word of all was the "yes" I said to you. The better half of this book is yours. You could have given me no more beautiful gift than the dedication of your fifth book, *To Make the Hands Impure*. I dedicate this first one to you—in reciprocity and abiding love. Long live heterochrony!

CONTENTS

PREFACE

"The sole *raison d'etre* of a novel is to discover what only the novel
can discover."

> —Hermann Broch, as cited by Milan Kundera in
> "The Depreciated Legacy of Cervantes"

It's a profoundly liberating thing when you stop trying to fix the Jews.

The emergence of Yiddish literature—and the Jewish literatures in other
languages that flowered alongside it—is a story of coming to grips with this
realization. (I hasten to note that I will privilege Yiddish cultural production here: not because I believe "Yiddish" to be synonymous or—heaven
forfend!—coextensive with "Jewish" but because during most of the time-
span under discussion, Yiddish was the Jewish language that commanded a
mass readership and exemplified the Ashkenazic "major" within the Jewish
"minor.") This account deals with the liberation of narrative energies that
followed from the radical shift in the Jewish thought world between Enlightenment and what came after it. The Haskalah, customarily rendered as
Jewish Enlightenment (1780–1900), was the engine that drove the rise of
Yiddish fiction; however, it sputtered at the turn of the twentieth century.
Until that time, Yiddish drama, narrative, and poetry performed the cultural work of raising readers' consciousness about Jewish social pathologies, modeling more robust models of personhood, and so attempting to
ameliorate the circumstances of Jewish peoplehood. In this respect, Yiddish
and other Jewish literatures hewed closely to the progress-oriented
nineteenth-century worldview that gave rise to the *Bildungsroman*, with its
assumption that the work of personal maturation complemented the task of
social integration. These stories centered on the *Bildungsheld*, typically a

young man from the provinces who migrates to a central city and there
gains an education, whether informal or formal, and assumes his place in
the (reasonably coherent) world around him. His (or less frequently, her)
private developmental arc was implicitly synchronous with his formation as
a national subject: to become a man was to become a citizen.

Yiddish literature reached its modernist apex just as such developmental discourses were falling under suspicion throughout the Western world,
but the reaction was rendered more acute throughout literary Yiddishland
by virtue of the deterritorialized status and murky national aspirations of
Eastern European Jewry. What took the place of realist developmental narratives in Yiddish and other modernist Jewish literatures? This study argues
that a poetics of the picaresque offers the most coherent generic critique of
the nineteenth century in this literary complex. This is not to say that most
works of Yiddish literary modernism were formally picaresque; they
weren't. But beginning with the relatively strict boundaries of a picaresque
"genre" and rippling outward into more diffuse but ever wider concentric
circles that illustrate a loosely configured picaresque character, we may
forge an understanding of how Yiddish letters entered and inhabited the
twentieth century. We gain a conceptual map for the movement from a literary model of development, improvement, striving, and repair—that is to
say, of *becoming*—to one of simply, or not so simply, *being*.

Within the Yiddish tradition that forms the spine of this book's range,
what I call the Jewish picaresque presents a form of resistance to totalizing
narratives, a cultural intervention that, in the words of high modernist
Samuel Beckett, "admits the chaos and does not try to say that the chaos is
really something else." The liveliest and truest path to the heart of this genre
is through its protagonist, a character type on whom I bestow the Yiddish
term *polit* (פּליט: refugee, fugitive), a Jewish cousin—several times (and
places) removed—of the original Spanish *pícaro*. The *polit* tends to be a socially marginal figure whose story is narrated episodically, usually by himself. The absence of a plot driven by linear causation, and on a more theoretical level, the substitution of the logic of metonymy over that of metaphor,
disrupts the dominant European master narratives of progress and reflects
a social reality in which integration is impossible. By tracing the fortunes of
this new kind of unheroic hero, we are able to discern a different pathway
for the development of Jewish literary modernism in its many languages:
Yiddish, German, Russian, Hebrew, and English enter into consideration in
this book. Moreover, when the analytic value of the *polit* surges beyond the

generic boundaries of the picaresque, we begin to make out the lineaments of a broader picaresque *sensibility*. The images I have put forward of rippling and surging bespeak an intentionally fluid approach to the term "picaresque" and the network of ideas at which it is meant to gesture. This fluidity honors the looseness of the works themselves, while flexible terminology enables me to articulate a mobile rather than a rigid demarcation of literary space that encompasses aspects of genre, poetics (literary form), and affect or sensibility. Essential features of this broader picaresque include contingency and uncertainty, peripatetic movement, the avoidance of linear plots, and the ironic puncturing of sentimentality. The ever-present germ of the novel, as Milan Kundera takes care to emphasize, is discovery. The picaresque returns the novel to its origins by letting discovery unfold on the plane of adventure even as it ushers the form forward into a pulsating and self-reflective modernity.

While this book is grounded in the study of Yiddish and modern Jewish literature, my field of specialization, its implications stretch toward genre studies in connection with modern and modernist fiction more generally. This account is intended to strike a chord not only with those who follow Yiddish and other Jewish literatures but also with students of narrative poetics and genre. Bearing in mind this potential range of readerships, I have sought to lay out concepts in the history and theory of the novel, while also explicating the relevant particularities of Jewish literary culture. In addressing the literary stylistics of a "minor" modernist literature, I seek to illuminate how the adoption of a picaresque sensibility allowed minority authors to write simultaneously *within* and *against* the literary traditions of Europe.

"IN LIFE, BUT NOT OF IT"
The Modernist Picaresque

"The rogue himself is therefore almost a convention, a pivot about
which a description of society in classes and manners turns; and in
the earlier Spanish romances of roguery we do not so much look at
the rogue as borrow his eyes with which to see the world."

—Frank Wadleigh Chandler, *Romances of Roguery*

"At last a form was found to portray the mode of existence of a
man who is in life, but not of it, life's perpetual spy and reflector; at
last specific forms had been found to reflect private life and make
it public."

—M.M. Bakhtin, "Forms of Time and of the Chronotope
in the Novel"

"Of course, as I've stated so many times, the whole of modernity
stands out from preceding epochs by its compulsive/obsessive
modernizing—and modernizing means liquefaction, melting and
smelting . . . But—but! Initially, the major preoccupation of the
modern mind was not so much the technology of smelting as the
design of the moulds into which the molten metal is to be poured
and the technology of keeping it there. Modern mind was after
perfection—and the state of perfection, hoped to be reached,
meant in the last account the end to drudgery, as all further change
could only be a change for the worse."

—Zygmunt Bauman, interview with Simon Dawes (2011)

The novel's first hero, Don Quixote, led a life ruined by literature.[1] The Spanish squire descends into madness through his addiction to books of chivalry, "which he perused with such rapture and application, that he not only forgot the pleasures of the chace, but also utterly neglected the management of his estate" (28).[2] A similarly dubious course of reading, this one comprising travelogues and Jewish folklore, has an equally distorting effect on the most direct Jewish heir to the Iberian knight-errant, one of the foundational characters of modern Yiddish fiction. Before embarking on our primary object of study, it is worth taking a moment to dwell on the misadventures of the character, and the quirks of the text, that together serve as precursor to the fully actualized modernist Jewish picaresque. S.Y. Abramovitsh's plucky Benjamin, the eponymous hero of his novella *The Brief Adventures of Benjamin the Third* (*Kitser masoes binyomin hashlishi*), resembles the Man of La Mancha in his thirst for adventure, his delusional misperceptions, and his failure to uphold broadly accepted social norms. Yet whereas Cervantes seems to present these delusions and failures as the idiosyncrasies of an outlandish individual,[3] Abramovitsh limns a questing *pícaro* whose social marginality is the *most typically Jewish* thing about him. Benjamin's keen interest in eschatology, metaphysics, and mythical spaces render him less a freakish outlier than an intensified version of a typical Teterevkan townsman, one who indulges in reading first-hand the extra-canonical books that flicker at the margins of his whole society's consciousness and help to shape its aspirations. While Quixote's madness is the singular product of his obsession with a literature that lauds a set of already outmoded values, the whole of Eastern European Jewry is implicated in Benjamin's lunacy.[4]

Realizing at last that there is nothing to prevent him and that, on the contrary, his wife's shrewishness offers every inducement to escape, Benjamin plans to light out for the Holy Land, crossing the mythical Sambatyon River to get there. In 1878, the year of the novella's publication, the actual locale of Palestine seems about as accessible as the stone-spitting, basilisk-infested, and wholly nonexistent river imagined to run in the vicinity. Even when the protagonist and his effeminate sidekick Senderl are derided by their fellow Jews, it is only their ability to complete their quest that is called into doubt, never its essential nature or social value. Benjamin is an outsider protagonist, a larger-than-life Jewish *pícaro*, conceived to represent (with biting irony) the yearnings, the illusions, and the pathologies of an entire civilization of outsiders. His literary heirs will wander from Lodz to Lublin to Lakeshore Drive in Chicago. A founding figure in modern Jewish letters, Abramovitsh not only proves himself with this novella to be a masterful architect of the picaresque[5] but also affords us an early, slightly premodern glimpse of a type, a form, and a sensibility that will prove essential to emerging Yiddish modernism.

If Abramovitsh sought to chronicle a society addled by its own literature—or by its relationship to its literature—where exactly did the madness lie? After all, most Tuneyadevkans and Glupskers (denizens identified by satiric toponyms that conjure, respectively, idlers and fools) do not spend their days, like Benjamin, perusing the esoteric *Shadow of the World* or even the more canonically familiar *Ein Ya'akov*. Yet according to Abramovitsh, the Eastern European Jews' story of themselves as a people out of place and out of time embroiled them in a kind of generalized pathology. Although he was by no means a doctrinaire or unreconstructed maskilic ideologue, Abramovitsh was formed by the Haskalah and wrote his way from its apex to its twilight. As a proponent of the "normalization" of Jewish society, he aimed to hold up an illuminated magnifying mirror to his readers, reflecting all blemishes the better to lance them. As with Don Quixote, wrong reading might account for Benjamin's illness, but the right reading, as Abramovitsh's career was calibrated to demonstrate, might hold out his society's cure. His overarching task was to illustrate *on the page* a life "ruined" by literature, the more forcefully to urge that *off the page*, the Jewish polity might be galvanized and ultimately redeemed by its reading.

This therapeutic ambition[6] marks the divide between Abramovitsh and the modernists who succeeded him and to whom most of this study will be devoted. Simply put, modernists were not committed to narratives of redemption or improvement. A discernible line, if not a straight one, connects Sholem Rabinovitsh to Isaac Bashevis Singer to Saul Bellow and even to a postmodern writer like David Grossman. That line cuts a trail through a characterological terrain whose landmarks have been designated with the labels of passivity and even nihilism.[7] Yet it also slices through a domain of laughter-despite, or in Sholem Aleichem's coinage, "laughter-through-tears."[8] It is the tightrope line of "never better!" that balances precariously between the insouciantly sanguine proclamation that things have never been better, so you may as well smile, and a rueful, even despairing resignation to the idea that things will probably never get better at all.

Who, then, inherits the spirit of Benjamin? Let us call him the *polit* (פּליט).

He is the quintessential protagonist of Jewish modernity. We might translate the term as escapee, or fugitive, although the original Hebrew from which the Yiddish word derives is lexically closer to "surviving"[9] than to "running." But the peripateia conveyed by the Latin *fugit* suits him well, for he is a figure in motion, lacking—or eschewing—repose. He is the indisputably Jewish cousin[10] of the *pícaro*, and he shares many traits with that sly hero of Golden Age Spain. Like the original, the *polit* is a socially marginal figure—a demobilized soldier, an emigrant, a man without family. His story is often told in the first person and—a hallmark of the genre—episodically. Like the *pícaro*, the *polit* is less of an agent, an actor upon the world, than he is a person upon whom the world acts. Things happen to him (and this protagonist is usually male) rather than because of him; stories collect around him. He is a magnet for the accumulation of narrative. The *polit* exists in an alternate temporality; his relationship with time is marked by irregularity. These tendencies help to distinguish *polit* from the *schlemiel*[11] on one hand and the Jewish gangster[12] on the other. While these character types exist purely on the thematic plane of representation, the *polit* renegotiates novelistic time, and in so doing enters into and helps to define questions of genre.

The Time-Space Discontinuum

Benjamin furnishes a useful example for understanding the relationship between space, time, and genre in Jewish modernity. Abramovitsh pushed his fellow Jews to confront what he considered their dysfunctionally mythologized relationship with space and time. The picaresque form, tracing a set of antiheroic adventures, organizes human experience laterally; the movement of the fiction is necessarily movement through space.[13] For the Jews of Ashkenaz, space was not a resource to be taken for granted. Subject to residency restrictions, corralled eventually into a Pale of Settlement, and lacking any sovereign borders of their own, these Jews' relation to space was often hidebound and therefore provincial. Immigration and inner migration were common enough (although both phenomena would peak shortly after the publication of the *Kitser masoes*), but these movements usually lacked a sense of volition and, in the Jewish imagination, partook less of a feeling of adventure than of an imposed ordeal, what Garrett calls "reactive movement" (50). In the course of their journey, Benjamin and Senderl trace a circle, and one of rather small radius at that. As Dan Miron reminds us in his seminal *The Image of the Shtetl*,[14] "Fidelity to an actual geography played a very minor part in the cultural framing of this space. . . . Essentially, the Jewish space of Abramovitsh's works is structured along schematic lines rather than in reference to 'real' space. Thus, instead of dozens of cities, provincial towns, townlets, hamlets, villages, estates and so on, Abramovitsh focuses on fewer than half a dozen symbolic places." (106).[15] Miron goes on to describe centrifugal rotating spheres organized around these Jewish centers, and all space that was not explicitly marked as "Jewish" being consigned to a catch-all category of "nature," which for Abramovitsh "remained a concept, a spiritual condition, rather than a commonplace reality" (*Image* 107).[16] The picaresque hero's most cherished point of reference is never really the Land of Israel or the fiery Sambatyon or Timbuktu, but rather homely Tuneyadevka. He doesn't so much want to *be* elsewhere as to *have been* elsewhere and made it back: "If only, he thought, my voyage were accomplished and I were already home again, world-honored and acclaimed, with rare tidings for my fellow Jews! Everyone in Tuneyadevka would then know who I am—yes, they would know what it means to be Benjamin" (318). Never does it (or could it) occur to the protagonist that after befriending foreign monarchs, as he fully expects to do, and being received as a hero by Jews in faraway lands, he might cease to care so much about opinion in his native town.

The picaresque emphasis on space matters—even if these works ultimately concern themselves with places of the mind over places on the map—because horizontal movement through space offers an alternative emphasis to movement "ahead" through time. Most nineteenth-century European fictions patterned themselves on the temporal logic of what Stephen Jay Gould[17] called "time's arrow," wherein

> history is an irreversible sequence of unrepeatable events. Each moment occupies its own distinct position in a temporal series, and all moments, considered in proper sequence, tell a story of linked events moving in a direction. (10)

This was just as true of "story" as of "history" from roughly the Enlightenment until the emergence of literary modernism. The direction in which the linked events were moving was ideally that of progress and generation: maturation, marriage, reproduction, enlightenment. These narratives of progress disseminated Enlightenment thought through the *Bildungsroman* and various forms of romantic plot.[18] Rather than writing such an exemplary narrative, in the *Kitser masoes* Abramovitsh took the opposite tack and wrote a satire, ribbing the Jews, for among other sins, their unyielding embrace of what has variously been called "messianic time" (Walter Benjamin) and "time's cycle" (Gould). In Gould's formulation,

At the other end—I shall call it time's cycle—events have no meaning as distinct episodes with causal impact upon a contingent history. Fundamental states are immanent in time, always present and never changing. Apparent motions are parts of repeating cycles, and differences of the past will be realities of the future. Time has no direction. (10–11)

Directionless time precludes the all-important desideratum of progress. By creating a travel narrative, Abramovitsh would seem forcibly to impose linear time on the cyclical: what is travel if not a linear progression from point A to point B, over time? But the circle that Benjamin and Senderl trace through space—or better yet, the widening gyre from tiny hamlet to the city of Kiev—makes a mockery of any progressive notion of time. Even the events of an apparently linear history—wars, Rothschild's financial ups and downs—are liable to become mutable nonevents in the baths and synagogues of Tuneyadevka and Teterevke, where torpid discussion can reverse their course. The society that Abramovitsh critiques has lost sight of the requisite balance between linear and cyclical time;[19] its myths and matrices allow it to function exclusively in cyclical time so that experience is "organized primarily through panhistorical patterns and vertical typologies" (Hasak-Lowy 17). Miron, to take another example, points out in his introduction to the *Tales of Mendele the Book Peddler*, that Abramovitsh criticized the Jews' lack of historical awareness in favor of a cyclical pattern of "sacred history," "which reduced all historical processes and vicissitudes to a single repeating pattern: sin, punishment by exile, persecutions, *gezerot* (evil decrees), brief temporary moments of reprieve bestowed by a merciful God due to the intercession of saintly religious leaders and miracle workers, and, of course, the ever-present but always deferred expectation of imminent messianic redemption" (xxxiii). This-worldly events shrink and recede when set against the cosmic scope of Grand Jewish Time, which was too firmly entrenched, as Benjamin's creator saw things, as Jewish Standard Time.

Abramovitsh sought to wrest from his readers this reflexive, timeless and placeless narrative of Jewish experience and to thrust them into the vicissitudes of a unidirectional history, M.M. Bakhtin's "national-historic time." The novella's climax, wherein Benjamin and Senderl face down the Russian army officials who conscript and then release them, represents the spectacle of the hapless hero's being "returned to history against his will" (Hasak-Lowy 19), or as another scholar puts it, "drafted into modernity."[20] But the encounter with "history" proves a fleeting one for these characters, who complete their circuit back home. The pathway that Abramovitsh devises out of this closed mimetic loop relies on his alter-ego character, Mendele the Book Peddler.[21] Mendele serves as an intermediary for the author in all of his substantial prose works: a traveling Judaica salesman whose peregrinations place him serendipitously in the way of a great many stories, for which he serves as compiler and conduit to the reading audience. The travels of Benjamin and of his chronicler Mendele are at pointed odds with one another: Benjamin appears to journey in linear fashion from point to point, but his departure turns out to be just a pretext for his coming home. On the other hand, Mendele, with his reassuringly traditional speech and dress, presents himself as a product of cyclical Jewish sacred time, emphasizing his status as a paterfamilias and a peddler of ritual books and objects: the eternal and therefore timeless Jew. Yet Mendele is the one moving forward through linear, secular-historical time. Among Abramovitsh's characters, he alone perceives and subtly calls attention—through irony that creepingly overtakes praise—to the calcified state of the Jewish community. Mendele is the quasi-maskilic hero of Benjamin's book, for the reader is meant to identify with the putative compiler and shaper of the tale rather than its protagonist. Every time some foible of Benjamin's evinces a chuckle, the reader affirms some rationalistic attitude or precept hazarded by Mendele. The bookseller's amiable but ideologically pointed presence in the text is the abiding clue that Abramovitsh was still trying to heal, cure, or otherwise fix the Jews.

Genre and Chronotope: Where (Progressive) Time becomes Visible

Viewed in retrospect through the prism of modernism, Abramovitsh's novella reveals itself as a prescient forerunner of the modernist picaresque. Within just over a decade of its publication, modernism would begin to change the literary representation of temporality, rendering time as a function of consciousness. Moments and hours would distend to fill pages, as authors attempted to register minute cognitive saccades, whether for Virginia Woolf's Mrs. Dalloway, Joyce's Leopold Bloom on the single day of June 16, 1904, or David Bergelson's disaffected Mirl Hurvits. Discontinuities, syncopations, and compressions of time would begin to matter as much as its unities and continuities. In part, this changing representation of time reflected a slackening belief in narratives of progress. Progress takes shape over biographical time, a span in which years and seasons matter more than moments and hours. Biographical time complements national-historic time, which in turn moves in tandem with what Jed Esty[22] calls "developmental time," a feature of whose representation is "reciprocal allegories of self-making and nation-building" (2). This kind of time passes in fairly uniform, orderly fashion, an armature on which developmental experience is hung. To Bakhtin, the essence of the realist *Bildungsroman* was the "image of *man growing* in *national-historical time*" ("The Bildungsroman" 25; his emphasis). But if a protagonist's growth is not what is being represented, then other kinds of time structures become more important than the linear sequence. Ursula Heise suggests,[23] for example, that modernist authors are more interested in simultaneous than sequential events as a means of organizing narrative, an argument extended by Esty to propose "that the generative and generational time schemes attached to the human life span or family saga in nineteenth-century fiction become compressed and syncopated in modernism" (215–16). Absent an ideal of progress, fictional time begins to behave in strange ways.

The literary experiments that we refer to broadly as modernism unsettled nineteenth-century narratives of progress. A robust critical discourse interrogates this turn from progress in terms of genre, but most of it grapples with changes within the *Bildungsroman* and the romance plot. As I indicated in the preface, this study maintains that a poetics of the relatively overlooked picaresque offers the most coherent genre-based critique of the nineteenth century in modern Jewish literature. In Bakhtin's account of the development of fiction, genres were defined[24] by the plotting of time and space in relation to each other and to event (FTC 250). Rather than a strictly neutral container for prosaic content, each genre expresses an implicit world view.[25] The special term for this plotting, for the intersection or interaction of time and space, is the *chronotope*; Bakhtin begins to define his neologism as "the intrinsic connectedness of temporal and spatial relationships that are artistically expressed in literature" (84).[26] There is a much-remarked vagueness to this definition,[27] which encompasses in Bakhtin's writings entities as disparate as an epoch and a doorway,[28] but his elaboration helps to clarify matters: "In the literary artistic chronotope, spatial and temporal indicators are fused into one carefully thought-out, concrete whole. Time, as it were, thickens, takes on flesh, becomes artistically visible; likewise, space becomes charged and responsive to the movements of time, plot and history" (FTC 84). Focusing on the chronotope extends our critical view beyond the strictly formalist and allows us to speak in the more richly textured terms of human experience, for the categories of time and space "constitute a fundamental unity, as in the human perception of every-day reality" (Bemong and Borghart 3). For our purposes, the chronotope will serve to organize this examination of the modernist picaresque over and against the *Bildungsroman* and other genres of growth and development. By the twentieth century, the picaresque is an old generic container just the right shape to be filled in a new way with modernism. As such, the modernist picaresque will have a different relationship to time, space, and interiority than its Golden Age antecedents.

This study does not concern itself with the picaresque *per se*, as a genre independent of all others. First of all, a rigid schema that places the pica-resque in its own hermetic box would run counter to the literary history and stylistics of the genre itself. What is more, my chief concern is with how the picaresque ebbs and flows around other literary currents during the emergence of Jewish literary modernism. The most important of these other currents is the *Bildungsroman*. Consider this schematic description of *Bildung*, by Piret Peiker:

> In a *Bildungsroman*, the protagonist negotiates his (and less often her) way through modern society, resolving in some form the basic oppositions between change and tradition, and between individual and collective. Typically, a young individual leaves home, frequently after a conflict between generations; he goes into the wide world, often travelling from province to metropolis, where he ex-periences and learns, develops and matures as an individual. Having become reconciled with society, or at least having consolidated his attitude towards it, he returns home, where he is recognized as an adult member of society with legiti-mate agency. The poetics of the traditional *Bildungsroman* is teleological and historicist in the sense that whatever happens serves the ultimate good and self-fulfilment of the protagonist—his or her rational progress in the world. (3–4)

The *Bildungsroman* conceives of time as linear and events as causally linked, the laying of a life's path brick by brick, tending toward the development of a hero who is endowed with a combination of exceptional qualities and deficiencies that form his unique subjectivity. The *Bildungsroman*, with its ingeniously crafted plot, and its linear causality between one event and the next, implies an ordered world in which "rational progress" may be made toward education, moral improvement, and social integration—all of which are possible if difficult to attain. While a *Bildungsheld* may fail tragically in his quest toward a happy adulthood, even his failure ratifies a coherence lacking in the picaresque and reinforces the basic patterns of *Bildung*: "The negative variations of this Grand Narrative of Enlightenment and Romanticism, for example a social mobility novel where the protagonist develops a critical attitude towards the social ladder he has climbed, follow the same structure of progressive development and maturation" (ibid. 4).

Above all, the *Bildungsroman* is a genre of progress, as Eluned Summers-Bremner explains:[29] "It was the *Bildungsroman* or novel of development whose ready cross-fertilization of, and by, the great nineteenth-century discourses of progress—Darwinian evolution, industrial and imperialist expansion, and their kind—helped retrospectively legitimize a heroic passage onward and outward" (308). The *polit* implicitly resists the master narrative of development suggested by the nineteenth-century European *Bildungsroman*, and his life's course undermines or even mocks the kinds of positivist nineteenth-century claims about progress that Summers-Bremner describes. The picaresque points instead to a world in which time may alternate between cyclical and linear, events are random, chaotic, and largely meaningless, and the hero is either an undistinguished everyman or notable only as a slacker or loser. Social integration is impossible for such a hero by definition, if not because of his own deficiencies, then because there is no functioning society into which he might integrate. The *polit* moves through a world of impossibilities and unpredictabilities, and his life choices do not necessarily lead to any overarching consequences. The episodic plot structure gives expression quite naturally to lives that do not progress along the linear path of actions that constitute more conventional novelistic plots. If the *Bildungsroman* portrays a kind of deistic world of interlocking social complexities, then the radical contingency of the picaresque plot perfectly suits a secular worldview in which there is no divine puppeteer secretly pulling the strings—not even the author. The secularism that is reflexive and rather obvious to the most typical of these characters bespeaks an age of disintegration, a set of circumstances offering a veritable petri dish for the growth of the picaresque:

> The picaresque novel affirms the primacy of individual experience—to begin with, the most basic aspects of individual experience—in a kind of existence where any larger order must be very much in question. It is a literary form characteristic of a period of disintegration, both social disintegration and the disin-

tegration of belief. Like Descartes, the picaresque writer finds any existing systems to be of the shakiest kind, and he, too, tries to effect a basic reconstruction by beginning again with the one self-evident fact of the experiencing "I." Chance rules in the picaresque world: the individual cannot really understand his world or control it. All he can depend upon is his own pliant resourcefulness with which he must learn to make the best of chance as it comes along. (84)

This observation is offered by Robert Alter in his compact and incisive study of the picaresque, *The Rogue's Progress*. Institutional decay or disintegration begets a renewed focus on the capacities and experiences of the individual. This characterization captures precisely the centrifugal situation of Eastern European Jewry as many Yiddish writers perceived it. Jews had long lacked the structures of governance from which other European nations drew or through which they expressed a sense of boundedness and security. However, the religious and communal superstructures that had compensated for this lack were rapidly crumbling, and the clashing, often mutually exclusive candidates for what ought to replace those structures (Bundism, communism, Zionism, neo-Orthodoxy, Polish nationalism, to name several) were individually and collectively insufficient for rejuvenation or even preservation. After unpacking the elements of picaresque poetics, we shall turn to a closer examination of Jewish reality in Europe at the dawn of the twentieth century.

The Picaresque as Structure and Sensibility

Because picaresque episodes begin and end without neat, causal logic, there has always been some difficulty in defining the genre and accounting for its structure. A late twentieth-century renaissance of picaresque studies was largely concerned with questions of definition and "its transcultural continuity across the centuries" (Ardila 4). Since we aim to extend the discussion of the picaresque to a new literary cluster (Yiddish and other Jewish modernist fictions), we require a delineation that is capacious without ranging so widely as to lose all definitional rigor. Howard Mancing, in his essay "The Protean Picaresque,"[30] sketches the chronological development of the genre itself (both in Spain and elsewhere), reviews criticism thereof,[31] and hazards a definition serviceable for our purposes: "A picaresque novel is a text in which a major character is a *pícaro* who usually tells the story of his or her own life; the text always displays some degree of generic self-consciousness;

it is a protean form" (281). Mancing's strong contention is that while almost every structural and thematic variable of a fiction may change within the picaresque, "The only unifying factor has been the authors' awareness of writing within this basically undefinable genre" (*College Literature* 183). In invoking authorial intent as a prerequisite for the picaresque, Mancing's otherwise insightful definition leaves something to be desired; however, its emphasis on the *pícaro* and on the protean quality of the genre serves our account well. Ulrich Wicks,[32] another cogent exponent of the diachronic sweep of the picaresque, echoes and expands upon Mancing's formulation, defining the *pícaro* as "a pragmatic, unprincipled, resilient, solitary figure who just manages to survive in his chaotic landscape, but who, in the ups and downs, can also put that world very much on the defensive. The picaro is a protean figure who can not only serve many masters but play different roles, and his essential characteristic is his inconstancy—of life roles, of self-identity—his own personality flux in the face of an inconstant world" (Wicks 245). Flux and inconstancy are strands of the picaresque ribonucleic chain that receive full expression in the modernist iteration of the genre. Some definitions suit the classical or premodernist picaresque, viewing it as a sort of proto-developmental genre. Critics like John Ardila[33] focus on earlier exemplars, so it is understandable (though perhaps nevertheless arguable) that he takes a progressive, teleological view of the genre that our study can hardly share: "A picaresque novel is much more than a narrative telling of the adventures of a roguish protagonist. Lazarillo and Guzman differed from previous and contemporaneous literature because they included an antihero but also because they presented a coherent narrative structure" (Ardila 4). Rather, our entire emphasis is on the picaresque as a vehicle for the incoherence of modern subjectivity. Claudio Guillén, rather than formulating one concise definition of the picaresque, drew up a list of eight characteristics that is rightfully still considered authoritative four decades after publication.[34]

It is important to emphasize that while almost all of the existing definitions treat the picaresque solely as a diachronically unfolding *tradition* (both publications in which Mancing's essay appear feature the word "tradition" in their titles), I wish to emphasize, along with Wicks, the always-available modality[35] of the picaresque. As I shall explain below, the picaresque intervenes against plot *structure* in the conventional sense of the term. Paul West argues that the main function of the picaresque is to "repudiate the organized mind" by providing "an ideal medium" to "the iconoclast, as well as the man who can connect nothing with nothing."[36] Although a few scholars of the genre have tried to discern a shapely structure within its episodic narration,[37] these efforts touch the premodernist picaresque.

Most accounts of the genre's development stop short of modernism or briefly evaluate a few twentieth-century examples as if to determine whether they "fit" the definition and merit inclusion in the picaresque "canon." Although these inclusions and exclusions are hotly debated, there is more general agreement that the picaresque begins decisively with the publication of the anonymous[38] *Lazarillo de Tormes* in the early 1550s.[39] Lazarillo spurred many imitators (Mateo Alemán's *Guzman de Alfarache*, Quevedo's *El Buscón*), and the fortunes of the picaresque, if not of the *pícaro*, ascended dramatically throughout the Spanish Golden Age. The seventeenth century saw these works translated, and that led to a surge of picaresque writing in France (*Gil Blas*), Germany (*Simplicissimus*), and England (*Roderick Random, Moll Flanders*). By the eighteenth century, the genre had peaked, and the nineteenth century was a relatively quiet one for the picaresque in Europe. Yet even during these relative doldrums, the picaresque flourished across the Atlantic: consider *The Adventures of Huckleberry Finn* (1884) and José Joaquín Fernández de Lizardi's *El Periquillo Sarniento* (*The Mangy Parrot*, 1816), commonly acknowledged as the first Latin American novel. Never entirely abandoned then, the picaresque springs to new vigor around the turn of the twentieth century.[40] Much-discussed examples include Thomas Mann's *Felix Krull*, Günther Grass's *Die Blechtrommel* (*Tin Drum*), and Saul Bellow's *Adventures of Augie March*. To these well-known titles, my own study adds Abramovitsh's *Kitser masoes* (*The Brief Adventures of Benjamin the Third*), Sholem Rabinovitsh's *Motl peysi dem khazns* (*Motl the Cantor's Son*), Israel Rabon's *Di gas* (*The Street*), Joseph Roth's *Hotel Savoy*, and Ilya Ehrenburg's *Burnaya Zhizn Lazika Roitshvanetsa* (*The Stormy Life of Laz Roitshvants*). Examples like these constitute a distinct subset: the modernist Jewish picaresque. They all hew to at least a broad definition of picaresque form; they will be joined in our analysis by several more modernist Jewish and Yiddish works that partake of a yet-broader but still discernibly picaresque *sensibility*. A portrait of its distinguishing features will emerge throughout our study, including the embrace of contingency and uncertainty, restless peripateia, a suspicion of linear plots, and an allergic distaste for sentimentality.[41] Only the last of these requires elaboration here, as it is the strand that links the modernist picaresque (which can be quite bleak in some instances) with the form's comic antecedents.

The twentieth-century picaresque is comic in the same sense in which a *scherzo* is a "joke": antic, frenzied, admitting yet somehow making sense of the chaos. It partakes of an honesty that can seem—and be—brutal. Few pieties survive the modernist (or even the earlier) picaresque: not only is there no angel in the house, but there usually isn't even a house. "The picaresque novel is fundamentally an antisentimental mode of representing reality" (Alter 78). In other words, the *pícaro* is radically alone in the world, a man without family, love, or even deeply held friendship:

> Sentimentalism is . . . a self-appointed protector of traditional values and traditional relationships. The picaroon, however, learns to take very little for granted. He may not consciously reject traditional values, but he is essentially an empiricist. He bases his actions and his estimate of people upon what experience teaches him. No relationship is a priori sacrosanct for the picaroon. (Alter 79)

The *pícaro* is subject to too much motion to form the kind of durable social webs of kin and friendship that dominate the nineteenth-century novel. If such motion is not imposed upon him absolutely by circumstance (emigration, war), then he manufactures it. Other people are experienced through encounters rather than in developing relationships. The *pícaro* need not be a solipsist but his relationships with others are ancillary to his core identity. Bakhtin's description chimes with Alter's: "As opposed to the hero of novels of trial and temptation, the hero of picaresque novels is faithful to nothing, he betrays everything—but he is nevertheless true to himself, to his *own* orientation, which scorns pathos and is full of skepticism" (Bakhtin DiN 408). To fully apprehend this scorn of pathos, including the pathos of one's own situation, is to behold a way of being in literature that extends beyond episodically structured picaresque plots and first-person narration by a *pícaro*. It becomes logical to place works that share these formal features next to answering works that do not. Given the distinctive conditions that constituted Jewish existence in Europe—statelessness, living under empire (Austro-Hungarian and Russian), multilingualism, immigration, belated and rapid secularization—it is tempting to speak in terms of a European-Jewish "chronotope." Though we might stop short of that designation, we can acknowledge that these peculiar time-space coordinates give rise to a breed of protagonist whose *sine qua non* is his isolation and his refusal of all of the traditional comforts of the psyche—and of narrative.

From Developmental Discourses to Modernism

However variously it has been defined, the picaresque has always protruded as a counter-genre. The picaresque represents a stepping back from nineteenth-century realism and naturalism, and in that sense its affinity is to a more primitive form of the novel. Therefore, in thinking about the contours of the genre, it is useful to consider Mikhail Bakhtin's typology of prenovelistic forms. Some caveats are necessary: the modernist picaresque is not a simple recapitulation of the Golden Age version or subsequent exemplars of the genre. Moreover, Bakhtin's account is denationalized and dehistoricized and involves no consideration of the specific torque of Yiddish and modern Jewish culture upon these fictional forms. Nonetheless, his anatomy of forms proves valuable, and we will attempt to bring it into conversation with the specific exigencies of modern Jewish literature.

In Bakhtin's roughly chronological typologies of the novel, the picaresque is one of several generic way stations on the path to realist nineteenth-century fiction, which he seems to regard as the apex of literary achievement. In his essay "Forms of Time and Chronotope in the Novel," Bakhtin traces fictional development from the Greek romance, to an intermediary form he calls the everyday novel of adventure (taking as his exemplar Apuleius's *The Golden Ass*), to ancient biography and autobiography, to the chivalric romance, to "The Rabelaisian Chronotope" (evidently an author so totalizing and paradigmatic as to defy categorization). The picaresque form and the picaresque hero float and dart throughout the first two discussions, with elements deriving from both the Greek romance and the everyday novel of adventure. These five categories are not bounded by bright lines but rather involve a steady if fuzzy movement from stylization, abstraction, and exteriority, to realism, mimesis, and interiority. Each phase of this progression is analyzed according to its chronotopic manifestations. One forebear of the *pícaro* is the hero of Greek romance, who collects adventures by moving laterally through an unmarked and unspecified but vast spatial expanse, and on whom time leaves no trace. Bakhtin emphasizes the flatness of his individual humanity to modern eyes, asking,

> How indeed can a human being be portrayed in the "adventure-time" that we have outlined above, where things occur simultaneously by chance and also *fail* to occur simultaneously by chance, where events have no consequences, where

the initiative belongs everywhere exclusively to chance? It goes without saying that in this type of time, an individual can be nothing other than completely *passive*, completely *unchanging*. As we have said earlier, to such an individual things can merely *happen*. He himself is deprived of any initiative. . . . In essence, all the character's actions in Greek romance are reduced to *enforced movement through space* (escape, persecution, quests); that is, to a change in spatial location. (FTC 105; Bakhtin's emphasis)

The Greek romance, like the picaresque, relies highly on contingency, and insofar as events have no consequences, it refuses linear, teleological plots. Bakhtin singles out the importance of the motif of meeting and the chronotope of the road as an adventurescape (98). An individual is not a distinctive, empowered agent but rather a screen onto which various events impose themselves. He can't "grow forward" but can only move through the world horizontally, and in the face of adversity hope with the Hebrew proverb that "changing place means changing luck." In the Greek romance, characters pass or fail tests, but they do not change their essential nature: "The hammer of events shatters nothing and forges nothing—it merely tries the durability of an already finished product" (107).

The adventure novel of everyday life pushes beyond the Greek romance with respect to characters' transformations. While "there is no evolution in the strict sense of the word," it nevertheless becomes possible to discern change in the characters through a process of "crisis and rebirth" (115), with moments of crisis assuming a disproportionate significance. This constitutes a step toward realist, biographical time. The Apuleian adventure novel contributes a great deal toward the picaresque, for instance, "the way it fuses the course of an individual's life (at its major turning points) with his actual spatial course or road—that is, with his wanderings. Thus is realized the metaphor 'the path of life'" (120). It is to this form of fiction that Bakhtin traces the introduction of a private life in the world of the novel. The wandering individual is poised to become "a 'third person' in relation to private everyday life, permitting him to spy and eavesdrop." The traveler comes upon life already being lived, interactions already in progress among others. The textual emphasis might at times be on his first-person experience, but he can be equally valuable as third-person witness. This privileged situation of participant-observer is precisely the métier of the *pícaro*, who typically narrates his own tale but serves to register the vicissitudes of social realities far beyond himself: "Such is the positioning of the *rogue* and the *adventurer*, who do not participate internally in everyday life, who do not occupy in it any definite fixed place, yet who at the same time pass through that life and are forced to study its workings, all its secret cogs and wheels" (124). Thus, the *pícaro* and his near literary relations are among the first private men, granted access to the privacy of others yet rarely yielding up their own secrets. Whether as cause or symptom of his lack of participation in everyday life, the *pícaro*'s high mobility is also an essential part of his profile. Embedded in Bakhtin's chronological schema is a separate discussion of "the Functions of the Rogue, Clown and Fool in the Novel." He regards these three types as a class apart, occupying "their own special little world, their own chronotope" (FTC 159)—and that chronotope is a proto-realist one. They are "life's maskers" (FTC 159), whose function, paradoxically, is to expose *internal man*, or human interiority (FTC 164). Bakhtin discusses these types in the earlier essay "Discourse in the Novel," where he traces the novel to two lines or tributaries and maintains that the picaresque ushers in the more sophisticated Second Line (406).

Many critics have observed that Bakhtin's typology stops short of literary modernism; indeed he draws from the canon of nineteenth-century realism to illustrate most of his points about polyphony, heteroglossia, and other centrifugal forces within the novel. Bemong and Borghart see an overarching teleological perspective in his work, noting, "The relative lack of critical attention to genuine chronotopic revival is more than likely the result of Bakhtin's teleological view of the history of narrative literature. The western novel . . . evolved from an initial state characterized by a total absence of historical time . . . to eventually arrive at the ideal of nineteenth-century realism and the conception of *real historical time* internalized by its attendant chronotope" (9). While acknowledging a heavy debt to Bakhtin's typology, our account begins in many respects where his leaves off. A major aim of the present volume is to reconceptualize the emergence of Yiddish and other Jewish literary modernism, as a shift in dominant sensibilities or modalities from the aims of *Bildung* (if not the form of it) to the picaresque. Though this shift is prominent and readily observable in Yiddish and other Ashkenazic Jewish literature, it is by no means exclusive to it. Acknowledging a similar debt to Bakhtin, Robert S. Stone asserts in his study of the Mexican picaresque "that the *pícaro* prefigures the hero of the bildungsroman—both are upwardly mobile and occasionally reprehensible representatives of an emerging class, torn between resistance and conformity" (371).[42] Instead of emphasizing the tension between picaresque and

Bildung, however, he stresses the continuity between the two forms as biographical exempla:

> Picaresque narrative is thus seen as educational in the sense of fostering evolutionary change through exemplary lessons in how to read the book of the world. If we take this genre broadly, as a narrative depicting the success or failure of an individual in a semi-fictional world, then we unite the picaresque with the bildungsroman. The attention to social learning and to the "reading" of culture through the experience of literature brings together two genres as biographical responses to volatile times. While the bildungsroman typically depicts the rise of the middle class into elite status, the picaresque novel, its more durable comic forebear, dramatizes the trials facing the middle class from its Spanish beginnings to its current global explosion. The Spanish picaresque is at base a narrative portraying an attempt to achieve stability either among the bourgeoisie or as part of a traditional elite and, again, it is this thread that binds it to the bildungsroman, the genre that follows the rise of its hero to his destiny. (ibid.)

The protagonists of the Jewish picaresques that we will consider do attempt to achieve stability, but not remotely as part of the bourgeoisie. With few exceptions, they are part of an irremediable underclass that can only look at bourgeois cousins, landowning neighbors, and married friends with admiring envy. They may or may not become educated in the art of survival over the course of the narrative. Stone is especially interested in the engagé possibilities for both genres, indicating that he wishes to analyze José Rubén Romero's 1938 Mexican picaresque "from the activist side of its genre heritage: as a conscious appropriation of the picaresque as a means to critique the dominant order in a time of change" (370–71). A similar spirit of social intervention, both in the scholarly retrieval of literary texts and in the aims of the fictions themselves, is evident in discussions of the feminist picaresque.[43]

Indeed, if we were to take the first-person narrator of the "original" Spanish picaresque, Lazarillo de Tormes, at his word, then the genre would have to be considered explicitly and heavily didactic from its inception. For an adult, fully formed Lázaro recounts to an unknown audience (identified obsequiously as "Vuestra merced") the zigs and zags whereby he came to be established as a householder and breadwinner. Few readers have been fooled by the narrator's unctuous pieties, grasping readily that the energy of the narrative is spent on relishing (and justifying) a career of petty thievery, opportunism, and the detection and practice of deceit. The novella celebrates the life of the rogue, justifying theft as necessary for survival, and countenancing perpetual wifely infidelity as the price of lasting financial security. Basic needs are at stake, and the methods for meeting those needs are not genteel. Yet as the picaresque genre continues to develop, its antinomianism falls away, its madcap energy is grounded and stabilized, and its delight in vice gives way to the expostulation of virtue. As Harry Sieber[44] explains, "By the end of eighteenth and nineteenth centuries, the *pícaro* had become almost exclusively a satirist or had been replaced by the anti-*pícaro*. In seventeenth-century Spain, as we have seen, the picaresque genre had prepared the groundwork for an 'anti-genre' in which repentance, virtue, stability and 'success' triumphed at the end of a life of roguery" (62). In turning the picaresque inside-out, the ground was being laid for the integrative developmental narratives that would dominate the nineteenth century.

We may trace this shift also in terms of a movement from anxiety about bare survival to the luxury of wanting more. Peter Brooks explicates the central, organizing role of ambition, which "provides an armature of plot" to the nineteenth-century novel. By that time, he writes,

> the picaro's scheming to stay alive has typically taken a more elaborated and socially defined form; it has become ambition. It may in fact be a defining characteristic of the modern novel (as of bourgeois society) that it takes aspiration, getting ahead, seriously, rather than simply as an object of satire (which was the case in much earlier, more aristocratically determined literature), and thus makes ambition the vehicle and emblem of Eros, that which totalizes the world as possession and progress. (39)

The nineteenth-century novel is populated by ambitious strivers, most of whom are assured the basics of survival and who can turn their attention to loftier aims. Through romantic and professional advancement, the *Bildungsheld* can unify his life as a coherent whole. If such achievement is plausible, then it is no laughing matter and may safely leave the province of satire, as Brooks indicates. The structural context for the expression of this ambition is the totalizing novel of vast, panoramic scope, multiple perspectives (authorial and narratorial omniscience), all woven into the unity of an immense literary tapestry. Saturated with Darwin's influence,[45] the latter half of the nineteenth century favored plots of growth in which time's arrow and the protagonist's developmental arrow shot inexorably forward.

Peering through their several lenses,[46] theorists and critics have sche-
matized differently the shift from the fictions of nineteenth-century Europe
to the modernism that succeeded them. A common denominator of the
various accounts is a sense of rupture or radical transformation around the
turn of the twentieth century.[47] The Great War intensified this sense of a
break with the past, ripping away any remaining shroud of gentility that had
covered naked survival with the cloth of ambition.[48] As Malcolm Bradbury
and James McFarlane write in the introductory chapter to their anthology,[49]
modernism presented "a problem in the making of structures, the employment of language, the uniting of form" (29). But so far, relatively little attention has been paid to the picaresque as a suitably fragmented form marshaled to accommodate the mess[50] of modernity. Rather than thinking of it
as a historically bounded genre, we do well to consider the picaresque as a
set of narrative possibilities available for the taking. This kind of narration
represents an intervention in structure, form, and unity. It interrupts and
destabilizes the totalizing work of the novel, as Bakhtin saw in writing about
the proto-modern picaresque: "what emerges first and most clearly is the
negating work of the picaresque novel: the destruction of the rhetorical
unity of personality, act and event. . . . A human being is, as it were, eman-
cipated here from all the entanglements of such conventional unities, he is
neither defined nor comprehended by them; in fact, he can even laugh at
them" (Bakhtin DiN 407–408). The picaresque negates, mocks, questions,
undermines. It emancipates. Modernism bends back toward the premodern, and its picaresque form returns characters to a more primitive state,
dialing the novel back to an earlier period in its development when it dealt
with mere survival.

The picaresque is a minor tradition of lightness,[51] whereas part of the
gravitas of the major *Bildungsroman* form owes to its coeval rise with the
nation-state; that form carried the nation's burden. As Timothy Brennan
explains, "the rise of European nationalism coincided especially with one
form of literature—the novel. . . . It was the *novel* that historically accompanied the rise of nations by objectifying the 'one, yet many' of national life,
and by mimicking the structure of the nation, a clearly bordered jumble of
languages and styles" (49).[52] Not only did the novel make meaning of spatial
limitations and borders, but it organized time in relation to the homeland.
Franco Moretti describes "the conclusive synthesis of maturity" in the life of
the individual, which chimes with or—to use a great trope of the nineteenth
century—recapitulates[53] maturation into nationhood. "Time," in Moretti's

pithy formulation, "must be used to find a homeland."[54] At the turn of the twentieth century, the Jews possess no such land, so it is only logical that the national form, the *Bildungsroman*, would be the exception rather than the rule in Yiddish literature.

From *pícaro* to *polit*

This is not to say that the European Jewish polity lacked national and even nationalist literary aspirations. The Western European age of nationalism coincided with the Haskalah, customarily translated as the Jewish Enlightenment but rendered with more nuance as the age of Jewish romantic nationalism.[55] Yiddish literature is still in its cradle throughout the seventeenth and eighteenth centuries, the bloom of other European romantic nationalisms. The debt of Jewish literature to the Haskalah is inarguable, as Miron[56] points out:

> Like much of modern Jewish culture, the central tradition of Yiddish literature had sprung out of the opposition to what appeared to be the inertia and passivity of the old, traditional Jewish way of life. . . . Modern Jewish culture and the new Yiddish literature as a whole operated under the assumption that the Jewish people, who had for centuries refused to take an active part in the formation of history, and had thus relegated themselves to the passive position in its most extreme sense (the position of the victim), must break out of their national passivity.
>
> When Yiddish literature sprang from the ideological soil of the Enlightenment (Haskalah) in the nineteenth century, or when it reflected, at the turn of the century, the birth of modern Jewish nationalism, or when it played a central role, later in the twentieth century, in the burgeoning Jewish socialist movements, its call to the Jewish people was a call for change and awakening. (8)

While Yiddish literature is a product of maskilic aspirations, the Haskalah does not manage to produce great Jewish *Bildungsromane* or sweeping romantic plots on the model of the foundational fictions that played a critical role in forging national consciousness in various Latin American countries.[57] Despite its debt to the maskilic revaluation of literary ambition and social commentary, Yiddish literature crests artistically just as the Haskalah is being superseded by Jewish nationalism, socialism, and other ideological movements; moreover, it comes to thrive precisely by casting off maskilic ideals of pedagogy and social meliorism. *Maskilim* had tried for a century and a half to instruct the Jews to adopt normative behaviors, so as to be perceived and actually to become "normal" Europeans. In the disruption of this striving lies the germ of this study, an alternate account of Yiddish modernism. Up to the turn of the twentieth century, according to Miron,[58] a hortatory sense that the Jews should be better than they were accounted for both the pedagogical and comedic tones of Jewish literature. Until Sholem Rabinovitsh (more widely known as Sholem Aleichem), the chief mechanism of Yiddish comedy was to highlight the discrepancy between normative and non-normative states, but the visionary Rabinovitsh embraced a dark, nihilistic humor that drew its force from the tacit admission that people—and implicitly, *The* People—could *never really become better* than what they already were. Thus, creating radically passive characters was a modernist response to a highly ideological time and a particular set of historical exigencies. As Miron observes, "Sholem Aleichem was alone in resisting this pedagogy and the tyranny of idealism." But he would not remain alone as the twentieth century progressed: his heir in this world view was to be Isaac Bashevis Singer, and his unknown (to Rabinovitsh) comrade and kindred spirit was Franz Kafka. The work of these authors, maintains Miron, showed "an acceptance of the condition of weakness, a rejection of heroic mode, and social meliorism." Yiddish literature finally came into its own artistically by leaving aside didactic aims and social interventions.

Yet this whole trajectory from didacticism to aestheticism—reminiscent of those of other European literatures—was launched belatedly. In relation to both *Aufklaerung* and contemporary sociopolitical events, the Haskalah arrived tardy. Robert Alter points to this "developmental delay" in his historical introduction to the anthology *Modern Jewish Literature*:

There was, for reasons that are not hard to imagine, a curious time lag in the mental world of the Haskalah. Its proponents still cherished the values of Frederick the Great, Voltaire, and Lessing at a point when cosmopolitanism and calm reason were forgotten dreams in European history and a fiercely assertive new nationalism was making itself felt everywhere. A full generation after the main wave of European Romanticism, some Haskalah writers do begin to produce idylls and to celebrate, decorously, the passionate aspects of life, but the more powerful themes—both in a literary and a political sense—of European Romanticism (like the engagement with the irrational and the occult, and the affirmation of organic national community) remain quite beyond the *maskilim*. (4–5)

When Yiddish authors undertake the kind of experimentation that falls under the heading of modernism, they do so under a different set of constraints than their coterritorial counterparts. Anita Norich acknowledges that Jewish and other European modernisms both privilege individual behavior, but they diverge over "ideas of history and causality." While other modernisms might appear dehistoricized, European Jewish modernism is always marked "by a terrible awareness of randomness, displacement, and a lack of causal connections." Anti-Semitism and revolutionary movements could not but figure prominently in any representation of the modern Jewish experience, and Jewish authors, Norich argues, were "inclined to temper the apotheosis of the self with a skeptical view of what the self could attain, given these surroundings"[59] (6). The picaresque form represents this historical awareness of limited horizons by foregrounding characters with defective or reduced agency: demobilized soldiers, emigrants and immigrants, starving artists, and actual or perpetual children. The *Bildungsheld* is a world-shaper, but the *polit* is acted on—harshly—by the world. As if to emphasize his lack of agency, the *polit* is sometimes juxtaposed to a more virile, empowered character, and thus rendered a "sidekick" in his own first-person narrative.

Both the *Bildungsheld* and the premodernist *pícaro* grow,[60] through a process of education, into formed persons, whose achievement of maturity marks the point of narrative closure. The simplest plot, and one of the most enduring, is simply growing up, with the implicit assumption that in literature if not in life, adulthood implies a plateau of stability. "In the traditional bildungsroman," says Esty, "youth drives narrative momentum until adulthood arrives to fold youth's dynamism into a conceit of uneventful middle age" (18). With his compromised agency, the *polit* (and his kindred modern *pícaros*[61]) has trouble bringing his tale to an organic, satisfying end point. If *Lazarillo de Tormes* reaches an artificial, too-stable stasis, then his modernist heirs end their tales *in medias res*. Even when the *polit* achieves a measure of education, he does not become *gebildet* in the encompassing sense intended by, say, Schiller, nor does his learning constitute the completion of his character. More typically, in the fictions we consider here, it is the *polit*'s lack of education or development that stands out. Development signifies as both a subjective, psychological term and an economic one, for the abnormal economics for which the *maskilim* took the Jewish polity to task continues to dominate the Jewish emergence into modernity.[62] Whether because he was as yet unproductivized (as Abramovitsh laments in the *Kitser masoes*) or because his prospects were compromised by war (as with Israel Rabon's demobilized soldier in *Di gas*), the *polit* could hardly participate in what Esty calls the "original magic of the [Bildungsroman] genre, which was to assimilate work into a narrative of education—to harmonize, as it were, production and self-production" (74). The hero's inability to harmonize production and self-production is a hallmark of the modernist Yiddish picaresque. It is a form for the ineluctably out-of-sync.

Feminism, Postcolonialism, and the Insufficiency of Traditional *Bildung*

Yiddish, so long dismissed by its own native speakers as a déclassé *jargón*, partakes of what has more recently been proudly reclaimed as a "Caliban aesthetic."[63] The literature to which this marginal, minoritarian language gave rise has certain affinities with other latecomers to the feast of literary scholarship. The intellectual kinship is especially strong with the feminist and postcolonial critics who have traced articulately the changes that overcame the *Bildungsroman* under modernism. Ventriloquized by female and subaltern speakers, this warhorse form of Western European patriarchy began to speak in a different register. In her tellingly titled study *Unsettling the Bildungsroman*, Stella Bolaki lays out the stakes of the female and feminist appropriation of the quintessential genre of development: "In its schematic representation, its primary function is to make integration into the existing social order legitimate by channeling individual energy into socially useful purposes" (Bolaki 12). With the nature of the existing social order undergoing transformation, legitimacy and social use become contested, so that the new feminist *Bildungsromane* "collide with normative conventions of the genre and grate against its naturalized assumptions, bending and stretching the form so that it reveals the multiple patterns and figures hidden under the generic 'carpet' that has served to define a largely Eurocentric and patriarchal form" (Bolaki 12–13).[64] Where Bolaki writes "European," Piret Peiker[65] might scruple to add "Western European," for Peiker offers a parallel analysis of how the conventional *Bildungsroman* is bent and stretched in the hands of Central European authors, who offer a "profound description of the non-western European experience, as a description of life without a belief in grand narratives" (5). The Estonian scholar Peiker sees a strong resemblance between the Central European experience of *Bildung* and that of postcolonial societies, where the classic elements of the *Bildungsroman* are systematically subverted, redirected, or otherwise transformed. Peiker argues that the logical grammar of the Western European *Bildungsroman* arose organically out of an Enlightenment metaphysics that posited "a firm sense of self and belief in rational agency" (2), but that, when exported elsewhere, hybridized only partially with "competing forms of knowledge and rationality." This incomplete synthesis gives rise to subjects who feel "no sense of security, no sense of personal empowerment and of being in control of one's destiny. Rather, there is a perception of fragmentation, of being 'constantly liminal' and forever incomplete" (2). These subjects might journey from the periphery to the metropole, but they cannot fully credit the socialization process that awaits them there:

> If the western European formation *Bildungsroman* "uncovers" or constructs the concealed order or wholeness of life, the eastern European one registers a journey towards such an order, which often is perceived as existing "elsewhere," but then with a second move restates scepticism about the existence of such an order, or at least a scepticism about the possibility of achieving it. The central European *Bildung* narratives share this trajectory with non-European postcolonial narratives. (Peiker 5)

Peiker's analysis chimes with Jed Esty's trope of unseasonable youth that cannot follow the customary arc of maturation, emphasizing as she does the postcolonial trope of "the longing for a *topos* of maturity and order, for a mythical realm of centeredness, that exists or existed somewhere, maybe in some ideal past, some Golden Age, maybe also in a contemporary metropolitan centre stylized as a capital of the world" (3). The bedrock of Western European metaphysics, the self, is rendered unstable so that, according to Peiker, "central European narratives of personhood generally convey the psychological stress of living without the ability to construct a coherent self. They associate self with feelings of immaturity, incompleteness, and impotence in dealing with what appears to be an equally fluid world" (5). The sense of compromised agency that typifies the *polit* also characterizes the postcolonial or Central European *Bildungsheld*. Most of Peiker's insights either apply to Yiddish modernism (without mentioning Yiddish among the literatures of Central Europe) or cry out for the analytic of the picaresque. I hardly mean to suggest a literary-historical arc whereby the picaresque supersedes or replaces the *Bildungsroman*; surely the modernist picaresque coexists with the modernist *Bildungsroman*, the difference between them residing in narrative strategies and chronotopic emphasis (time-space coordinates). But Peiker's analysis, without invoking the term, shows clearly how the Central European modernist *Bildungsroman* bends toward its picaresque cousin. If these compromised *Bildungshelden* manage "to construct a 'life story' of any coherence, it is a record of stressful negotiations through many particularized small narratives, rather than the teleological revelation of one grand narrative" (Peiker 6). Is this not the pathway of the modernist *pícaro*?

Scholars of Yiddish and Jewish literature have begun to employ the analytic framework offered by postcolonial thought.[66] Marc Caplan does so deftly in his recent study of peripheral modernisms in Yiddish and African literatures,[67] noting that, "The field of postcolonial studies offers a politicized consideration of the ways in which one establishes subjectivity both in relation to, and at the expense of, the object-position of other subjects" (8). Surging beyond the original historical context of "liberated" colonies, postcolonialism has morphed into a larger cultural and literary analytic category, yielding insights about marginality, subalternity, alterity, land, nation, minor, major, metropole—all of which have precedents that antedate colonialism and certainly postcolonialism. Thus scholars may apply "postcolonial" analysis to medieval texts.[68] Caplan makes the case directly for a postcolonial study of Yiddish, establishing that postcolonial theory "demonstrates that for both colonizers and the colonized, the moment of self-recognition confronts the subject with his or her essential doubleness" (ibid.), and then pressing on the significance of Yiddish as "a crucial means of making apparent the doubleness of Jewish identity otherwise effaced in contemporary, monolingual Jewish cultures conducted in English or Hebrew" (9). Discerning in Yiddish and African writers "similar genres, rhetorical gestures, and thematic dilemmas," Caplan dwells on the spectral, deterritorialized status of the languages of composition as being central to both of these literary clusters. To the discourse of postcolonialism, then, let us add the analytics of genre and specifically of the picaresque.

Partials

> "Art is limitation; the essence of every picture is the frame."
>
> —G.K. Chesterton

Bakhtin made no secret of his delight in the great realist fictions of *becoming*, writing that "The large epic form . . . including the novel as well, should provide an integrated picture of the world and life, it should reflect the *entire* world and *all* of life. In the novel, the entire world and all of life are given in the cross section of the *integrity of the epoch*" ("Bildungsroman"; Bakhtin's emphasis 43). He admired such fictions in their *totality*. This account must be equally frank about its fascination with an epoch whose chief characteristic was that it had no integrity; what is offered here, reflecting this time of radical centrifuge, is *partial* in two respects. First, there is the nontotalizing nature of the fictions themselves: they unfold over a period of a few weeks or months and might stretch as far as a few years.[69] They do not remotely attempt to account for the grand arc of their protagonists' becoming. Limited as they are in time and scope, it would be incongruous to write a totalizing, compendious account of them; indeed, it seems truer to their own spirit to say, "The picaresque is one especially salient form taken by Yiddish and Ashkenazic Jewish resistance to nineteenth-century fictions of progress." This brings us to the second sense in which *partials* are on offer here. This book will not argue that the Yiddish novel moved from the *Bildungsroman* to the picaresque, nor that all—or even most—Yiddish modernist fiction partakes of the picaresque form or the yet-broader picaresque sensibility. Instead, we will consider the conspicuous *lack* of *Bildung* narratives in Yiddish modernist fiction and analyze the picaresque as presenting the single most coherent alternate worldview, or chronotope, to the *Bildungsroman* in the modern Jewish literary cluster. Taking our cue from the metonymic logic of the picaresque,[70] we shall pursue a synecdochal approach, aiming at careful consideration of several representative texts rather than exhaustive description of all the relevant ones.

So profound is the imprint of history upon the study of Jewish literature that it is rare to find a book on the topic that is not organized chronologically. Interested mainly in poetics and literary stylistics, I have taken up the challenge of structuring a book that is respectful of chronology without being enslaved to it. Thus, I have ordered this account according to three prominent avatars of the *polit* figure: the mobile modern subject, the demobilized soldier, and the new Soviet citizen. The first section concerns narratives of mobility, both of the geographic variety afforded by the railroad and the concomitant social mobility that followed in its wake. The freedom to move about brought with it license to deceive, whether by perpetrating the minor prevarications that inhere in a friendly card game or the profound metaphysical lies that lurk in demonic seduction. This mobility—and its accompanying moral lability—both spelled and reflected the attrition of the *shtetl* as a plausible habitation. The *polit* and the phenomena he epitomizes assume robust form in immigrant narratives including Sholem Aleichem's *Motl peysi dem khazns* (*Motl the Cantor's Son*) and Isaac Bashevis Singer's great New York novels *Soynim, di geshikhte fun a libe* (*Enemies: A Love Story*) and *Shotns baym hodson* (*Shadows on the Hudson*). The central section proposes demobilization as a trope for post-Haskalah Jewish existence and offers readings of I.J. Singer's *Shtol un ayzn* (*Steel and Iron*) as a counter-picaresque *Bildungsroman* set against two quintessential *polit* narratives: *Hotel Savoy* by Joseph Roth and *Di gas* (*The Street*) by Yisroel Rabon. The third section, following the fortunes of the *polit* under the new Soviet regime, seeks to explain the workings of a picaresque poetics not only at the level of event but at the level of discourse. This examination builds on the formally picaresque early novel by Ilya Ehrenburg *Burnaya Zhizn Lazika Roitshvanetsa* (*The Stormy Life of Laz Roitshvants*) and extends beyond the boundaries of the form to consider Isaac Babel's *Odessa Stories* as avatars of the picaresque sensibility. The epilogue, following the *polit* beyond the borders of Yiddishland, considers alternative forms of Jewish emplacement in the diaspora and in Israel, by juxtaposing Saul Bellow's *The Adventures of Augie March* and David Grossman's *Yesh Yeladim Zigzag* (*The Zig Zag Kid*). What was impossible in Europe becomes inevitable in Bellow's America: a fusion of the picaresque with the *Bildungsroman*.

Affixed as an epigraph to this introduction are the words of Frank Wadleigh Chandler, who maintains in the first modern study of the Spanish picaresque form (1899), "We do not so much look at the rogue as borrow his eyes with which to see the world." This formulation takes the *pícaro* as a cipher, a roving device for entering a series of social milieux; his significance inheres not in his own person but in the perspective he can bring to bear on the world(s) around him. As Marc Caplan[71] reminds us, "the picaresque, both in its original Renaissance manifestations and its reconfigurations in nineteenth-century Yiddish fiction, is fundamentally a sociological genre, formulated in order to represent early modernity's politics of dislocation and social disruption" (76). In its twentieth-century form, the Jewish picaresque will still gather energy, of course, from the era's politics of dislocation, but it will also grow into something more character-driven and recognizably modern. The choice between bird's eye view and worm's eye view is ultimately an incidental one: in either case, the author surveys the terrain with the mastery of distance. Here the modernist *polit* must part ways with his older European cousin, the *pícaro*. His creator has been vouchsafed no grand or grandiose vision of society, even the Jewish part thereof. But spared the tasks of the roving device, the character of the *polit* becomes more centrally important as a distinct *person* with his own subjective interiority. Emerging in tandem with the revocation of Enlightenment promises of *Bildung*, his partial view would come to stand both against literary realism's totalizing narratives and nationalism's totalitarian effects.

PART 1

The *Polit* on the Move

CHAPTER 1

SHARKS AND MARKS[1]
The Swindles and Seductions of Modernity

"The World Invites Deception."

—legend of the Joker on a deck of Bicycle Ghost cards

"Ingenious philosophers tell you, perhaps, that the great work of the steam-engine is to create leisure for mankind. Do not believe them; it only creates a vacuum for eager thought to rush in."

—George Eliot, *Adam Bede*

"True ambivalent and universal laughter does not deny seriousness but purifies and completes it. Laughter purifies from dogmatism, from the intolerant and the petrified; it liberates from fanaticism and pedantry, from fear and intimidation, from didacticism, naiveté and illusion, from the single meaning, the single level, from sentimentality. Laughter does not permit seriousness to atrophy and to be torn away from the one being, forever incomplete. It restores this ambivalent wholeness."

—Mikhail Bakhtin, *Rabelais and His World*

While Yitskhok Bashevis (later to become known as the phenomenon Isaac Bashevis Singer) began to publish within just over a decade of the passing of Sholem Rabinovitsh (also to be enduringly known as a phenomenon: Sholem Aleichem), their total corpora span more than a century. Written nearly at the temporal poles of modern Yiddish *belles lettres*,[2] the work of these two authors marks, respectively, the starting and ending points of the *polit*'s journey through Yiddish modernism. Rabinovitsh's fictions represented a structural departure from much of the contemporary European fiction that his fellow Yiddish authors had tried to emulate, and in many instances, a thematic departure as well. He very rarely composed a full-length novel with a third-person, omniscient narrator, preferring instead monologues, linked or freestanding short stories, and epistolary novels—all genres that fall under the heading of the "partials" elaborated in the introduction to this volume. While some of these narrative techniques, such as epistolary storytelling, harkened back to an earlier and perhaps more primitive moment in the development of the European novel, they could equally be claimed as the province of the forward-looking early modernist who would eschew linear plots and straightforward narrative presentations.[3] On the thematic plane, Rabinovitsh revels in the contingency, uncertainty, and peripateia that mark the transition from the nineteenth century to the twentieth, and having embraced all this whirling movement, his fictions logically enough disdain the sentimentality that attends a settled, comfortably bourgeois existence.

Bashevis's novels and short stories are more structurally conventional, and indeed he scorned any fictional form that smacked of the experimental.[4] However, I would claim that as an *antimodernist*, Bashevis used the form of the novel against itself. Indeed, his fictions illustrate the impossibility of growth or progress: master narratives that the European novel evolved, in part, in order to illustrate and embody. Intervening, then, in a literary tradition that "cast its lot with individualism, change, will power, and 'the courage to transform,'"[5] both Rabinovitsh and Bashevis dismantled many of the conventions of Yiddish fiction and redirected its energies. With respect to Bashevis's work, Dan Miron places this stance against striving in the framework of passivity and nihilism, citing that author's "deep distrust in human will power and an absolute aversion for both the Nietzchean 'will to power' and the liberal faith in 'progress'" (ibid.). What about the apparently more comic case of Rabinovitsh? Sholem Aleichem, he acknowledges, also "presented archetypes of Jewish passivity," but in Miron's account, Bashevis inverted these monologues even as he imitated their verbal richness. While the Bashevian speakers have utterly surrendered to their fates, resigning any lingering sense of agency, Rabinovitsh's (variously pitiable and risible) monologists digress and zig-zag with a nervous energy that resembles "the scuttling from wall to wall of the prisoner who knows not how to break through the prison walls" (341) but who still hopes his antics, if sufficiently audible and gripping, might lead to his release. However, in discussing the *Railroad*

Stories, a fairly late specimen of Rabinovitsh's work, Miron argues for the "uncannily smooth, relaxed, albeit ironic, surface, as if the writer had reconciled himself to the chaos and absurdities of existence" (202).[6] We might distinguish, then, between the "hot" Sholem Aleichem of antic, desperate speakers (as in "*Dos tepl*"/ "The Pot" and "*A nisref*"/ "Burnt Out") and the cool, collected Rabinovitsh of the *Railroad Stories*. The kinship between Rabinovitsh and Bashevis as two ironists, cool customers with an exceptionally[7] bleak view of Jewish—and human—perfectibility, is so strong and so potentially illuminating as to disrupt a strictly chronological exploration of our subject. In this section, I shall attempt to tease out the particulars of their literary affinity and to understand how those particulars might fill in significant swaths of this portrait of the modernist Jewish picaresque.

Neither Rabinovitsh nor Bashevis made extensive use of the picaresque *form*, but both authors crafted fictions into which a picaresque sensibility is woven indelibly. The two intertwined threads of their picaresque poetics are a preoccupation with delinquency and a disdain for sentimentality. The delinquency that traditionally marks the picaresque is considerably softened in the Jewish milieu, or at least off-loaded from the protagonist to other characters. Thus, we have the fly-on-the-wall narration in stories like "Knortn" ("Cnards") and the *Railroad Stories*, whereby a mild-mannered first-person narrator withstands a brush with the criminal, the pathological, or the merely distasteful. Bashevis takes the opposite approach but to similar effect: far from an affable cultural translator, his first-person narrator may well be one of the devil's own minions, a figure so extremely odious as to bend back to a certain sympathetic likability. Neither Rabinovitsh nor Bashevis, though, is ultimately interested in delinquency for its own sake, as were the classical picaresque writers of Western Europe. Both of these Yiddish authors are fascinated with deception as a way of deflating sentimental pieties.[8] For each of them, the quintessential human interaction involves the exploitation of differential power dynamics between characters, between speakers. In Rabinovitsh's vast collection of novellas, short stories, linked story collections, and a few novels, this means a recurring focus on the swindle or heist story. Monologic speakers or *rasskazchikn*[9] are always trying to elicit or wring something from their immediate and putative audience ("Sholem Aleichem") or from their secondary audience (the reader), be it sympathy, absolution, or expert advice. For Bashevis, over his similarly wide-ranging novels and short stories, this interest takes the form of a dogged obsession with the drama of seduction. In placing these advantage-taking units of action at the heart of their narratives, these authors restore to modern Jewish literature an element latent in the picaresque: the insouciant swindle.

Seduction is a staple of the classical picaresque, so it is hardly surprising that James Wesley Childers's *Tales from Spanish Picaresque Novels: A Motif Index*[10] should offer several pages of entries on seduction and deception. Lazarillo de Tormes and his literary progeny are constantly on the make, establishing a series of more-or-less trusting relationships that cost them at times and confer benefit at others. That is to say, trust is rarely mutual in these texts, but rather it serves as a currency to be wrung from one party by the other. The *pícaro* only furnishes one of literature's starker instances of the persuasion to the will of another that lies at the heart of seduction. Yet this kind of encounter might be regarded as central to an account of fiction in general, a case Ross Chambers begins to make in his study *Story and Situation: Narrative Seduction and the Power of Fiction* (1984) and develops further in *Room for Maneuver* (1991).[11] In the earlier book, he argues that the narrative relationship is an essentially erotic one and that the act of seduction is a metaphor for narration—a provocative, slow undressing of events that prompts the narratee (whether a character within the fiction or the reading audience) to pantingly ask, "What happens next?" For Chambers, seduction and authority present ways to address differential power relations in acts of storytelling but also in hermeneutic transactions. Operating not only within the story but also *between* texts and readers, "such seduction," in his formulation, can allow for "producing authority where there is no power, is a means of converting (historical) weakness into (discursive) strength. As such, it appears as a major weapon against alienation, an instrument of self-assertion, and an 'oppositional practice' of considerable significance" (212). Insofar as they radically accepted the Jewish condition of historical weakness rather than trying to mitigate it through their literary efforts, the authors under consideration here were content to revel in whatever discursive strength they could marshal. They could sit back and expose, in a blithely picaresque spirit, the human comedy as an essentially unwinnable confidence game.

The *pícaro* moves through fluctuating, even labile circumstances, with his confidence—or outward projection thereof—as the only constant currency at his disposal. Although it might at first appear that his task is to win the trust of the stream of other characters that he encounters, as well as of the reader of his first-person narrative, the seductions that he must carry off in order to survive are most effectively pursued by means of an inversion. A savvy con in David Mamet's 1987 film *House of Games* pithily describes the necessary reversal, lecturing another character (his mark, of course), "The basic idea is this. It's called a *confidence* game. Why? Because you give me your confidence? No. Because I give you *mine*." This imparting of one's own confidence smoothes the transits of desire at the center of these fictions and abets processes of seduction that might be singular or serial, as in the case of the fully realized picaresque.

Instead of focusing on the fully realized picaresque in this chapter, I will focus on two "partials" as adumbrated in the introduction: the discrete units of action that recur so frequently in the respective corpora of these two authors as to crystallize a set of key concerns for each. This concentrated interpretive opportunity is presented by the game of chance in Rabinovitsh's fiction and by the verbal seduction in that of Bashevis. Representative texts will, in each case, enable thinking through the mechanics of a relational transaction (the game and the seduction) and how these confidence games give rise to what I would call an epistemology of the picaresque. To wield power over someone, it is necessary to consolidate one's knowledge of them, but most knowledge is divulged indirectly, through moves rather than through direct verbal communication. Indeed, the swindlers and seducers take advantage of inaccurate proxies for knowledge of other people, such as speech mannerisms and costume. In these stories, the consistent failure of some characters to gain accurate knowledge of others casts into doubt the idea that such knowledge is even possible.[12] The picaresque sensibility rebukes maskilic positivism and suggests that skepticism is the only reasonable posture in a world whose people are fundamentally unknowable.

I.

Two stories about playing cards, "Knortn" (1912, translated, serendipitously, as "Cnards") and "A zeks un zektsik" (1911, "A Game of Sixty Six"), focus our attention on a number of Rabinovitsh's preoccupations central to our study of the picaresque sensibility: the swindle, games and play, social anonymity, and the interaction with casual strangers enabled by the mobility of the railroad. In Lazarillo's time, one had to be an exceptional figure to enjoy (or risk) journeying continually from city to city and through the countryside. By the twentieth century, such travel had become the norm, at least for an

expanding population of middle-class merchants and salesmen. The peregrinations of this upwardly and geographically mobile group gave rise to
frequent, short-lived interactions, especially in railway cars that moved
travelers and through which travelers moved in relative anonymity.[13] From
1880 to 1906, the Russian empire more than doubled its miles of railroad
track. Increased railroad traffic led to the diffusion of "picaresque" situations and interactions across many different kinds of social contexts and
helped foment the development of a picaresque sensibility that lodged in
allied literary forms even when the actual form of the picaresque was not
used. These kindred forms might include the short story, with its possibilities for narrative fragmentation, and first-person monologues, which replicate the first-person subjectivity of the traditional picaresque. With sufficient mobility, one might swindle others and move on without any
uncomfortable consequences; stuck at home, however, one is perforce the
swindled.[14] This is even true of more benign and soft-edged transactional
relationships, such as that of the scapegrace *luftmensch* Menakhem Mendl
and his homebound wife, Sheyne Sheyndl.

The card game furnishes Rabinovitsh with an ideal device for probing
the ludic possibilities of deception. In both stories we shall consider, the
point of the game is the con, but the game setting renders deception socially
acceptable. The card game constitutes a ritualized attempt at seduction in a
framework of play, transposing social norms enough so that to object to
foul play becomes a breach of sportsmanship or etiquette. Turn-taking
games such as cards and board games involve "moves" that reveal what each
player is thinking far more reliably than speech or even body language.[15] It
is often in the best interest of each player to maintain silence or even to attempt to disguise the emotions provoked by one's hand. As Peter Bernstein
explains, the founder of game theory,[16] John von Neumann, established that
in many gaming situations, the central strategy is not to guess an opponent's
thoughts but to conceal one's own, and the chief object should not be to win
but to avoid losing (234). The unknowability or uncertainty of other players'
plans and motivations is of central importance to a successful strategy.
"Earlier theories accepted uncertainty as a fact of life and did little to identify its source," notes Bernstein. "Game theory says that *the true source of
uncertainty lies in the intentions of others*" (Bernstein's emphasis; 232). In
games of turn-taking, there is a decisive moment to act, and then one must
wait. The prudence of waiting to see what others do within the game constitutes a strong argument for passivity, the instinctive posture of the *pícaro*.

According to one theorist of games,[17] play serves as an embellished mimesis of ordinary life. In this case, one sphere of life that is being illuminated through these stories is Rabinovitsh's economics of passivity. Representing the game for stakes concentrates and intensifies Rabinovitsh's basic view of Jewish economic activity as redistribution rather than production.[18] In this view, illustrated vividly through a character like Menakhem Mendl, life is one big gamble[19] in which hard work may be necessary but is never sufficient. But it is equally true of less playful characters. Even in "Tevye Strikes it Rich," a story about coming into new money, the first paragraph is a protestation of the futility of human effort or agency in acquiring wealth. No new capital has been created over the course of the story; the affluent family's generous reward to Tevye merely redistributes existing capital. Indeed, the first sentence insists, "If you're meant to strike it rich, Pan Sholem Aleichem, you may as well stay home with your slippers on, because good luck will find you there too" (3). Of course Tevye's industry will stand him in good stead as he launches his dairy business, but he goes out of his way to emphasize rhetorically the role of dumb luck and divine blessing, which—as twin stances against human striving—amount to much the same thing. This economics is deeply antithetical to the maskilic ideal of productivization as part of a program for perfecting, or at least normalizing, European Jewry.[20]

Focusing on the trope of card playing in the work of a Yiddish writer at the turn of the twentieth century also registers for us a shift in the social significance of that activity in different cultural and temporal milieux. Games of whist, preference, and the like had been depicted in the European novel, whether English, French, German, or Russian, since at least the eighteenth century. There they functioned as a marker of class, whether it was the aristocracy (often portrayed as dissolute in its gambling) or the ascending middling classes (more amiable and contained in its habits of play).[21] In these stories by Rabinovitsh, playing cards signifies characters' increasing secularization. Whether moving from the drawing room to a Jewish *shtetl* living room known to the players, ironically, as "*dos klayzl*" (the chapel) or to the railway car, social card playing changes from signifying socioeconomic nobility to socioreligious mobility. The circumstances framing the card games are culturally specific as well. Both tales are set at Hanukkah, when the rare authorization to gamble on the dreidel seems to have carried over to games of chance in general, especially cards. Specific rationales for permitting card games on the eight festive nights are articulated fairly late in Jewish legal discourse, and tend to vary.[22] "A zeks un zektsik" has the more "secular" setting, but Rabinovitsh mentions having completed it in a letter dated 6 December 1910, and he requests that it be printed for Hanukkah.[23]

"But the train was already moving": "Knortn" (1912)

Although "Knortn" was published a year after "A zeks un zektsik," we consider the later story first because it is more narratively straightforward. Like several other Sholem Aleichem heist tales that do not involve cards, "Knortn" recounts a picaresque situation from the perspective, not of the sympathetic *pícaro*, but of the stationary dupes. Set in an unidentified *shtetl* very similar to Kasrilevke, this Hanukkah story unfolds among the town's "avant garde" and rapidly secularizing youth. The narrator, a participant-observer, seems attached to the fringes of "our secular aristocracy" (373), a crowd who chafe against the strictures of provincial religiosity and find consolation in each other's company and in such "scandalous" behaviors as playing cards and nibbling on *treyf* sausage throughout the year and even on fast days. The setting for their rather tame debauchery is the home of a young and evidently childless couple, the Ramshevitches, the daughter and son-in-law of the town's cantor. Their circle is not an ideologically engaged group of Bundist or Zionist youth, or an artistic band of writers and actors; they are a motley crew of locals who just want to have a good time. Despite claims to being more culturally "modern" than the town's old-fashioned Jewish establishment, their modernity does not extend to maskilic ideals of productive labor; this aspirationally aristocratic sect prefers to extend its leisure over days as unseen others pay the bills. This idleness is enabled by their generation's being caught between the norms of an old economic structure that rewarded young men for Torah study (an activity that "produced" no discernible goods) and new, more conventionally Western economic arrangements that have not yet fully come into being.[24] Thus, it is possible for "silken" sons-in-law still on the *kest* system, whereby the bride's parents support the couple during the newlywed years, to fritter away their days at cards and to lose their dowries and their wives' pearls in the bargain. By the time the story is recollected, the economic transition has implicitly taken place, for the events are described as having transpired "in those days."

The narrator divides his story into two parts: first a series of anecdotes establishing the taboo against playing cards except during Hanukkah,[25] and then the swindle that forms the main story. The story's temporal signature is left fuzzy (at least in linear, national-historic time; its setting in relation to the cyclical time marker of the winter holiday is quite clear). "Modern" mores predominate in the narratorial present, and the ban on card-playing, together with the outmoded *kest* system, are recalled as features of a distant but still-remembered past. As the narrator explains, "Nowadays a game of cards is an everyday affair. . . . There was a time, if you know what I mean, when we used to play cards only once a year—at Hannukah" (372). Back then, his "secular aristocracy" was the exception: "That is, if you want the whole truth, people used to get together for a game in those days too—a real game, a hot game! But where? In a secret chamber, behind locked doors" (372). Raymond Williams situates the "knowable community" in an idealized, never-was past. In this case, that past was an imagined time of innocence when upstanding citizens didn't so much as recognize a playing card—much as storied Talmudic scholars were reputed not to recognize the face on a coin. After recounting the shock of the matronly *gabbai's* wife at finding a curious foreign object—a king of clubs—at her place in the synagogue's women's section, the narrator explains, "I merely wanted to show you what a forbidden thing cards used to be and how carefully we had to hide our knowledge of them" (374). Her distress seems overplayed, as will the amazement of the visitors who perpetrate the main swindle; there is a tacit consensus on the part of the townspeople, it would seem, to hide their conversance with secular modernity.

The quintessence of that modernity is mobility and the anonymity it can confer. The synagogue is a place where everyone's identity is known and associated metonymically with a particular customary seating location. For this reason, the scandalized *gabbaite* takes the presence of a playing card at *her seat* quite personally. But playing at the Ramshevitches' affords an anonymous interaction in a town that appears fully known and knowable; this unaccustomed anonymity rivals even that granted by the railroads. While the train offers physical mobility, the card game yields social mobility by redistributing wealth. Holding out the potential for a life-changing transaction and interaction, all among virtual strangers, gambling on cards establishes a form of mobility-within-stasis. As the narrator recounts, "May my enemies have as many plagues and I as many lucky years as the number of times we played with people five nights and five days in succession, and then broke up without ever knowing who they were or what they were or where they had come from. A game of cards is not a marriage contract. You can play a very good game without knowing your opponent or his pedigree"

(377). *Yikhes*, or pedigree, was a crucial basis for social relations and marriage alliances in the *shtetl*, standing in as it did for social knowability not only within a single generation but over the historical sweep of several generations. A modernity of railroads and card games played with strangers opens up new economic opportunities even as it undercuts the safety net constituted by social knowability. In the absence of true knowledge, characters are forced to rely on proxies.

A leitmotif running throughout much of Rabinovitsh's short fiction is the assessment of character according to dress; people who "look *frum* (pious)" are assumed to be reliable when they are not ("Chabne," "Der oyrekh" / "The Guest"), or a sartorial accoutrement dictates social relations to preposterous effect ("Iber a hitl" / "On Account of a Hat"). In "A Game of Sixty-Six," the main or external narrator notes but is not ultimately swayed by the fact that his interlocutor looks like a commercial traveler "like myself." In "Knortn," the visiting charity collectors, who are "fairly up to their eyebrows in pious whiskers" (108), have impeccable sartorial credentials. One early warning sign, almost too subliminal to register, is the way that their Hasidic garb and facial grooming commingle the pious with the thuggish: "One of them was a tall man—long and thin—in a long, black silken coat; earlocks—long and narrow, curly, reaching almost to his belt; a fur cap on his head; and a long beard and a pair of whiskers so thick and black that if you had met this man on a dark night on a deserted road, you'd want to say your prayers" (378). But his voice and manner of speech offset any foreboding in his appearance: "Speaking slowly, one word at a time and with a delicate sweet smile that came out of his thick and frightful whiskers (he did not even seem to be talking to us, but looked rather as if he were deep in prayer, in humble communion with the Lord)" (379). The two men manage to look so agog at the sight of the scattered playing cards ("'What sort of thing is this—on the table here?'" [380]) that they create the impression of having never before seen the like. Thus, the "secular aristocrats" are taken in by the same virtuous pretense they themselves affect in relation to the rest of the town! Indeed, the story's humorous title is predicated on the idea that these two lily-pure charity collectors can't even accurately assimilate the *word* for cards into their vocabulary.

The worldly wise youth of the "*klayzl*," so intoxicated with their own iconoclasm, prove the true gullibles. Unwittingly, they carry out their prescribed role in relation to the visitors: to marvel at the outsiders' ignorance, and to gently educate them about the goings-on: "And Ramshevitch helped her out by explaining to them briefly and clearly the meaning and the use of cards; concluding with the observation that cards were both a diversion and a vocation. In short, you could say that cards were a trade. A trade like any other" (381). Thus the unsuspecting dupes end up explaining the con men's own trade to them! The posture of pious ignorance is essential to the exchange. The nub of the cardsharps' deception lies in convincing the marks that they are too innocent to inveigle anyone. The swindle that takes place within the game is secondary to the meta-swindle of luring others to the game in the first place. This lopsided exchange will find its parallel in Isaac Bashevis Singer's seduction stories, where his demons' most daunting task is to convince human beings to converse with them altogether. The ostentatious display of innocence is an elegant example of the con's necessary inversion: the interlopers impart confidence to the Ramshevitches and their habitués, leading their marks to stake all and lose all.

The visitors' finesse extends beyond their systematic trouncing of the "aristocrats" at the card table. A resentful Velvl Ramshevitch exacts on them a petty revenge, and they turn even that moment to their advantage. He insists that they partake of his sausage and then gleefully informs them that they've eaten *treyf*, still imagining them to be pious enough to care. The narrator recalls the measure of comfort, of Schadenfreude, the company takes in this small counter-deception: "Our vengeance was so complete that we almost forgot how much we had lost that night, forgot the depths to which we had sunk, and looking at each other we laughed and laughed and laughed" (387). Yet here, too, the visitors play the gulls for all they are worth, exploiting the shock and drama of the moment in order to make their escape: "Before he could finish the sentence our two visitors clutched their heads in terror, opened their mouths wide as if to spit everything out, and then with a bitter groan sprang for the door and swept out of the house like a cyclone" (387). Unwittingly and witlessly, Ramshevitsh has furnished the visitors with a pretext to run out. It is only after their departure that Chayale Ramshevitsh discovers the stacked decks they have mockingly left behind. The group is slow to understand how pointed was the swindle, how intentionally *they* have been targeted. They assume at first that the con men might be "collecting for charity" elsewhere in the town and proceed to search every synagogue, chapel, and prayer house. Only then do they move on to the railroad station. This shift represents, finally, their dawning realization that they are the unique and specific dupes of these calculating criminals. The "aristocrats" recognize, too late, that the cons are defined by their dexterity and mobility, not their costumes. When the interlopers are finally glimpsed, it is hardly surprising that they are smooth-shaven, giving the lie to their sham pious whiskers. The "silken" son-in-law Rafalski is first to spot them:

> "There they are!" he cried. "There they are! The two cnard players—as sure as my name is Rafalski!"
>
> But the train was already moving. (388)

Indeed, Rabinovitsh implies, the train of modernity—with all its lurching forward motion, dangerous social anonymity, and eager thought—is already clacking along at full speed and has been for some time.

The swindle plot is simple enough, but the story's satisfying complexity, like so many of Rabinovitsh's fictions, owes to the ambiguous position of the first-person narrator. How much did he know about the unfolding events, and when did he know (or suspect) it? The conceit is that he suffered equally along with his townsmen in the drubbing, yet there are hints all along of a detachment from his peers; the narrator seems closer to the author than to the other characters. He doesn't bemoan the loss of any personal wealth. At the least, he is a perceptive participant-observer, noting with anthropological cool,

> I am afraid that I was the only one who really kept an eye on them. From time to time I looked up and I began to think that to them we must look even stranger than they did to us. We and not they were peculiar, involved in a strange pursuit, speaking a wild language and conducting ourselves in general like savages: sitting bareheaded, inhaling smoke, exchanging little squares of paper, throwing money into a plate. And talking to each other in a language that might have been Turkish or Greek. For who could understand the meaning of *pass, deuce, pair, flush, jack, queen, king, ace,* and other such words that belong to the language of cards? (382)

Intriguingly, he imagines the aesthetics of secular dissolution from the vantage point of the traditionally religious, registering the silliness, decadence, and insolence of their pastime in equal measure. Here is a bit of irony at the earnest narrator's expense, since his critique rings true even as the imaginative ventriloquism whereby he voices it rings utterly false. Far from regarding the "strange pursuit" with pious wonder, the visitors are agile criminals wondering only at the provincial naiveté of these small-scale sinners. They justify the rueful lament of Isaac Bashevis Singer's bypassed demon that modern-day Jews are capable of sinning only in a small way.

The character "Sholem Aleichem" does not figure formally in this tale, but the narrator is a more-than-decent approximation, with his close attention to peculiarities of language (cataloguing the specialized argot of card play) and of mores, as well as his intense yet ultimately futile attention to detail. "I am afraid that I was the only one who really kept an eye on them," he confesses, but his vigilance avails nothing on behalf of his boon companions. A friend of questionable loyalty, he fixes his gaze on many details unflattering to the "secular aristocrats," such as the Chayale's "pockmarked face" and "large, stained teeth" (375), "uncombed blond hair, with the tired, puffy eyes" (377). He also records unflinchingly the moral ugliness, the pettiness of tricking the visitors into eating *treyf.* Like the Sholem Aleichem persona who appears in other fictions, the narrator sees all and does little.

The argument for this story as a representative instance of the picaresque antinostalgia may be discerned in two small matters of diction, the sorts of verbal tics that inflect the speech of many of Rabinovitsh's monologists. As mentioned above, the temporal signature of the story is left vague. Yet the narrator seems to recollect the events being recounted from a significantly later date than when they occurred, repeatedly opposing "those days" to "nowadays," and thus intimating that the story could never take place in the narratorial present.[26] Does he mean to imply that he and his contemporary readers live in a more rational, discerning era? Does the narrator quietly yearn for a time when it was plausible that the town's leading citizens wouldn't even recognize the face of a playing card? If the narrator, into whose care we are entrusted, is a closet nostalgist, then that is Rabinovitsh's subtle con on the reader. He lulls us into nostalgia only to puncture it, much as the con men lure the townsmen into a game of Hanukkah cards. The harshest aspect of Rabinovitsh is that he denies his readers the comfort of an idealized past:[27] it never *was* any better. Echoing the sensibilities of four centuries of *pícaros,* Rabinovitsh and his kindred spirit Bashevis were two of the most determined antinostalgists in Yiddish literature.

The second verbal tic that infects and inflects the speech of this story's narrator is his use of the tagline "*oyb ir hot in dem a gefil*," which may be translated literally as "if you have a feel for it (what I'm saying)" or more colloquially, "if you catch my drift." This phrase recurs multiple times, especially as he recounts the anecdotes that form the preamble to the main swindle. "If you catch my drift," the narrator keeps hazarding, with the verbal equivalent of a cocked eyebrow and pursed lips. What, then, when the swindle is revealed and the train is acknowledged to be already moving? If you catch my drift, dear reader, then you will have already understood that the esteemed secular aristocracy could only be deceived insofar as it has been deceiving itself all along. Left untranslated in Julius and Frances Butwin's English, the recurring phrase calls our attention to the phenomenon of the tagline in Rabinovitsh's monologic stories.[28] Ranging from the pedestrian to the chilling, its very superfluity demands interpretive attention. The tagline is a marker of the authorial alter ego, the author/storyteller split that Rabinovitsh inherits from his mentor S.Y. Abramovitsh and then modernizes. Mendele's tagline *"nisht dos bin ikh oysn"* ("but that's not what I'm talking about") followed him from work to work and served to playfully undermine itself; every such demurral indicated that—bingo!—the putative digression was precisely the matter to which Abramovitsh wished to call the reader's attention. As such, Abramovitsh's tagline carried out a unifying, centripetal function.[29] It gathered in disparate material under the aegis of a singular narratorial consciousness. By way of contrast, Rabinovitsh's multifarious taglines, distributed among several one-off speakers, perform a centrifugal function across his fictions. They fragment the act of storytelling, a modernist maneuver that thrusts narrative energy outward and stymies all attempts at concentration or totalization. The fragmentation reaches its apex in the *Railroad Stories*, which, as Sidra deKoven Ezrahi observes, are "the most sinister of Sholem Aleichem's fictions" because Sholem Aleichem "himself" is absent from them (113).

The Rise of the *komivoyazher*

The train offered the quintessential *topos* for the broken promise of mobility and therefore of modernity. It is no coincidence that the maskilic hero Fabi in Y.L. Gordon's verse tragedy "Kotso shel ha yod" ("The Tip of the Yod") is a railroad engineer; the Pale knew no more potent symbol of progress. This idea reaches its fullest expression, as Harriet Murav[30] documents, in Soviet Yiddish literature, where authors such as David Bergelson would figure the revolution as a speeding express train. The railroad seemed to constitute, literally, a vehicle to somewhere else, but its capacity for meaningful transit is vitiated factually and discursively in the *Railroad Stories*. Rabinovitsh's train has no destination, click-clacking its way neither back to the *shtetl* nor

forward to anywhere else (Ezrahi 115). Y.Y. Trunk famously observed that
the train is Kasrilevke on wheels; Dan Miron disagrees, averring that the
Railroad Stories are quintessentially of the road, not home, transitory not
permanent. Moreover, Miron insists, Rabinovitsh's trains "always embody
an extrinsic and foreign entity that pulls the protagonists out of the confines
of their intimate world and hurls them onto an alien one" (*Image* 274).
Whether figured as essentially homey or essentially foreign, though, the
railroad offers an apt representation of deterritorialized Jewish space within
Europe.[31] As Sidra deKoven Ezrahi points out, the bathhouse in *Benjamin
III* is akin to the railway car in *Railroad Stories* (112) as a place for political
discussion and a site of homosocial intimacy, warmth, and competition. It
should not escape us that in Abramovitsh's proto-modernist picaresque,
this site was a static location rooted in each town and originally attached to
a nominally religious function (ritual immersion), but three or four decades later, those social functions are carried out on a moving train.

The twenty stories that an ailing Rabinovitsh eventually designated the
Azynban geshikhtes (*Railroad Stories*) were originally known as *Ksovim fun
a komivoyazher* (Writings of a Commercial Traveler). The term for traveling
salesman, a portmanteau that Russian borrowed from the French *commis
voyageur*, bespeaks modern efficiency and suggests a new berth for Jews in
a changing economy. Following the advice dispensed by Rabinovitsh's
komivoyazher in his final tale, these commercial travelers often sat in the
"democratic" third-class cars, where a wide-ranging "social promiscuity"
accustomed them to question prevailing hierarchies of "estates, ranks, and
order" while creating a "new sense of space and time" (Brower 51).[32] The
continent effectively shrank, and ambitions grew inversely. From the mid-
nineteenth century to the middle twentieth, the vocation of the traveling
salesman kept pace with expanding railroads in Russia, Britain, and the
United States. In America in 1870, there were seven thousand "drummers"
(salesmen who traveled far afield to drum up business), but a mere twenty
years later, their ranks had ballooned to sixty thousand.[33] Geographically
smaller England and Wales kept up with and perhaps even outpaced this
explosive growth, leaping from 20,730 traveling salesmen in 1871 to 98,428
by 1911.[34] Given the numbers involved in this new economic niche, it stands
to reason that the associated lifestyle would give rise to an entire subculture
and would figure prominently in a number of cultural artifacts, including
the *Railroad Stories*. According to a perspicacious analysis of the workings
of this subculture in the British Isles, Michael French and Andrew Popp[35]

chronicle a "distinctive masculine and fraternal culture among salesmen from the 18th century onward" (791). That culture was solidified in sites that either did not exist in Russia or that would likely have been implicitly closed to Jews, such as commercial rooms of hotels and travelers' associations. Nevertheless, such locales could have been approximated by Jewish merchants and salesmen on their own terms. The *komivoyazher* stood (or, when he was lucky, sat) at the nexus of several preoccupations and anxieties about onrushing modernity, and thus was a compelling figure for literature:

> A series of tensions are evident: between masculinity, fraternity, and respectability; between morality and drink and other temptations found on the road; between travelers' changing roles as agents of modernization; and anxieties over class and social mobility. These were concerns not only for travelers but also for the wider society. Travelers' peripatetic life had long made them conspicuous objects of interest, jealousy, or even fear, which led to their often being made subjects of cultural representation. (French and Popp, 791–92)

An occupational type associated early on with loose morals and deceit advanced between the late eighteenth century and the mid-twentieth along an arc of professionalization. A trade that had been hospitable to gambling, whoring, and cheating was gradually cleaned up so that, "In 1909 the commercial room was reportedly less lively than it had been fifty years earlier; card-playing was less common, and bibles were more available" (French and Propp, 799). But that was in England, whereas Rabinovitsh writes about a Russian Jewish milieu where, on one hand, the dissolution was never as extreme as among English and American drummers, but neither was the clean-up so rapid or so marked. To judge by the *Ayznban geshikhtes*, during the same time in the Pale, the vocation remained the backdrop to a certain kind of easy lifestyle rather than the increasingly demanding profession that Walter Friedman describes in *Birth of a Salesman*. In fact, Rabinovitsh says little to nothing about the work of the *komivoyazher* as such.

What he describes, with playful indirection, is the traveling salesman as a lackadaisical but nonetheless exacting writer—or more precisely, literary entrepreneur. The con men and cardsharps who roam the Russian rail lines are merely an intensified version of the *komivoyazher* himself. The con man imparts his confidence to lure you into a losing card game, while the salesman also imparts his confidence to sell you literary wares you don't really need. This correspondence was heightened by the fact that Rabinovitsh

composed the railroad stories while convalescing from pulmonary tuber-
culosis in various European sanatoria, but most of the raw material had
been collected during his recital tour of 1908. Thus the creator of the narratorial *komivoyazher* was literally riding the rails in order to hawk his literary
compositions to an adoring public.[36]

Con-volutions: "A Game of Sixty-Six" (1910)

Dan Miron reads the *Railroad Stories* as a sustained treatment of the arts of
obfuscation and failed communication. While his readings are convincing,
our understanding of some of the stories might be pushed yet further by
considering them in the light of a double figural and narratorial game (between characters and between storyteller and audience), in which various
proxies are the only means available to assess other players' otherwise unknowable motives and strategy. The ripest tale for this kind of analysis is "A
zeks un zektsik" ("A Game of Sixty-Six"), which exposes the volutions—or
turns—of the con-that-is-a-game both as a subject and a mode of representation. The plot is simple: our commercial traveler recounts verbatim a series of mis-adventures "which I heard on the train from a dignified gentleman of about sixty whom I took to be a commercial traveler like myself"
(207). The embedded yarn culminates with that gentleman's swindle at the
hands of a couple of slick cons posing as father and son who entice him into
the game by pretending to play badly with each other. Ruefully shaking off
the bad memory, the teller ever so casually proposes a game of sixty-six
right then and there, in honor of Hanukkah. Like narration-by-monologue,
sixty-six is a card game for two players, and when the "original" *komivoyazher* politely refuses the proposed game, the reader understands that he
has successfully parried a con's advance. Noting its textbook unreliable interior narrator, Ken Frieden[37] groups this story among Sholem Aleichem's
"monologues of mastery," those tales featuring powerful speakers in which
a "manipulative character uses storytelling to entrap his audience" (203).

Compared to "Knortn," this story features a more daring and perhaps a
more manipulative attempt at the meta-swindle of luring the other player
into the game. Whereas in "Knortn," the con-men disguise themselves as
benevolent and even pious charity collectors, the only "disguise" here is the
relatively understated self-presentation as another commercial traveler
"like myself." Every player in a game is confronted with the fundamental
unknowability of his opponent's strategy (recall: *"the true source of uncer-*

tainty lies in the intentions of others"), but in this story the proxy-for-knowledge is not really a disguise at all, but rather the logic of empathy. That is to say, the swindler asserts his victimhood at every turn, implicitly reasoning that if he knows a victim's pain, then surely he could never inflict the like on someone else. Sharks and marks, he implies, are sharply delineated from each other and assumed never to swim interchangeably in the same waters. A seasoned player, the internal narrator (the con-man) anticipates skepticism and defuses it by being the first to reckon with other people's unknowability and anonymity, acknowledging, "you never know who you're getting involved with. . . . Whoever knows what goes on inside another person?" (207). This insuperable uncertainty is hazarded as a possible explanation for some people's taciturnity, but it could explain equally other people's obfuscating loquacity.

But playing the game and making moves diffuses knowledge. Now, retrospectively, the internal narrator can declare, "Oh, I know them, I do! And I've paid dearly for the privilege." With these words, the *soi-disant* commercial traveler marks himself at once as victim, expert, *and* retailer of stories. He trots out a series of nuggets about other people's losses—"each of these sad stories begins and ends the same way—and no one knows it better than I do." By the end of the tale, the reader cannot help wondering whether he came by this material all too honestly, as the one who "liberated" each of these poor suckers from the burden of their funds. This reading is reinforced by his mock-sympathetic but actually derisive use of diminutives ("*yungermantshik*" and "*studentl*" [Y 159]) to describe the other victims. Yet the more impressive swindle might be to scoop up this anecdotal material at second-hand and then to sell it at retail—a feat left to the mild-mannered and unassuming external narrator.

The reflexive and self-referential play extends so far that the internal narrator warns about cardsharps (like himself!), "It's not all that easy to tell one of them from an honest man. In fact, most of those fellows make believe they're poor innocent saps themselves. They'll pretend to be more dead than alive, or moan and groan over each bad hand—but it's all just an act to get you into the game" (209). But he fails to lure the vigilant external narrator into *his* game: "I watched him cut the deck; he did it a little too skillfully, a little too fast. And his hands were a little too white. Too white and too soft. Suddenly I had a most unpleasant thought" (217). The surefire sign of the con is his disappearance, and as if on cue, "He vanished at the next station. On a whim I walked up and down the train twice, looking for him everywhere—he was nowhere to be seen." The *komivoyazher* refuses the offered game of cards, but he plays with aplomb and even bests his rival at that other game for two: conversation. He works as a passive agent and lets the stories come to him, for as Miron points out, "People will tell one their stories not because they trust one, but because they must speak, and there is nobody else who would listen" (275).

In watching and waiting, the commercial traveler proves himself the subtler con artist. After all, he is not what he appears but rather a writer in disguise. Is a writer so very different from a cardsharp?[38] By biding his time and waiting his turn (to play or speak), he succeeds at expropriating the cardsharp's tale for his own purposes. It becomes raw material for *his* literary product.[39]

No *Mitsve* Goes Unpunished: Jewish Cultural Specificity

Witnessing and/or perpetrating many scams has left the internal narrator chary enough to adhere to "a strict rule besides: no card games with strangers! I wouldn't sit down to play with you if you offered me the world . . . except, that is, for a little two-hand game of sixty-six." Sixty-six is different, he asserts: harmless, *heymish*, Jewish. The whole enterprise of cards is quintessentially non-Jewish, but he Judaizes it, confiding, "Just as a good Jew takes his tallis and tefillin with him everywhere, so I always have my cards" (210). Then he elaborates on the sociological reality of card play among Jewish traveling merchants: "It's a Jewish game, your sixty-six is. I don't know about you, but I like to play it the old way, with marriages worth twenty and forty. If I've won a trick, I can exchange the nine of trumps for the deck trump, and if I haven't, I can't. Fair enough, no? That's how we Jews play it everywhere, at home and on the road" (210). How unlike the elaborate protestations of social stigma that attach to gambling at cards in "Knortn"! He sandwiches his rather technical disquisition (a tipoff to his suspect mastery of the game, according to Miron) between assertions that "It's a Jewish game" and that Jews play it "everywhere" according to the rules he has laid out. In fact, according to him, the "Jewish" method of playing sixty-six is more consistently reliable than Yiddish newspapers or other Jewish cultural institutions. Just as "Cnards" captures a moment of economic transition, so "A Game of Sixty-Six" freezes a moment of changing social relations, whereby the meaning of Jewish affiliation shifts from a shared sense of religious norms and obligations to the seeking out of tribesmen with whom it is "safe" to socialize. It would be so unthinkable to play cards with non-Jews that the internal narrator can remark, "Well, there I was, sitting that winter day all by myself. I don't mean I was alone in the car; there were other passengers too, but none of them were Jews. What good did that do me? There wasn't a soul to play a game of sixty-six with" (212). The self-contradiction is more pointed in Yiddish, to greater comic effect: "*zits ikh mir azoy, heyst es, eyner aleyn. Dos heyst, nit eyner aleyn. Es forn nokh pasazhiren, nor nit keyn yidn*" (Y 163). I'm alone . . . I'm not alone . . . I might as well have been alone.[40] There are no casual social relationships with Gentiles on the train. Indeed, part of the frisson of train travel is the anonymity it affords and the liberation from a static, known community where "*yikhes*" trumps all; the attempt to "pass" fuels the comedy in more than one story, and indeed, it is a point of pride for the commercial traveler and many of his comrades to be able to recognize a fellow Jew, though he be dressed up "like eighteen *panies*."

One vestige of the commercial travelers' shared Jewish heritage is the moral vocabulary that envelops a deeply antinomian, *petit-bourgeois* relation to time, wherein it must be "killed." The internal narrator enumerates the problems with reading newspapers and holding conversations, insisting, "There's a better way than that to kill time on a train, and that's with a good game of cards. I mean with a game of sixty-six" (209). The Yiddish phrase is "*Di tsayt tsu fartraybn*," a violent verb meaning to "drive out." He goes on to say "that cards are the Devil's own invention—but on a long train ride they're a godsend" (209). The Yiddish juxtaposes the terms "*a yeytser hore*" (evil impulse) with "*a gan-eydn*" (a paradise). Whereas traditional religious Jews would recoil from wasting time (*bitl zman* or "idleness" is considered a sin, an affront both legal and moral) and maskilic Jews would seek to maximize and productivize their time, these economically and culturally transitional figures are content to playfully beguile the hours of the train ride.[41] Travel is like Hanukkah, when special rules apply and such frivolity is implicitly permitted. The idea of time as an empty expanse needing to be occupied shows how far these characters have moved toward a secularized consciousness, and it also reflects a picaresque temporal sensibility of formlessness, as opposed to the shapely time required for development and progress.

Rabinovitsh embeds his harshest expressions of skepticism in stories that turn on some deceitful manipulation of a Jewish ritual or a legally mandated act of communal or individual generosity. In "Knortn," it is the commandment to give charity. In "Der oyrekh" ("The Guest"), it is the injunction to extend hospitality to the stranger (who then absconds with the silver and the maidservant alike). In "Baranovitsh Station," the *mitsve* is redeeming the captive from the Gentile authorities, and in "Chabne," it's the whole set of legally mandated torts surrounding the guarding of another's property. The codes that have governed normative social behavior for this civilization across millennia have been rendered, everywhere Rabinovitsh turns his narratorial gaze, a liability.

II.

Seduction, which relied on the exploitation of a differential power dynamic between two parties, was the form of delinquency that most steadily preoccupied Isaac Bashevis Singer. His fictions invite us to consider the picaresque as a series of more and less successful acts of seduction. From the failed swindle in "A Game of Sixty-Six," it would be a relatively short jump to the failed seduction in Bashevis's *Mayse Tishevits* ("The Last Demon"). Indeed, the failure of the ruse in each of these "cool" monologues exposes its seams and calls for analysis. But in Bashevis's fictional worlds, both fantastic and realistic seduction most usually succeeds, so it makes sense to begin with a garden-variety case at the hands of an imp bent on destruction. Like some Emma Bovary of the *shtetl*, Tsirl of Krashnik is accustomed to repose nude before her mirror "for hours on end delighting in her beauty" and imagining that the bolted door of her sanctum "opened to admit either a prince or a hunter or a knight or a poet." So observes the narrator of Isaac Bashevis's short story "The Mirror,"[42] whose original title, "Der Shpigl: A monolog fun a shed," is far more informative. As the Yiddish title suggests, this story is a demon's first-person account of his advancement through the ranks of the underworld by successfully tempting a coquettish provincial bride. "Like a spider in its web," he installs himself in the mirror of her boudoir and waits, knowing that his prey is vain and, being childless, has ample time to sit and admire herself. After observing her ways, the narrator finally reveals his presence to Tsirl, who "was so surprised that she forgot to be frightened." A dialogue ensues, with the demon oscillating between romantic and playful tones. He quickly moves to disarm her fear of his frightful body—which is "black as tar, long as a shovel, with donkey's ears, a ram's horns, a frog's mouth, and a goat's beard"—by candidly admitting that his power is not physical but verbal: "'Fear not,' I said. 'I am an imp (*shretl*), not a demon (*shed*). My fingers have no nails, my mouth has no teeth, my arms stretch like licorice, my horns are as pliable as wax. My power lies in my tongue.'" He continues without pausing, "'I am a fool by trade, and I have come to cheer you up because you are alone'" (61). He implies that whereas a powerful body would be threatening, a powerful tongue poses only a negligible danger. This disingenuous reassurance is followed by what can only seem like a non sequitur in the English translation—how does a powerful tongue relate to being a fool by trade? Yet the treacherous connection between these clauses is readily apparent in the fuller Yiddish text: "*Mayn koyekh iz nayert in di leftsn. Kh'bin a badkhn, a lets, a freylekh-makher, an ibergedreyt shlesl.*" The phrase, "I am a fool by trade," compresses a whole catalogue of badinage: a wedding jester, a clown, a merry-maker, and a virtually untranslatable term of mischief that can only be rendered literally as "an upside-down zipper." The demon's verbal power is inextricably bound up in his persona as a joker. In his article on Bashevis's monologue stories, the great Yiddish critic Khone Shmeruk[43] lauds the author's use of demonic narrators who combine the jokeyness of the traditional Jewish wedding jester, the *badkhn*, with the erudition of the religious scholar. He writes,

> Such combinations give the speakers of these monologues that element of humour and buffoonery which belongs to the nature of demons who do not act from malice towards man. In this way we feel that behind the demonic, there is a touch of clowning and cleverness, corresponding to the use of the word *shed* in Yiddish as applied to human beings. (xix–xx)

Shmeruk is right enough in pointing out that the usage is *generally* benign, akin to calling someone "impish" or "puckish" in English. However, with respect to his observation that "behind the demonic, there is a touch of clowning and cleverness," I must argue that when it comes to the work of Isaac Bashevis Singer, the formulation is more accurately reversed: behind clowning and verbal cleverness, the author places a touch of the demonic.

The humor and litheness of such demonic speakers has led many critics to misapprehend a fundamental aspect of Bashevis's work. Elsewhere,[44] I have described how several critics have flattened these robust demonic speakers with psychological readings of these tales, in which a figured world[45] of externalized evil is reduced to the pathology that fits between a pair of human ears. Neither believing literally in demons himself nor expecting that his readers would, Bashevis nonetheless used the language of demons to illustrate something very real about the malevolent power of speech. Indeed, Tsirl of Krashnik falls so thoroughly under the verbal spell of her seducing imp that she zealously carries out his minute instructions in committing the sins that will most surely and swiftly earn her a place in hell. The story leaves her tormented in the underworld, at last fully cognizant of how much power lies in the tongue.

Tsirl is not alone in her misfortune. Bashevis gave free rein to his clever demonic seducers in a series of stories published in the early 1940s. In introducing the first of these, "Zeydlus der ershter" (translated as "Zeidlus the Pope"),[46] he anticipates publishing a collection to be known as the "Yeytserhore mayses" or "Memoirs of the Evil One"—mostly monologic tales told by demons about their verbal exploits among human beings. Four of the tales eventually appeared together, also in 1943, bound with a reissue of *Der sotn in goray*; surely these stories narrated by demons in the first person benefit from being read as a corpus. Together, they forge a distinctive vocabulary for discussing the besetting crises of Jewish modernity, including secularization, urbanization, and assimilation. The demonic lexicon satisfied Bashevis's aesthetic criteria for a Yiddish fiction set squarely in the precincts of the European past, as elaborated in his polemical essay "Problemen fun der yidisher proze in Amerike" ("Problems of Yiddish Prose in America"),[47] which also appeared in *Svive* in 1943. More immediately and more strikingly, they afford a way of speaking indirectly but nonetheless trenchantly about the cataclysmic destruction to European Jewry wrought by the Holocaust—while setting this monstrous new act of demolition over and against a process of communal crumbling already generations in the making. For Bashevis, the *khurbn* differed more in scale than in kind from previous instances of human evil. So many of his fictions are arranged as lopsided contests between various forms of positivism (religious, Spinozan) and the nihilism that quietly yet insistently negates them. In the manner of the modernist picaresque, he posits "a human existence that runs from birth without will to a death without choice" (Miron "Passivity and Narration" 345).

If the essential directive of modernism was Pound's injunction to "make it new!" then the antimodernist Bashevis understood the subversively shocking power of embedding the ancient, the venerable, the seemingly antiquated, in an ultra-modern literary landscape. It would take the minions of Satan and their "*Yeytser hore mayses*" to register—if only by the unspoken yet arresting contrast—the mid-century's efficient and sophisticated new technologies of evil. With its deep conceptual roots in rabbinic litera- ture as "the evil impulse," the *yeytser hore* develops in Yiddish literature into a moniker for the devil. Satan is often a clever conversationalist in the Yid- dish canon,[48] but Bashevis points to his speech *itself* as the distinctive means of evildoing. Human wickedness is not the result of an internal flaw or of imitating poor behavior, but rather of a relentless series of overpowering verbal seductions perpetrated by an endlessly clever and bottomlessly re- sourceful demonic speaker. Rather than inciting passion directly through visual or tactile stimuli, these minions work through the medium of speech. The demon stories are driven less by temptation, as some have argued,[49] than by seduction; that is, less by the dangling before the mark of desired outcomes than by the particular conversational pathways by which the devil seeks to make his case and consolidate control over his victim. Seduc- tion is a dual form of speech that constitutes both an act *of* saying some- thing and an act *in* saying something—to borrow the terms of J.L. Austin's classic discussion in *How to Do Things With Words*.[50] That is, the conversa- tional exchange attending a seduction is simultaneously *representational*, it's "about" something—philosophy, the beauty of the seduced, the palace of Lilith and Asmodeus, or the sin of adultery—and *executive* or "doing" something—namely persuading the seduced to the will of the seducer. Se- duction creates the appearance of a dialogue, which in turn implies the par- ity of the speakers. But in the case of demons who can harness the omni- science and near omnipotence of Satan, the exchange is just as lopsided as the mark's game of sixty-six with a cardsharp. To seduce literally means to "lead aside," an etymology underscoring the fact that seduction is really about the creation of a differential power dynamic rather than the adultery, blasphemy, or other sins that are its proximate and putative aims. Seduction works not only because the delights that it promises are compelling, but also because its representational qualities mask its executive power. The ap- parent neutrality of conversation, the assumed dichotomy between talk and action, offers persuaders a kind of immunity as they pose provocative ques- tions and utter sweet blandishments. The imp in Tsirl's mirror could indeed have appeared to her as a prince or a hunter or a knight, but he chose the guise of a homely beast with a potent tongue.

In the rabbinic view, with its injunction to "guard your tongue," speech is a critical realm of action independent of belief or intention. Both the le- galistic and the ritual emphases in this cultural framework tend toward full recognition of the illocutionary nature of utterance, which manifests itself in clearly prescribed and proscribed forms of speech.[51] The rabbis espoused a vibrant notion of *lashon hara*—slander—and its malevolent power, writing in a well-known Talmudic passage[52] that *lashon hara* kills three: the speaker, the hearer, and the subject of the slander. In the course of the same discussion, the rabbis imagine God sternly adjuring the human tongue to behave, reminding that wayward organ that it has been purposely immured behind the double protective wall of teeth and lips.

Employing his deft demonic speakers, Bashevis sets up a perfect contest between this cautious ethos and the seductive word fully unleashed; it is as if he had mentally parsed the phrase *lashon hara*—*loshnhore*, it would have been to him—and sketched with his pen a literal instantiation of the evil tongue. His human speakers are hapless, caught up in and trapped by their use of language. Correspondingly, his demons are peculiarly, even overweeningly, verbal creatures. The first-person narrator of "Mayse Tishevits" / "The Last Demon" refers to himself as "the master of speech" (185) and summarizes his task as *onredn tsu shlekhts* or persuading to evil, leading Martha Glicklich and Cecil Hemley, in their English translation, to render his self-characterization as "*der letster tsvishn di nisht-gute*" as "the last of the persuaders" (179). Suasion is related etymologically to sweetness, and indeed the demons' rhetoric is an aesthetic treat: sweet, pleasurable, voluptuous, and powerful. Playful masters of what might be called sleight of tongue, the demons employ rhetorical strategies including comedy, irony, equivocation, wordplay, antithesis, and flattery. The goal of this artistry is seduction, which Bashevis regarded as the quintessential human speech-act and one of the core varieties of interpersonal encounter. Verbal seduction is at once locutionary and perlocutionary, aiming to effect a form of capitulation, whether sexual, spiritual, or otherwise. It exploits and widens a differential power dynamic between two speakers. In the mouths of Bashevis's *shedim* and *shretlekh* (demons and imps), it usually succeeds.

It is especially instructive, therefore, to consider the unusual case in which the demons' methods fail. In "Mayse Tishevits," translated as "The Last Demon,"[53] a minor devil, more of an imp really, is sent from his normal beat in the small city of Lublin to the backwater of Tishevits, a village so small he says, that "Adam didn't even stop to pee there" (179). Dreading the anomie of provincial life, his only hope for making it back to the big-time is to corrupt the soul of a pious and brilliant young rabbi. The demon is a frustrated *pícaro* whose agency is limited by enforced stasis. As a delinquent, he more properly belongs with Rabinovitsh's charlatans who escape on the train and enjoy the free run of Jewish Europe. However, his boss has confined him to the purgatory of Tishevits until he can prove his powers of seduction. The only form of mobility—or agility—available to him is verbal. Things look bleak for this emissary of Satan. According to another imp, who has been subsisting idly in Tishevits for two hundred years disguised as a spider, the rabbi possesses a daunting combination of erudition and ascetic discipline:

> He's not yet thirty, but he's absolutely stuffed with knowledge, knows the thirty-six tractates of the Talmud by heart. He's the greatest Cabalist in Poland, fasts every Monday and Thursday, and bathes in the ritual bath when the water is ice cold. He won't permit any of us to talk to him. What's more he has a handsome wife, and that's bread in the basket. What do we have to tempt him with? You might as well try to break through an iron wall. (181)

Such an individual would seem proof against seduction of any kind, demonic or otherwise. His kabbalistic mastery presumably includes knowledge of how to ward off "the evil ones." A handsome wife completes the picture of contented virtue, depriving the devil of another foothold. To carry out their seductions, the demons require an opening; the three snares that work "unfailingly" by the demon's own account are "lust, pride, and avarice" (183). The *shed* from Lublin decides to start with the former. He and his newfound associate visit their target in the midst of his Talmudic studies. Taking his cue from the very phrase the rabbi is translating and explicating, the *shed* plays on *rokhl*, Hebrew for the name Rachel and a common noun meaning "lamb." After the first rebuff, he begins riffing on the *rokhl* theme, making his badgering more and more overtly sexual. The imp guides his mark through a set of word and concept associations (sheep~wool~girl~hair~pubic hair) that mimic the free association of an idle mind.

Perturbed, the mark resists his seducer:

> "Rascal. *Shaddai kra Satan*," the rabbi exclaims. Grabbing both of his sidelocks, he begins to tremble as if assaulted by a bad dream. "What nonsense am I thinking?" He takes his ear lobes and closes his ears. (182)

From the English translation, it would seem that the unnamed rabbi experiences the encounter as his own thoughts,[54] even as the awareness dawns on him that they may be the result of demonic temptation. He seems to take the blame on himself, wondering, "What nonsense am I thinking?" (182). In fact, though, the translators have elided the conversational nature of the encounter and rendered it as internal thought: the Yiddish reads, *Vos faln mir epes ayn azoyne shtusim?* The rabbi's question is actually not, "What am I thinking?" but rather, "What is happening to me?" The drama is staged not in the internal arena of thought but in the external one of event. Perhaps the best proof for this reading is in the earlobes. By stuffing his earlobes into his ears, the rabbi makes it clear that he experiences the crisis as an audible assault from "out there." Were it an internal, mental event, he might clasp or shake his head, but it would be pointless to block his ears.

The gradations of the rabbi's conversational responses prove illuminating. He initially answers without leaving the Talmudic register of speech. Jewish law is traditionally studied in pairs as a mildly adversarial spoken discourse. His questions "So?" and "Therefore?"—presumably spoken aloud—are terms with which one study partner might goad or draw out the logic of the other. This rationalistic legal discourse proves inadequate, however, to squelch the voice that continues to distract him. He angrily dismisses the *shed*'s evocation of an explicitly sexual image but is willing to argue calmly against the attempted calumnies of Biblical heroes for their alleged sexual misconduct. Finally, realizing the identity of his adversary, the rabbi abandons the sedate language of reason and adopts a kabbalistic formula with magical efficacy: "*Shaddai kra Satan.*" This phrase, which may be translated as "Lord, rend [the power of] Satan," was a kabbalistic acronym for the prayer "*kabel rinat amkha sagvenu, taharenu nora,*" or "Accept the prayer of your people, strengthen us, purify us, O Awesome One." It staves off the tempter, at least for a while. For now, the rabbi's language has won out over the imp's language.

A week later, the *shed* renews his efforts, setting aside lust in favor of vanity. There is no longer any pretense that the rabbi is thinking his own thoughts; now he clearly converses with a supernatural interlocutor. But which one? The demon poses as Elijah the Tishbite, the prophet charged with ushering in the messiah. Arguing that the rabbi of Tishevits is a scholar and saint of cosmic proportions, the demon encourages him to abandon the anonymity of his small-town post and take his rightful place as rabbinic leader of the generation. Needless to say, certain sacrifices will be required in the pursuit of greatness. But for one trained to humility and the vitiation of personal desires for the sake of heaven, the devil's rhetoric presents a genuine quandary:

"Who are you and what do you want?" the rabbi asks in terror. "Why don't you let me study?"

"There is a time when the service of God requires the neglect of Torah," I scream. "Any student can study the Gemara."

"Who sent you here?"

"I was sent; I am here. Do you think they don't know about you up there? The higher-ups are annoyed with you. Broad shoulders must bear their share of the load. To put it in rhyme: the humble can stumble. Hearken to this: Abraham Zalman was Messiah, son of Joseph, and you are ordained to prepare the way for Messiah, son of David, but stop sleeping. Get ready for battle. The world sinks to the forty-ninth gate of uncleanliness, but you have broken through to the seventh firmament. Only one cry is heard in the mansions, the man from Tishevitz. The angel in charge of Edom has marshaled a clan of demons against you. Satan lies in wait also. Asmodeus is undermining you. Lilith and Namah hover at your bedside. You don't see them, but Shabriri and Briri are treading at your heels. If the Angels were not defending you, that unholy crowd would pound you to dust and ashes. But you do not stand alone, Rabbi of Tishevitz. Lord Sandalphon guards your every step. Metatron watches over you from his luminescent sphere. Everything hangs in the balance, man of Tishevitz; you can tip the scales."

"What should I do?"

"Mark well all that I tell you. Even if I command you to break the law, do as I bid."

"Who are you? What is your name?"

"Elijah the Tishbite. I have the ram's horn of the Messiah ready. Whether the redemption comes, or we wander in the darkness of Egypt another 2,689 years is up to you." (184)

Much of the story's ironic humor turns on the absurdity of casting the rabbi of Tishevits in the central role in this cosmic drama. The rhetoric is terribly overblown: a host of notorious demons, named individually, lie in wait for this innocuous small-town rabbi, and a corresponding host of angels stands ready to protect him? *Him*? At just this moment, humanity has reached the nadir ("the forty-ninth gate of uncleanliness") that will summon the messianic savior? As if this pomposity weren't enough to tip off the reader, the *shed*'s speech ricochets from the flippant to the august and back again. The irreverent rhyme *onev gramt zikh mit zonev* suggests that nice guys finish last. An additional joke is the punning replacement of the Tishbite (the place-name that identifies the biblical Elijah) with the Tishevitser. "Only one cry is heard in the [celestial] mansions, the man from Tishevitz." Yet this inflated, mock-heroic tone—so obviously (to the reader) parodying such rhetoric—is credible language to the pious believer sitting at his book stand.

The demon has only to tap the available eschatological language[55] that is a genuine and deeply rooted part of Jewish tradition, which he does here with his endorsement of Abraham Zalman, a shadowy figure promulgated by Sabbatai Zevi as the "Messiah, Son of Joseph" or forerunner who, according to rabbinic tradition, must precede the advent of the ultimate "Messiah, Son of David." Abraham Zalman, who was in fact from Tishevits,[56] died a martyr's death in 1648.[57] The dark aspect of the joke lying just beneath the surface is the ludicrousness of the proposition that Jewish salvation could conceivably come from a small *shtetl* in Poland; instead of renown as hometown to the people's savior, this town is destined only for anonymity and finally, annihilation, to which "the last demon" will eventually bear witness. Bashevis drives home this joke by having the demon repeatedly refer to his mark as "the man of Tishevits" or "the Tishevitser Rabbi"—playing off the smallness of Tishevits against the gravitas such a phrase would seem to demand. This talk of imminent messianic salvation is euphonious music to the devout rabbi's ears, just as the devil's flirtatious blandishments were to Tsirl's.

Unlike all the other protagonists in this set of stories, the rabbi successfully resists his seducing demon. While humility plays a role, what ultimately saves the rabbi of Tishevits is the hold exerted on him by *talmud torah*, the study of holy writ. This activity constitutes the linguistic matrix in which he lives, and it is simply inconceivable to him that he should be asked to abandon it. Could any plan requiring him to forsake the Torah really be the will of God? Doubt niggles:

> Suddenly the rabbi says, "Forgive me, my Lord, but I require another sign."
>
> "What do you want me to do? Stop the sun?"
>
> "Just show me your feet."
>
> The moment the rabbi of Tishevitz speaks these words, I know everything is lost. We can disguise all the parts of our body but the feet. From the smallest imp right up to Ketev Meriri we all have the claws of geese. . . . For the first time in a thousand years I, the master of speech, lose my tongue. (185)

Although the demon has recourse to sweet-talk, clever rhymes, and many ornate Hebrew phrases, he is finally foiled by the rabbi's simple request. From a protean magician who was all tongue, the devil is reduced to being all feet. As Ken Frieden notes, "The demon's predicament is both subtly and profoundly comic: in Yiddish, the word *gendzn-fislekh* means both 'goose's feet' and 'quotation marks.' Asking for proof of the demon's authenticity, the Rabbi discovers that it is a mere quotation, an unsatisfactory imitation of sacred texts" (267). Because the rabbi is a true expert in traditional Jewish rhetoric, he possesses the ability to distinguish between the authentically sacred and the demonic pretender. As soon as the sage of Tishevits unmasks his interlocutor, he suspends the conversation, conclusively frightening away his potential tormentor by brandishing the kabbalistic Book of Creation. "What devil can withstand the Book of Creation?" (186) asks the narrator. Not through mental exertion, nor through moral amendment does the holy man of Tishevits vanquish his opponent, but by waving words before him.

Demonstrosities: Bashevis's Narrative Frame

Now we are free to remove to the framing story, which offers a fascinating counterpoint to the tale embedded within it. Just to review the mechanics of the whole narrative's construction: the tale of attempted seduction of the rabbi of Tishevits, totaling almost exactly half of the story, is embedded within the chronicle of the demonic narrator's arrival in town, encounter with an imp disguised as a spider, and eternal condemnation to remain in place (not going beyond the *tkhum-shabes*) after his failure. From this enduring and lonely captivity, the demon witnesses the Holocaust and liquidation of the town's Jews. The historical chronology is left intentionally indistinct, buttressed rhetorically by the fact that, as the narrator acknowledges, "I speak in the present tense as for me time stands still." There are two concrete if inexact temporal markers in the story: the Enlightenment and the Holocaust. The demon, when recently arrived in Tishevits, explains to the back-bencher imp disguised as a spider, "Enlightenment! In the two hundred years you've been sitting on your tail here, Satan has cooked up a new dish of kasha. The Jews have now developed writers. Yiddish ones, Hebrew ones, and they have taken over our trade. We grow hoarse talking to every adolescent, but they print their kitsch by the thousands and distribute it to

Jews everywhere" (181). So the attempted seduction of the rabbi of Tishevits takes place sometime between *Haskole* and *khurbn*, in a kind of mythic, present-tense time out of time. Perhaps it is something of a temporal equivalent to the kind of mythic space occupied by the burnished and warmly lit *shtetl* in the collective psyche of Bashevis's first readers.

In the 1980s, several narrative theorists thought a great deal about the significance of narrative framing or embedding stories within other stories. Conventionally, in the eighteenth- and nineteenth-century novel, the frame story suggests enhanced verisimilitude, shoring up a truth claim for embedded material whose veracity might otherwise be subject to doubt. By contrast, Bashevis's explicitly—and ironically—supernatural conversation between demons can hardly be thought to carry out this authenticating—or authorizing—function. Indeed, the narrator's aggressively diagetic nature implies that the idealized, armored-against-sin protagonist of the embedded tale is just as mythic and unreal, even as vulnerable, as his would-be seducer. Angela S. Moger[58] articulates the relationship between the two levels of narrative rather pointedly: "The function of the frame, then, would be to undercut the framed, to make clear that the central narrative's appearance of substantiality is an optical illusion, and to mock the pretensions of the conventional reading of such a story" (134). The existence of two narrative levels, argues Moger, redirects readerly attention so that "the frame compels the understanding that the story is *about* the telling of the story" (136). In the case of "Mayse Tishevits," the embedded story that the narrator recounts certainly does not redound to his credit; indeed, his entire aim in seducing the rabbi was to secure for himself a promotion to the Sin City of Odessa, all hope of which has now been lost, given a destruction so complete as to extend even to his dark employer. Moger's logic would suggest that Bashevis emphasizes the surviving demon's (he even denominates himself a *polit*, a survivor) recounting of an old exploit, not because of the psychodrama involved in the confrontation between demon and rabbi, but rather to call attention to the total—and now perpetual—isolation and desolation of the teller. Even the arachnid imp who presented himself as an interlocutor and coconspirator at the story's beginning has fallen wordlessly away by its end. In attempting to register the horror of the Nazi annihilation, then, Bashevis foregrounds not violence but silence: there are no partners left for conversations either conspiratorial or adversarial, no gullible marks to

be ensnared in verbal seductions. The Holocaust has amplified the demon's greatest frustration, articulated in miniature in the embedded story,
namely that "he becomes absorbed in a difficult passage and there's no
longer anyone to speak to."

Ross Chambers has been especially precise in delineating two kinds of
embedded narratives: narrational and figural. The former refers to placing
"narrative act within narrative act" so as to give rise "very frequently [to]
the mirroring within a story of the storytelling relationship itself" between
narrator, narration, and narratee (*Story and Situation* 33), a relationship that
in Chambers's broader account may be figured as a love triangle. We quoted
Chambers above as saying that narratorial seduction is capable of "producing authority where there is no power," and "is a means of converting (historical) weakness into (discursive) strength." The historical weakness that
pervades Bashevis's indirect rendering of the European cataclysm is palpable, but what discursive strength is marshaled here in this tale of Tishevits,
written in New York? Quite simply, it is Bashevis's authorship in the wake of
the Holocaust. This in turn brings us back to Chambers's second form of
embedding, which is figural and involves the replication of a figure or trope
in both the frame and embedded stories. In "Mayse Tishevits," that dupli-
cated figure is the Jewish book. The rabbi fends off his would-be seducer
with the *Sefer Yetsirah* and with his broader commitment to a life of Torah
study; as he cries out at his moment of near-capitulation, "Oh, but my soul
yearns for Torah!" At the end of the framing story, we are left with the corresponding image of the desolate *shed* sucking out a bare sustenance from
the Hebrew/Yiddish letters of a maskilic book discarded in an attic:

> I keep on reading gibberish. The style of the book is in our manner; Sabbath
> pudding cooked in pig's fat: blasphemy rolled in piety. The moral of the book is:
> neither judge, nor judgment. But nevertheless the letters are Jewish. The alpha-
> bet they could not squander. I suck on the letters and feed myself. I count the
> words, make rhymes, and tortuously interpret and reinterpret each dot. (186)

Some unspecified number of years after the *khurbn*, what remains? *Fort
yidishe oysyes*: true Jewish letters. Bashevis's indirect framing of the
narrative—this act of demon-stration (and demon monstration)—was the
best means the author, sequestered throughout the war in the heated rooms
of the Upper West Side, could fashion for showing rather than merely tell-

ing what had been lost. The Jewish book, however scandalous or heretical—the book in his readers' own hands—would have to suffice. The alternative lay in an attic in Tishevits, where

> *When the last letter is gone,*
> *The last of the demons is done.* (187)[59]

Stop-time; Animation

Allison Schachter describes the frame story as a staple of diasporic Jewish modernism, a device that draws attention to itself "in order to point to the representational limits of literary narrative" and so "capture the alienation of Jewish writers and readers" (12). In the rather leaden frame story surrounding "Mayse Tishevits," Bashevis paints a portrait of unyielding stasis not susceptible to amelioration of any kind. There can be no movement beyond the walls of the attic, and the *shed* will remain trapped in post-Holocaust time-out-of-time. If such a suspension of temporality and mobility seems extreme, consider that it was already implicit in Rabinovitsh's Kasrilevke stories, with their "nonlinear and therefore anti-modern conceptualization of time" (Caplan 128). Marc Caplan argues that

> The Kasrilevke stories invert and subvert all the conventions of the modern novel: they are static, drama-less descriptions, focused on a spatial collectivity, possessing neither individualized characters, other than the author's own modern yet folksy narrative persona, nor internal psychology; they are generally short, and even relatively longer examples from the genre . . . fragment into discrete episodes, instead of developing a thoroughly dramatized plot. (132)

This fragmented mode of storytelling bears out the picaresque vision of both Rabinovitsh and Bashevis. What mobility there is in the train stories is a tool for deception or a pitiless self-cancellation. Forward motion as most Yiddish authors conceived of it was deemed by these writers an impossible dream, one to be refuted with scenes of stasis or parodied with devices like Rabinovitsh's "Slowpoke Express." "In its stasis," argues Caplan, "Kasrilevke enables Sholem Aleichem's readers to see modernity for what it is, by exposing the illusory nature of modernity as a self-contradictory myth of progress" (133). Far beyond the Sabbath boundary of Kasrilevke, progress remained a risible notion to these most pitiless of Yiddish writers. If they distorted or stopped time, it was as if to insist that their readers scrub the past of nostalgia, the future of hopes founded on progress, and the present of sentimentality. Yet that is not to say that they limned inertial worlds lacking all dynamism. The card game, the swindle, the seduction—these are the loci of energy and animation in a picaresque world missing only the *pícaro*.

CHAPTER 2

LIVING SERIALLY
Neoteny and the *Polit*

> I have heard what the talkers were talking, the talk of the
> beginning and the end
> But I do not talk of the beginning or the end.
> There was never any more inception than there is now,
> Nor any more youth or age than there is now,
> And will never be any more perfection than there is now,
> Nor any more heaven or hell than there is now.
>
> Urge and urge and urge,
> Always the procreant urge of the world.
> —Walt Whitman, "Song of Myself" III

The comedy of Sholem Rabinovitsh, especially when read through Soviet critical lenses, was easy to misapprehend; to wit, the generally incisive critic Meir Viner[1] saw a body of work "imbued with faith in man and his future" (42). Regarding Rabinovitsh's formally picaresque novel, *Motl peysi dem khazns* (*Motl the Cantor's Son*), Viner discerned in the rollicking treatment of dislocation and immigration the author's testimony to "a faith in the progress of the human race, a hope for a better, more intelligent social order. He exhorted his readers to strive hopefully, not to submit to the obstacles before them, but to grasp hold of life, to work and demand their due" (43). Cheerful Motl is the most "light, bright, and sparkling" of Rabinovitsh's major characters, and Viner did not err in his sense of the novel's sanguine warmth. But *Motl* is about the joy of *letting go,* so all of Viner's effortful, tendentious (in the sense of holding on) vocabulary—"strive," "grasp," "demand"—is woefully misplaced. Educating his readers to strive for progress was decidedly not Rabinovitsh's aim.

In a 1968 interview with *The Paris Review*,[2] Bashevis left no room for doubt on his feelings about the same subject. Setting himself apart from other Yiddish writers, he observed, "Most of them believe in progress. Progress has become their idol. They believe that people will progress to such a degree that the Jews will be treated well, they will be able to assimilate, mix with the Gentiles, get good jobs, and perhaps be president one day. To me all these hopes are very little and very obsolete and very petty." In novel after novel and story after story, Bashevis dramatizes the paralysis of Jews who can see no fulfilling way "forward" into a secular modernity aiming at progress and no meaningful or intellectually satisfying way "back" to a traditional religion aimed at serving a God who may not exist and who certainly does not reveal His will to humans. Where other writers and thinkers might embrace the humanistic ideal of progress under the guise of communism, Zionism, or even scientific positivism or spiritualism, or sidestep it by way of aestheticism, Bashevis steadfastly refused all these expedients as half-measures at best.

In "Sharks and Marks," we began to explore the affinity between these two authors who wrote against the grain of the reflexive progressivism that animated most Yiddish literature. The juxtaposition continues now with an in-depth examination of Rabinovitsh's and Bashevis's presentations of time and how their alternative temporalities inform their respective deployment of the *polit* figure. By representing the course of human life in serial rather than progressive fashion, they disrupted the most basic plot: the child growing up. Whether understood as an ascending line from folly toward rational adulthood (the developmental view) or a descending line from innate wisdom to pedestrian knowledge (the Romantic view),[3] the process of maturation was imagined throughout the nineteenth century as a linear progression that could literally be plotted.[4] Modernists, on the other hand, embraced heterochronic depictions of a life's span, experimenting with novel means of representing the no-longer stable relationship between childhood and adulthood. Among a wide range of narrative strategies for resisting the linear plot progressions that correspond to progressive ideologies, these two celebrated Yiddish authors relied on such heterochronic or achronic techniques as the use of vignettes and "stills," iteration and repetition instead of development, and an emphasis on proliferation of persons and experiences instead of linear sequences charting growth and inner change. The essence of Rabinovitsh and Bashevis's modernist picaresque register is that it resists neatly arcing narratives of progress and development. But the fictions to which we turn in this chapter lay the strongest claim to the picaresque label because they are built around some variation of the *polit*, or Jewish *pícaro*. In each case, the *polit*'s relation to childhood colors and even drives the plot.

The authors under consideration here propose alternatives to conventional "coming of age" stories, such as a series of adventures that remain within the world of the eternal and changeless child (*Motl*), or else the *Tin Drum* or *Pinocchio* world of the perpetual man-child (Menakhem-Mendl, Hertz Dovid Grein, Herman Broder, and Yasha Mazur). This arrested development[5] in the modernist picaresque chimes with the unseasonable youth that Jed Esty associates with the colonial *Bildungsroman*, a narrative situation where, "In open and sustained violation of the developmental paradigm that seemed to govern nineteenth-century historical and fictional forms, such novels tend to present youthful protagonists who die young, remain suspended in time, eschew vocational and sexual closure, refuse social adjustment, or establish themselves as evergreen souls via the tender offices of the *Künstlerroman*" (3). These instances of narratorial heterochrony find their parallels in the realm of evolutionary biology, where the term refers to the slowed down, sped up, or otherwise anomalous development of an organism. One dimension of biological heterochrony is *neoteny*, a "holding on to youth" that complements and enriches the clinical but somewhat pejorative Freudian idea of "arrested development."

A tendency to manifest traits typical of the young of the species, neoteny is thought to confer a selective advantage in many organisms. A neotenous appearance signals vulnerability and thus may call forth extra care, protection, and even useful tutelage from mature members of the species. Aggressive behaviors that might be harshly repressed or defended against when enacted by adults are tolerated more patiently and corrected more gently in those who appear younger. Evolutionary biologists[6] have theorized that in humans, a prolongation of childhood arose in tandem with bipedal locomotion and increasing brain size; longer periods of juvenility meant a more sustained opportunity for education.[7] Ironically, when neoteny (also known as juvenilization) has been considered in relation to literary texts, it has pointed in almost the opposite direction: instead of underscoring the juvenile's dependency, it has posited preternaturally wise or able children or gestured at a privileging of the child-like on a scale of social values or as "the key

to child power—mutiny by mutation" (Honeyman 348). Either way, a re-
tarded or fitful developmental curve (or line or scatter of hard-to-connect
dots) means a long apprenticeship consisting of many episodes. I propose,
then, that neoteny is a defining feature of the *polit*—and a deeply held assumption of his social milieu—as imagined by both Rabinovitsh and Bashevis. Continuing to braid together their picaresque worlds, I shall focus in this
chapter on the titular characters of Motl (who remains suspended in time)
and Menakhem-Mendl (who refuses vocational closure and remains an (a-)
sexual enigma), as well as on the character systems dominated by pedomor-
phic man-children in *Shadows on the Hudson* and *Enemies: A Love Story*.
Thus, while exploring narratives that undermine notions of linear progress,
my own analysis will nonetheless follow a line of regression from child, to
child-like, to childish. The connotative continuum of these terms from neutrality to opprobrium underscores how maturity is measured against expec-
tations correlating to biological age.

Motl: And a Child Shall Lead Them

From the start of the novel that bears his name, Motl the cantor's son is set
on a typical picaresque course. At home, there is little money, an ailing father, and an emotionally wrecked mother. According to picaresque convention, these straits require his expulsion from home; but in this genial milieu,
he is not sent far away but only to the home of another cantor in town. Ostensibly, the boy is to serve as a cantorial apprentice, but he is mostly assigned to care for the host family's hunchback toddler. Motl's particular
dream of escape reveals the core difference between him and Lazarillo, or
any other classically conceived *pícaro*: "I have to get away. How? Where?
Home, of course" (112). While other *pícaros* dream of fleeing into the great
world, Motl dreams of running back to his family. When his picaresque
wanderings begin in earnest with the sojourn that will lead ultimately to
New York, he travels *en famille*. His individuation comes not through striking out on adventures of his own but through harboring a radically different
perspective than everyone else, a rapscallion child's view of the world. The
charming pastoral opening scene in *Motl the Cantor's Son*, where the eponymous hero frolics outdoors with Menye the calf, may be reconsidered as an
instance of play between two neotenes. The sympathy between boy and
beast is born of their synchrony, but with a pathos-inducing difference:
Menye the calf will be sentenced to death while Motl will be initiated into

life. Dan Miron has placed this biological theme of "death and rebirth, as connected and interdependent phenomena" (*Image* 226) at the center of the book's first unit.

The first two episodes—Motl frolicking with Menye the calf (for which he is smacked and teased) and the sale of the empty cupboard to raise money for his father's care ("Of all the things we sold, the glass cupboard was the most fun" [109])—are calibrated to illustrate how deeply Motl's desires and values diverge from those of the adults who surround him. Motl's differing scale of value owes more to his status as a child[8] than to any aspect of his individual character. Noting his role as a foil to the more "mainstream" grownups, Naomi Sokoloff[9] perceptively links this function with the picaresque tradition:

> [T]he status of the child as someone on the margins of adult activity recalls the marginality of the picaroon (who also often starts out on adventures at an early age, and whose naivete or incomprehension helps him cast social convention in an unfamiliar light). Mottel fulfills comparable functions of undermining established values and ways of speaking. By quoting adult words and transforming them into his own, the boy allows for a highly ironic view of the foibles and moral unsoundness in his society. (61)

The most significant transvaluation of values that Motl performs for his extended family is his embrace of the new—economic arrangements, technologies, entertainments, architecture—all without directing much animus toward the old. By dint of the child's plasticity and adaptability, "this narrative allows a more affectionate, less bitter satire of society than is characteristic of the picaresque novel proper" (Sokoloff 61). Sidra de Koven Ezrahi, who argues that "the Jewish migratory course throughout time and place is the very essence of Yiddish prose" (104), explains that Motl exchanges the curse of Jewish wandering for the blessing of Jewish mobility (105, 116). Lachrymose *golus* gives way to safe and prosperous Diaspora[10]—for those who intuit how to let go and enjoy the ride. Not yet in thrall to adult illusions of exerting control over one's life, a child can more easily summon the necessary measure of passivity. A still-developing brain is also more adept at learning the new language and assimilating new habits. Thus youth tend to be uniquely empowered in stories of immigrant experience,[11] inverting the customary subordination of children to adults.[12] In this way, immigrant novels recall the adolescent science fiction that Honeyman has analyzed, replacing "the associations of recapitulation (by which children represent our evolutionary past) with neoteny (by which children represent our evolutionary future)" (352). Both genres offer "emancipatory models" that view "children as evidence of evolutionary advancements" (Honeyman 348). Moreover, we might note that both also figure strange new worlds and thrive on tensions between the familiar and the "alien." In both of these genres of rapidly altered reality, children must perforce lead the way forward.

If the ideal vision of the fully formed adult is a clear one, then an immigrant narrative might map very neatly onto the basic developmental story of maturation.

> With the modern interest in individual development (expressed in literature through the popularity of *Bildungsromans*, or "coming of age" stories), nature and nurture conflated conveniently in popular discourse as well. Increasing literacy and organized education in the 19th century enabled further categorization of children in a seemingly measured linear progression from irrationality to rationality, concrete to abstract thought, immediate gratification to deliberate civility, all in service to a rationalist ideal of adulthood. (Honeyman 349)

However, modernist authors placed little faith in any "rationalist ideal of adulthood," so their immigration fiction could not be counted on to bear the child safely through adolescence and into adulthood. Motl is a boy in amber, no discernibly older or wiser after grappling with the loss of a parent, ongoing financial distress, tense peregrinations throughout Europe, a sickening sea voyage, witnessing other children's mortality, or tenement living in the Lower East Side, than he was during his initial gambol with Menye. Without the analytic instrument of the *polit*, Naomi Sokoloff nonetheless sees that this lack of inward development qualifies Motl as a Jewish *pícaro*:

> The picaroon's recasting of the world generally entails no internal agony of consciousness, and this point distinguishes the picaresque from the Bildungsroman as a genre . . . the picaroon learns but does not change. That is to say, the protagonist wises up, figures out how to play the game and to survive as a self uprooted and alone, but does not develop into a figure of complex psychological interiority. (62)

The plotting logic of *Motl* substitutes movement for growth.[13] Immigration or emigration might seem to promise a new beginning, whether a contented or tumultuous sense of *Aufbroch*.[14] But for Rabinovitsh, departure and arrival are circular, and a set of experiences that seem to demand narratives of progress (featuring movement, geographical change) are reinscribed in a circular loop that cannot be exited. To Ezrahi, this looping quality suggests a parody of the quintessential Jewish journey of epic return: "Its parody, the picaresque voyage, though ostensibly linear, is episodic in form and circular in direction . . . it issues in an implicit rejection of any utopian or epic resolution" (103). One of the aims of this account, of course, is to demonstrate that the picaresque is not "just" parodic in relation to the Jewish journey of return, but that it has a straightforward, modernist manifestation as well.

Sadly, Rabinovitsh died in 1916 before the novel could be completed, so it ends abruptly with Motl's family in New York, on the verge of upgrading from running a street kiosk to a more established corner "kendy staw." Nonetheless, one puzzles over how it might have even been possible to bring the family's adventures to full narrative closure,[15] for the book is inexorably concerned with middles that come to defy time. As Miron observes, "Instead of biography, the book is structured around patterns that violate the expected chronological and seasonal sequences and are governed instead by repetitions, analogues, and alternations between different rhythms. All of this points to movement as the ultimate reality of the work: movement rather than development and therefore perpetual movement" (253). There is no need—and no room—for the sort of reflection that comes with stasis, for recollection in tranquility.

Rabinovitsh intended Motl as a portrait of the artist as a young man, and that artist was originally supposed to have been a musician rather than the visual artist whose skills are blossoming as the narrative stops.[16] Had Rabinovitsh carried out his original plan, the novel would have joined *Stempenyu* and *Yosele Solovey*, and *Blonzhende shtern* (*Wandering Stars*) in probing the artistic formation and early lives of young Jewish musicians. Music functions, according to Miron, as "the residue of Jewish eastern Europe basking in the rays of its setting sun" (185); drawing, on the other hand, opens up a new chapter of freedom from such ancient ties as the proscription against graven images. Yet in another sense, the visual arts cannot represent unfettered, forward-looking freedom. After all, drawing leaves behind an artifact, and representational art of the kind Motl pursues *fixes* a moment in time. Thus, the visual arts register the anxiety of hurtling into the new, even for adaptable Motl. His doodles, an occasion for punishment in Europe, elicit more frequent and deeper laughs in America and come to be punished less and less severely by his brother Elye. Not only does Motl sketch and doodle, but like a true artist, he visualizes that which he cannot execute immediately. A lack of materials may stay his hand for the moment, but it cannot shut his eye. Tableaux like this one freeze the frame in a world of frenetic motion:

> If I had a fresh sheet of paper, I'd take some charcoal and sketch. This is what I'd put in my picture:
>
> A table. At the head of it sits my mother, her arms crossed on her chest. To one side of her is Brokheh—big and tall, with monster feet. To the other side is Taybl—a skinny little quarter of a chicken. Both are at work, one sewing and one knitting. My brother Elye sits at the table's end, a grown man with a beard. In one hand he's holding ah bahntsh kahdz and in the other some dahleh bilz. They're what he kehlehkted today.
>
> Pinye is hunched across from him, smooth-shaven, a real American. He's emptying his pockets of kvawdehz and nikelz. Being nearsighted, he brings every kvawdeh and nikl to his nose. Two piles rise high on the table, one of kvawdehz and one of nikelz. Pinye goes on counting. He reaches into his pockets for more coins. You can see that his pockets are still bulging. They look ready to burst. (305)

The passage quoted above constitutes a subsection unto itself. As if to underscore the fixative function of his artistic vision, the very next paragraph ushers in a new subsection with the declaration, "Nothing lasts forever" (ibid.).

The consciousness of the visual artist is necessarily the consciousness of the outsider, the participant-observer. A degree of abstraction is necessary in order to render a scene of hugs, smacks, and conversational exchanges in terms of line and composition. Motl's visual recording of the scene focuses our attention on Rabinovitsh's own mimetic tendencies, although these were more typically acoustic than visual. "His sentences are directed in the first place not to the eye, but to the ear" (Viner 46). Miron describes how Rabinovitsh felt pulled between the opposing poles of the emotive-lyrical mode of music and the satirical-mimetic one of visual art, a tendency that played out in his movement between comedy and lyrical pathos (183). The middle section of this novel, unfolding in cities across Europe and during the passage to New York, constitutes an album of stills or snapshots or a series of postcards ("moving pictures" in Miron's parlance, 250), their images filtered through a softer, warmer light than much other writing by Rabinovitsh. The episode or vignette is the rhetorical form that "fits" on these postcards. The commercial traveler of the *Railroad Stories* rues his inability to get a visual fix on the tragicomical "happiest man in all Kodny," reflecting, "It's a pity I'm not a photographer and don't travel with a camera. It would have been a great thing to have taken that Jew's picture" (151–52). In *Motl*, Rabinovitsh has found a way to take and display one picture after another.

Menakhem Mendl: Rabinovitsh's King of Iteration

By drawing—on paper and in his head—Motl isolates moments in time and so privileges the synchronic over the diachronic and progressive. His portraits and snapshots correspond to the narrative strategies of iteration and repetition, which elevate the serial over the sequential and developmental. Iteration and reiteration lie at the heart of the double-edged ethos of *never better!*: the comic buoyancy (here we go *again!*) coexisting with the tragic inability to, as the Soviet Yiddish scholar Max Erik[17] put it, "show a way out" or even to imagine one. The comedy that inheres in repetition owes to the energetic and mildly transgressive interplay between "a repressed feeling which goes off like a spring, and an idea that delights in repressing the feeling anew."[18] The rhetorical use of reiteration features prominently in almost every significant work of the fully fledged Rabinovitsh in his modernist mode, not only in *Motl* or the Kasrilevke stories but also in the Tevye cycle (which Meir Viner summarizes as five iterations of the same basic story),[19] the *Railroad Stories*, and various other monologues. *Wandering Stars*, which would seem to be a *Bildungsroman* on the Russian[20] and Western European model, is also protracted by iterations of experience. Menakhem-Mendl, as we shall discuss further, is a veritable king of iteration. Bashevis also trades heavily in iteration and repetition, featuring serial seductions, proliferating wives and mistresses, and redundant plots.

Citing Rabinovitsh's "rhythms of repetition" (138), Marc Caplan probes the way fragmentary, episodic forms reinforce that author's critique of ideological progress in his "sub-genre" of stories set in Kasrilevke. It is not surprising that he adopts the terms of the visual arts, noting, "Kasrilevke's function in these stories is to freeze the shtetl landscape in the instant of modernization" (133). The contrast between static Kasrilevke and careening modernity is rendered most glaringly in the epistolary novel that records the correspondence between scapegrace and *luftmensch* Menakem-Mendl and his loyal harridan, Sheyne-Sheyndl. With very few exceptions (where one episode might lead into another or build on a previous one), it would be possible to reshuffle the order of the episodes endured by the eponymous hero without any harm to the sense of the story.[21] Since each chapter involves another fruitless attempt to make a living, the book has lent itself to economically driven readings;[22] however, the episodes cry out just as urgently for a more genre-driven stylistic analysis. Taken together, they exemplify Sheila Ortiz Taylor's bead image, mentioned in the introduction, whereby the structure of the picaresque forms a bead necklace whose non-uniform episodes are strung together to constitute the plot. Menakhem-Mendl, who seems to finger the string of these beads without ever trying on the necklace, remains blessedly, hilariously unaware of the circularity of his own predicament. Sheyne-Sheyndl is the one blessed and cursed with longitudinal memory, writing, "Have you forgotten your Odessa Lumdums, and your Pottyboils and your Lilyfoots, and all your golden opportunities that are ashes in my mouth?" (40). The book's recurring joke is that Menakhem-Mendl believes each gleaming, new bead (the golden opportunity of an investment scheme or a questionable occupation) can supersede and outshine the last; he sees almost no accumulation. He instantiates Bakhtin's adventure hero on whom time (to say nothing of toil or wifely frustration) leaves no trace.

Menakhem-Mendl resembles the young of the species not in his readiness to be educated (as the biological theory of neoteny would posit) but rather in his perpetual ineducability. He moves about (and eventually beyond) the Pale in a self-created bubble, out of time and not susceptible to the teachings of experience. Although Kasrilevke is supposed to be the place whose temporal congelation is juxtaposed to the liquid onrush of modern development taking place "out there" beyond its borders, *The Letters* contrive to reverse this polarity. Family life marches on in "real time," without Menakhem-Mendl's participation. There could be no Menakhem-Mendl without the counterweight of Sheyne-Sheyndl, who reminds him ceaselessly if pointlessly of the procreation that ought to pull them both "forward" in linear time. Family life is centered, after all, around the growth and maturation of the children that parents have engendered. Seen from a distance, family life might manifest a cyclical aspect, but the fact of genetic recombination makes it new. Yet the *polit* cannot advance to fatherhood, as he must remain himself the child. In the case of Menakhem-Mendl, whose age is unspecified but who has already sired (three?) children, this requires a dereliction of paternal duty. This abandonment is the main bone of contention between husband and wife, and the tension grows yet tauter in *The Further Adventures of Menakhem Mendl*,[23] where his political screeds edge out any thought of the "merely" personal and familiar. In that sequel, he fails to even respond to the intelligence that Sheyne-Sheyndl's father has died.

As it is for the boy Motl, "Only the present is real" for man-child Menakhem-Mendl (Miron, 171). He is, as Miron avers, "a character singularly unaware of or unwilling to talk about his psychological underpinnings" (178). Even so, he cannot help a dawning awareness of himself as "a man with a story." As if independent of his agency or volition, events simply accumulate to him and, lubricated by his ongoing loquacity, become a form of capital. By the time he makes his pitch to the insurance inspector-general, Yevzerel, he knows at least that there is a "whole story" to be told:

> Well, I told him everything, the whole story: how I was bound from Kishinev, and ended up in Odessa, and dealt in Londons until I moved to Yehupetz, and worked on the Exchange buying and selling Putivils and Liliputs and other stocks & bonds, and traded in sugar, real estate, and lumber, and tried my hand at matchmaking, and even had a fling at writing. There was nothing in the world, I told him, that I hadn't knocked my brains out doing and I still had nothing to show for it. Once a loser, always a loser! (98)

Although Menakhem-Mendl's own rhetoric flattens out and devalues his experience ("nothing to show for it," "loser"), his interlocutor listens at the meta-level and sees possible utility in his gift of the gab. Yevzerel responds, "I like you. I like your name and I like the way you talk" (98). With some refinement and guidance, Menakhem-Mendl's status as "a man with a story" might even be helpful in selling insurance. This interaction sets the pattern not only among characters within the book but also the dynamic between character and reader. The psychological richness and depth inheres in the work, but not in the character or in his self-awareness. "One must develop a Menakhem-Mendl grammar," urges Miron, "and regard the letters as exercises in a new language in order to see how, in this char-

acter, Sholem Aleichem seemed to be able to do something and its opposite at one and the same time" (178). Without undergoing an "internal ag-
ony of consciousness," Menakhem-Mendl points the way to one for his
readers. In this respect, he is a transitional figure to a more fully imagined
modernist picaresque.

Shadows on the Hudson: The *Polit* Out of Time

Isaac Bashevis Singer's long novel *Shadows on the Hudson* ran twice weekly
in *Forverts*, from January 1957 through January 1958.[24] Set a decade before
its publication, this panoramic yet intimate book follows a group of European Jewish refugees loosely bound together by social and familial ties but
doubly isolated by traumas resulting from the Holocaust and the strain of
the immigrant experience.[25] In economic terms, Hertz Dovid Grein, the
character at the novel's center of consciousness, is a tragically actualized
Menakhem-Mendl:

> Grein regarded this prosperous business of his, like everything else that had
> befallen him during the years he had been connected with the firm, as a sort of
> perpetual and self-renewing miracle. He had gone into investment brokering
> after teaching in Talmud Torahs had driven him into a depression, and at a time
> when he had been so ignorant about financial affairs that he had no idea of the
> difference between stocks and bonds, capital shares and securities. The oppor-
> tunity had arisen as if the powers who watch over each individual, and for
> whom no trivial detail is unimportant, had decided that the time had come for
> his rehabilitation. (194)

But this effortless financial success—which forever eludes his Kasrilevke-
born forbear—affords Grein little happiness. Prosperity only enables a set
of romantic entanglements that ought by right to be practically, if not morally, impossible. In fact, the serial quality of Menakhem-Mendl's vocational
life, always on the cusp of success but never quite reaching it, chimes with
the asymptotic love life of the transplanted stock broker.[26] Neither character
matures into a stable adult, and both lead lives dominated by the arrested
aspects of their development. *Shadows* serves as the blueprint for several of
the novels Bashevis will write in and about America.[27] It is the most fully
realized portrait of the disillusioned, love-seeking, tormented, and finally
repentant émigré—his version of the *polit*.

"Regression may be a balm for the disappointed,"[28] and the characters that populate these postwar New York precincts are nothing if not disappointed. Grein, fortysomething, married, and already fitfully attached to a longtime mistress, has spent the past year fantasizing about thirtysomething Anna, herself trapped in a desultory second marriage, to a Warsaw barrister unemployed in America and considerably her senior. Setting the plot in motion, their romance gathers momentum at a party hosted by Anna's widowed businessman father, Boris. After Hertz drives the estranged couple home from Boris's Upper West Side home to their own Lexington Avenue apartment, he and Anna end up absconding to a hotel in the wee hours and consummating their mutual attraction. The rise and fall of their adulterous romance, which includes a months-long sojourn in Miami Beach, defines the book's first part. The love affair, promising to restore to both parties their youth in interwar Warsaw, is a nostalgia expedition, an indulgence in regression, and a willful abrogation of adult responsibilities to spouses, children, and parents alike. There is a childish quality that asserts and reasserts itself in each of them, especially in relation to the other. This is borne out by recurring rhetoric[29] that dwells on the juvenile traits of both actors.

Based in nostalgia, their relationship reverses the natural sequence of time; instead of maturity, they seize what seems like a chance at a do-over on youth. Early on in the story, Anna is barely aware of her own heterochronic impulses: "She was bashful, but not in the way adults are bashful. She seemed to have lain down to sleep as a young girl and mysteriously woken up a mature woman. Meeting Grein after a separation of twenty-three years had brought both hope and bewilderment into her life. Layers of time had been inverted and confused by a harrow that plowed up and turned over the earth of ages and epochs" (16). Time is figured as sedimentary, so that its harrowing represents a disruption of geologic scale. The usual hegemony of passing time is indeed challenged and even rendered absurd for these characters: Anna's stepmother is not much older than she, and she has an affair with a friend of her youth who has children of marriageable and childbearing age—to whom she herself might ostensibly become a stepmother. It stands to reason that Grein, who will show himself over the course of the novel to think more spontaneously and with less advance planning than Anna, experiences heterochrony more locally, as he starts "kissing her with childlike eagerness and the heedlessness of those for whom day and night have been turned upside down" (54).

Curiously, there is little imagery that speaks to Hertz and Anna's re-experiencing childhood or adolescence together, as peers; instead, they are cast as parents and children to each other. This is true not only of their affair but of several other romantic relationships described in the novel. Bashevis's women are either forbearing "mommies" to their men or self-indulgent libertines. Grein regards his long-suffering wife Leah as "his ideal of what a wife should be. She was like his mother and grandmother, who were the pattern for the image of the virtuous woman he took with him from his father's house" (75). Watching her in their kitchen, "Grein gazed at Leah, observing her every movement. He felt like a child sitting and contemplating his mother" (83). Leah, Grein reflects, "had always been the mother, even before she had children" (140). It is striking that selfish, girlish Anna had borne a similar relation to Cesare, the Italian Jewish youth with whom she enjoyed a fling between her first and second marriages. "He never stopped calling Anna 'Madre' or 'Mamma'" (144), she confesses, and "I was left with the feeling that I was his mother, even though I was only six years older than he was" (122). Grein's mistress Esther, who is generally presented as a well-educated, articulate Scheherazade, nevertheless falls into sarcastic maternal blandishments when welcoming Hertz for the first time since he has taken up with Anna: "Here he is, the great Casanova! Well, little boy, come closer. Don't hide by the door. Mommy won't spank you!" (92). But the roles are fluid, and Esther can play the petulant girl who demands that Grein tell her bedtime stories so she can sleep (95). In introducing the concept of neoteny, we noted that part of its selective advantage may lie in the tolerance that a neotenous appearance elicits for immature behaviors that would otherwise be suppressed or punished. A resigned Esther captures perfectly the various dimensions of Hertz's neoteny, fuming, "I ought to be angry with you Hertz. I ought to be your worst enemy, because you've ruined me. . . . But one can't hate you. You're just a big, helpless child. You trample on people the way children step on toads or worms" (97). In this compressed effusion, she articulates the pedomorph's heterochrony, helplessness, and unwitting power without corresponding judgment or self-control. This mother-son dynamic obtains even in the book's most serene and fruitful union, the nonromantic but very high-minded self-arranged marriage that Boris forges with the widow Frieda Tamar. When Boris confesses a business reversal involving a bad investment that threatens to destroy their financial security, his wife responds less as peer than as forbearing mother: "Frieda's face retained the amiable expression of tranquility and mild reproof of a mother whose child confesses to her that it has lost a toy or broken a bauble" (337). Male-female partnership is deeply imprinted as a displaced parenting relationship.

Never the Procreant Urge of the World

The task of fatherhood cannot be central to the identity of the *polit*, who either remains childless (pointedly *choosing* to do so in the work of Bashevis) or else takes such a lackadaisical or distant attitude toward his existing children as to vitiate his paternity. Menakhem-Mendl, Hertz Dovid Grein, and Herman Broder are all indifferent fathers. In Bashevis's survivor novels, the lack of desire to procreate is elevated to a principle ("What for? So that the Gentiles will have someone to burn?" Herman parries when Tamara urges him to have a child with Yadwiga; *Enemies* 101[30]). In the 550 pages of *Shadows*, Grein evinces almost no recollections of fatherhood. His daughter Anita seems to swim into his consciousness only when he becomes aware of her as a sexual being entertaining a lover—and then it is only to deplore her promiscuity! It is telling that he experiences this moment as the ultimate heterochrony, a complete reversal of generational roles: "The tone of voice she employed made it seem as if she, the daughter, had through some kind of witchcraft become the adult and he, the father, had been reduced to a clumsy boy" (367). He has no psychic resources on which to draw *as a parent* in a situation that casts his own choices in such a glaring light.

The women attached to Bashevis's *polit* figures almost always want children. Tamara Broder states as an axiom to Herman, "If a woman loves a man, she wants to have his child" (*Enemies* 103). Indeed, when Masha believes that she *is* pregnant with Herman's child, she becomes "inappropriately babyish" (ibid. 135).[31] Anna initiates a conversation with Hertz about family planning by appealing to their (ostensibly) shared maturity and noting, "We're not children." Her point is that they need to plan for economic security in order to raise a family, a goal Hertz resists (124). Esther expresses regret at not bearing Hertz's child and acidly predicts that he will have children "with Boris Makaver's daughter," to which he replies just as darkly, "I won't have any more children with anyone" (220). Anna makes herself a similar promise early on in the novel (114), but by its end is contemplating establishing a family with her first husband, Yasha Kotik. The fact that the desire is mutual owes to Kotik's crassness; he concedes that although his once and future father-in-law loathes him "as if he were a cockroach[32] . . . if he gave the crabby old bigot a grandchild, he'd come around" (495). Morris Plotkin, the equally crass but far more genial hedonist who is married briefly to Esther, goes so far as to proclaim, "One ought to have kids. Since we take from the world, we oughta give somethin' back to it" (357). Kotik muses blithely, as he envisions a future with Anna, "He'd give her a child or two so that a couple of new souls could wander about" (428). Engendering children, the novel seems to imply, is well and good for men too shallow to care much about anything anyway, but more refined souls like Hertz recoil at the thought. The only man of any moral seriousness to bring forth life is Boris Makaver, who dispels some of his depression at financial reversals by reassuring himself, "If my wife expects a child, it's a sign that heaven wants me to live" (338). Yet even earnest Boris is shown in a more crassly jokey mood than usual when he winkingly refers to grandchildren as "profit."

Endless Flight

At the center of this long novel chronicling a two-year period is a chiastic exchange whereby the omniscient narrator underscores the process of immature Anna coming into her own, as Grein remains essentially changeless but perceives himself to be declining. The contrast is stark, as Anna matures into a steely, savvy woman who "had lost all her uncertainty, her terror, her feeling of being trapped in a dead end or an inescapable impasse" (341). The narrator goes on to cite her release from the mésalliance with her second husband, the helpful inheritance of his death benefit, and the acquisition of new practical skills such as driving and an education in the rudiments of the American real estate business. Anna is no longer willing to accept situations that don't accord with her sense of *comfort*, an axiom equally germane to money matters and matters of the heart:

> The chief rule was to do whatever one did as comfortably as possible. Talking had a different effect when one was sitting in a comfortable chair from when one was standing in a filthy telephone booth choking for breath; one did business one way when one had money in the bank, and another when one grasped for every penny. Even in love, one dared not be totally dependent on the person one loved, Anna reflected. If he thinks you're dying because of him and he's everything in the world to you, he walks all over you, even if he's in love with you. One must always keep a trump card in reserve. (343)

In short, she has discovered the American idea that nothing succeeds like success. The trump card she holds in reserve is Yasha Kotik, who abused and sexually humiliated her during their first marriage in ways about which even this most risqué of Yiddish novelists remains coy. Shorn of illusions, she fully expects him to cheat on her should they remarry. But this time, she reasons, she would drive a different sort of bargain: "She would pay him back in the same coin. As long as she was comfortable with him, she'd stay with him; if it became too difficult, she'd get rid of him. Meanwhile, she'd snatch a few years of happiness" (491). Eventually, the novel will find Anna cohabiting with Yasha Kotik in the "old" apartment on Lexington, the home she made with Luria during their union. Where her father's West Side apartment seeks to recreate the heavy furnishings of his Warsaw rooms, Anna's décor is a study in modernism with "everything chosen for the comfort of the guests who smoked, drank, and did not remain long in the chairs assigned to them" (34).[33] Such entertaining—and such comfort—may have been merely aspirational during her years with Luria, but Kotik's reentry into her life and her living space actually brings about the planned-for and dreamed-of party.

Neither superficial happiness nor true maturation is available to Grein, however. All he can hope for is the fantasy of flight: "Well, I'll just disappear, Grein told himself. I'll leave everything and run away" (351). It is no accident that Anna begins to amass her fortune and to rebuild her father's through real estate. Newly self-possessed and confident, she goes in for all things solid and immovable, while Grein has built his bit of prosperity, in true Menakhem-Mendlesque *luftmensch* fashion, on stocks. Finally (or perhaps only cyclically) cut loose by the end of his affair with Anna, Grein embraces dream of flight that has been "an idée fixe" for him since boyhood:

> Very often he had tried to calculate the minimum a person needed to get by, reading with particular interest articles about the diets of different peoples and about families forced to live on a limited budget, counting every penny. Grein often imagined that he lived alone in a dirt cheap apartment without heating or a bath, owning nothing but a bed, a table, a few utensils, some books. His clothing consisted of a pair of inexpensive denim trousers, a sweater, a pair of stout shoes, a few shirts that he himself washed in the sink. He ate black bread, potatoes, porridge with milk, and occasionally a piece of fruit or some vegetables. Everything—food, clothing, expenses—was reduced to the essential: He went nowhere, telephoned no one, wrote no letters, visited and received nobody. He

needed only two thousand calories per day, a blanket to cover himself, a piece of soap, and a library card so he could borrow books. He had settled his accounts with the world and had even learned to control his sex drive. He had saved enough to eke out an existence and be free from all care, all haste, all competition. (351)

Where others might dream of luxury, Grein wallows in fantasies of abstemiousness and isolation. Although the physician Solomon Margolin expresses skepticism about Grein's ability to live out such a fantasy ("You'll run away for a year or two, and then that, too, will become boring. That's because there's nowhere to run to" [448]), we do well to consider how close the protagonist comes to having executed this vision in the book's epilogue. Yet for all the novel's exhaustively enumerated specificities, an unanswerable question lies at its center: is the reader witnessing a unique chain of events in Grein's life that lead to a conclusive break with his past and an enduring new life cut off from the New York émigré world, or are we simply catching him along one stretch of an endlessly repeating cycle or spiral? In other words, upon reaching the book's end, what happens next? An aspect of the book's picaresque sensibility is its lack of closure, despite its heavy-handed, authoritarian ending.

Proliferation, Repetition, and Interchangeability

Shadows on the Hudson is, in formal terms, a twentieth-century realist novel rather than any kind of picaresque. Yet we may make a further claim for reading Grein as a *polit*[34] given how proliferation and interchangeability order—or disorder—his life. He commits himself to three women simultaneously, desiring flight *with* two of them and finally *from* all of them. He inserts each partner in turn into the never-ending, self-involved fantasy of escape that plays ceaselessly in his own psyche: "He had always wanted to hide away somewhere: in an attic, in a cellar, in a cave, on an island. Over the last few years he had fantasized about living on a yacht moored near a deserted reef somewhere in the Pacific. There had been a time when he wanted to have Esther on board this yacht with him, but now he wanted Anna" (85). Women and locales revolve for Grein on a sort of lazy Susan of the mind, as the omniscient narrator reflects, "This same fantasy repeated itself with variations. Sometimes he imagined himself in New York, on the

East Side; at others on a farm in Canada or South America, where every-thing was cheap and life was quiet, full of timeless repose. Sometimes he planned to settle on a tropical island somewhere, like Gaugin; at others in Palestine on a kibbutz" (352). For Grein, as for the adventure hero of Bakh-tin's account of the premodern novel, time and place are "highly intensified but undifferentiated" (FTC 90). To this spatial and temporal interchange-ability, this modern character adds the interchangeability of persons. Time, place, and persons collapse together, as when Grein squeezes in a visit to Esther on the eve of his Miami Beach departure with Anna and muses on the subway, "Wasn't the whole of life a trip exactly like this one? Wasn't Anna just another subway station on an undeviating journey through time?" (89). When Grein later enacts a similarly impulsive flight with Es-ther on the eve of Rosh Hashana, this time north to the Berkshires, the re-iteration is so absurd as to seem darkly humorous. Grein's actions are never as nuanced as his thoughts. In a moment, he turns rigidly pious *and* vege-tarian, but in the span of a single weekend is completely given over (once more) to hedonism and libertinism. Again there is the matter of the epi-logue, which finds him living in Jerusalem's Meah Shearim, willing himself to replicate his father's pious behavior without actually believing in its theo-logical underpinnings.[35] Peter Herman characterizes Grein's eventual mo-dus vivendi as "chilling" (167), which may be too Protestant and belief-driven a view for this drama of action-driven Jewish identity. But Grein's choices are certainly extreme and antinomian, and his "re-becomings" turn the drama of becoming—the basis of the traditional *Bildungsroman*—into an absurd joke.

The novel's insistent heterochrony builds toward an overwhelming sense of belatedness, which culminates at a birthday party for Boris and Frieda's one-year-old at which the birthday boy is the only child present. The gathering recapitulates the party that opened the novel, set two winters before, but all is now transposed to a tragic register.[36] Grein is absent, of course, Luria is dead, and Professor Shrage's meager existence has been snuffed out, by age and sorrow, like the candle that his name would suggest. The bleakest moment, though, is when Frieda pulls Dr. Solomon Margolin into the nursery to examine her son, in whom she has noticed the signs of Down's syndrome. She is filled with regret over her decision to bear a child in her forties, dreading the pain his condition will cause her husband. In fact, the phrase "too late" (*tsu shpet*), runs like a leitmotif throughout the novel and defines its desultory mood.[37] Ironically for a novel of the Jewish experience set in 1947–48, these characters have not, in Franco Moretti's formulation, used time to find a homeland.

The looping, undifferentiated quality of Grein's time calls to mind a temporal category that Mikhail Bakhtin associated with the Greek romance, but which he allows to have entered the subsequent European novel via historical fiction.[38] The "adventure-time" that Bakhtin contrasts with national-historic time unfolds when "the normal sequence of life's events is interrupted" (FTC 95), and it implies a passive attitude typical of the *polit*:

> These points provide an opening for the intrusion of nonhuman forces—fate, gods, villains—and it is precisely these forces, and not the heroes, who in adventure-time take all the initiative. Of course the heroes themselves act in adventure-time—they escape, defend themselves, engage in battle, save themselves—but they act, as it were, as merely physical persons, and the initiative does not belong to them. Even love in unexpectedly sent to them by all-powerful Eros. In this time, persons are forever having things happen to them . . . ; a purely adventuristic person is a person of chance. He enters adventuristic time as a person to whom something happens. But the initiative in this time does not belong to human beings. (FTC 95)

Granted, the character of Hertz Dovid Grein is hardly an unreconstructed Greek adventure hero, but for all of his modern subjectivity, he does bear a striking resemblance to the sort of premodern person that Bakhtin describes. Ricocheting from woman to woman and from locale to locale, he behaves as a merely physical person to whom love is "sent" and to whom things happen by chance or *as if* by chance. His attempts to seize initiative are mostly risible and merely launch him, with the convert's zeal, on new regimens that he cannot maintain. Insofar as this worldview devalues human initiative, it also decenters the human being in relation to worlds much smaller and larger than he. Traditional religion of the kind that Grein struggles to believe in is conceived on a human scale in relation to a superhuman deity. But, he muses, "What if, God forbid, the unbelievers were right? the profane thought flashed through his mind. According to them, there was nothing: no God, no World to Come—merely atoms, electrons, blind forces. One was born and one died, to no purpose. Human beings were no better than dust" (489). Until the twentieth century, Bashevis implies, the alternative to religion was humanism. But modern physics threatens, as has every scientific revolution,[39] to relegate human beings to a marginal place in the universe, and it is this threat that terrifies Grein. He perceives his soul to be assailed by boredom, and he muses darkly, "Boredom begins in the atom." Under quantum theory, the atom "throws itself about like a demented thing, twisting and turning without stopping," an unrest that he takes as "the ultimate symbol of man today" (183).[40] Apprehending the unrest encoded in the most basic atomic building blocks of the universe, Grein is thrown back on his own kind of ineluctable, unpredictable motion through space and time. Rather than imitating God, he imitates the atom, which lands him in a farcical update of adventure-time. As Bakhtin points out, "Greek romance-time does not have even an elementary biological or maturational duration" (FTC 90). Grein is on the lam from individual maturation.

At the same time, Grein speculates on the Jewish collectivity—rather than the individual—as the more fitting subject of developmental or maturational discourses. Grein's existence has negated itself, he believes, because it has not fructified forward into a Jewish future: "Whether Grein himself became an observant Jew again or not, he had snapped the chain of generations, mixed his blood with the blood of the enemies of Israel. He, Hertz Dovid Grein, was a last twig on the Jewish tree. Whatever might happen to Jews in general no longer had any bearing on him" (418). He implicitly imagines "Jews in general" as a sort of collective *Bildungsheld*, subject to maturation and improvement; the mythopoeic Jewish story is a *Bildungsroman* of uncertain denouement. For his own family, he imagines, it is too late, announcing resignedly to Margolin that, "The future of the Jews no longer has anything to do with me. My grandchildren will be Gentiles" (445). In historical retrospect, Grein and Herman Broder appear to have embraced an unwarranted fatalism about the future of Judaism in America. Their authorial creator seems to have been aware, albeit perhaps suspicious, of the hybrid vigor that could be infused into the community through marriages to women like Jack Grein's Patricia and even to Herman's Polish Yadwiga, women who are unambivalent about motherhood, inquisitive about the religion, and determined to raise their children within its consoling if demanding framework.

"Swindle, swindle, bubble, bubble": Two Picaresque Yashas

We have considered several aspects of Hertz Dovid Grein's claim to the mantle of the modern *polit*: his inability (or refusal) to mature into settled adulthood, his undifferentiated or heterochronic experience of time, his indifference toward fatherhood, his idealization of flight, and above all, his resistance to being educated by experience. Yet he is an attenuated *pícaro* who has enjoyed, perhaps, just a little too much personal safety and material security to fully represent the figure in question. A more full-bodied, classically picaresque character lurks in Bashevis's fictions, traipsing from Manhattan to Coney Island, from *Shadows on the Hudson* to *Enemies: A Love Story*. That is the comic actor and war refugee Yasha Kotik. His role is more prominent in *Shadows*, but he serves some critical plot functions near the climaxes of both novels, and it is worth looking more closely at how Bashevis uses him, for he may be the true *polit*.

It stands to reason that Grein flees with traveler's checks and stock certificates, while Kotik carries wads of cash, stashed on his person. Kotik must remain totally liquid because he is, first and foremost, an *agent of circulation*. He insinuates himself into all kinds of company, moving comfortably among and beyond subgroups of European Jewish immigrants, artsy theater folk, and the prosperous patrons who fund their ventures. Dickens might have written such a character, slipping in easily among high and low alike. In *Enemies*, word of Masha's death comes to him in a dream. He links Masha with Pesheles, and thus with Herman's peasant wife Yadwiga, who has visited the Broders in Coney Island. In *Shadows*, he has been married to Anna Makaver, and he regains entrée to her circle when he acts in a play being produced by Morris Plotkin, who marries Grein's longtime mistress Esther. He facilitates contact, whether desired or not, and thus also carries contagion. He attends (or throws) every party; circulating, he sows fear in a world of men with something to hide. Grein and Broder are serious men with serious sins, the kind of which Kotik makes light of as both a matter of conviction and profit; to him, nothing is sacred.

Despite his appearance as a clown ("outlandishly dressed in a variety of loud colors," *Shadows* 247), Yasha Kotik is the rare man in these pages who remains virile without being a man-child. He might give off the initial appearance of a neotene, but as a performer engaged in physical and verbal comedy, he rather calculatingly commodifies his humor and child-like lack of inhibition. Anna catechizes Grein in the importance of "having a plan" as a marker of maturity, and Kotik surely has a coherent if self-serving plan. He can contemplate fatherhood because he is so blithe about everything, including procreation. He has truly played the Scheherazade, repeatedly staving off death through his clowning:

Everything about him moved with acrobatic agility. His face was in constant motion, grimacing and mimicking simultaneously. He raised one eye in mock surprise while the other one drooped as if crying. He inflated his nostrils. Herman had heard a great deal about him from Masha. It was said he told jokes while digging his own grave and the Nazis had been so amused by him that they let him go. Similarly, his buffoonery also stood him in good stead with the Bolsheviks. He had been able to overcome countless perils with his gallows humor and comic antics. (*Enemies* 219)

By nature and by vocation, Kotik is a clown or *komedyant*. Pleasure-seeking, verbally adept,[41] and willing to exploit others, he is morally bankrupt and yet somehow appealing—at least to a disillusioned fatalist like Anna. If there are to be New Jews in America, they will arise from the combination of Kotik's insouciance with Anna's drive. As if to confirm Bashevis Singer's disdain for the *komedyant*,[42] the author awards this figure the last place in his catalogue of modernity's evildoers. Reciting a similar catalogue, the penitent Joseph Shapiro excoriates his assimilated brethren, who "revere all kinds of murderers, whores, false prophets, clowns."[43] In the passage from Europe to America, the seducer par excellence has metamorphosed from Satan and his minions to popular culture and the entertainers who promulgate it.

Bashevis's most formally picaresque fiction, *Der kuntsnmakher fun lublin* (*The Magician of Lublin*),[44] also places a *polit* named Yasha at its center. The eponymous Yasha Mazur gazes into his beer early on in the novel and murmurs, "swindle, swindle, bubble, bubble" (E 15; Y 14). Over the novel's course of travels from Lublin to nearby Piask to more distant Warsaw, we will see Yasha deflate from a man bubbling and brimming with activity, virtuosic skill, and desire to one nearly inert. Unusually for the picaresque genre, *The Magician of Lublin* is a *re*visitation tour, a story of seductions already transacted. Magda the assistant, Zeftel the procuress, even Emilia the hard-luck aristocrat, and certainly Yasha's long-suffering wife Esther—have all already come securely into Yasha's seductive thrall. Rather than presenting the picaresque in real time, the novel offers a kind of retrospective of journeys already made. The seventeenth-century picaresque would have comprised the tale of how all these seductions were accomplished in the first place, but this latter-day version has done all the legwork in advance, a fact that accounts for the novel's tired quality. Only the degree of the protagonist's attachment to (Christian) Emilia threatens to disturb the equilibrium of his (un)settled domestic life with Esther. By merely letting the reader tag along to places Yasha has already been, Bashevis ups the ante on the picaresque and bends the form yet further away from *Bildung*: we don't get to witness the protagonist being educated. Rather than toeing a line, Yasha traces a circle from home, into the world, and finally, with his resigned self-immural, back home for good.

PART 2

The *Polit* as Demobilized Soldier

CHAPTER 3

THE *POLIT* AT THE
WANING OF HASKALAH

Demobilized Soldiers, Demobilized Jews

> The trains resembled a multinational fair. Demobilized soldiers
> and civilian refugees clung to all the wagons. Hirsute, starved, pale
> from years of detention, wearing wooden clogs instead of shoes
> and leggings of rags tied with string or telegraph wire, with sacks
> and bags slung over their shoulders, they had to beg a little food
> to stay alive. There were White Russians, Caucasians, Chuvashes,
> Kalmucks, Yakuts, Uzbeks, Kirghiz, Jews and Ukrainians, Tatars,
> Circassians, Cossacks, Georgians, and Armenians.
>
> —Israel Joshua Singer, *The Brothers Ashkenazi*, 393

"Demobilization is just as much a part of the war game as mobilization. It requires the same soldierly qualities. So play the game out to the end."

So runs the avuncular patter of Major William Brown Meloney, American journalist, historian, soldier, and author of a 1919 handbook called "Where Do We Go From Here?"[1] and subtitled, confidingly, "This Is The Real Dope." In order to guide American doughboys through the details of their demobilization, the War Department published five million copies of the manual. Including sections on all of the veterans' financial, vocational, and educational entitlements, the publication chummily but exactingly instructs returning GIs on how most swiftly to reintegrate into peacetime American life. Meloney places great reliance on his readers' willingness to view the *spiel*-like possibilities of total war and its aftermath,[2] referring throughout the publication to "the war game," "the education game," and even the helpfulness of the American Library Association in "the book game." Playing the game "out to the end" means being a good sport, whether that entails making the best of whatever work is available or meeting with martial stoicism the specter of unemployment. But if demobilization is a soldierly task that constitutes the last phase of war, then when does it end?

For Meloney and those who commissioned him to write his "Handy-Andy" compendium, successful demobilization concluded with the occupational placement of returning veterans—ideally in "Your Old Job or a Better One," as one section of the pamphlet is headed—or else on track to new employment as farmer, tradesman, or professional. He urges enlisted men to mechanical training, railroad or civil service work, college men back to their studies, and all men to the utopian farm settlements that were conceived as a wistful dream-scheme to forestall dizzyingly rapid urbanization. "Where Do We Go From Here?" is the soldier's point of access to a vast complex of government-sponsored and private initiatives designed to ease his homeward passage. The pamphlet bespeaks an upholstered society in which the going might be rough, but there was somewhere *to* go. Soldiers could go home again, and their return to the nation that they had rendered, in Lloyd George's formulation, "fit for heroes" would be heralded with gratitude.

No such social upholstery cushioned the demobilization of soldiers returning to the nations where the Great War had actually been fought. A ravaged Europe, east and west, seethed with civil unrest generally and with labor strife more specifically. Britain saw almost fourteen hundred strike actions in 1919, affecting 2.5 million workers. To put this number in perspective, the year 1912, which had previously been considered the "benchmark for labor militancy,"[3] saw 1.46 million workers affected. Farther to the east, military defeat combined with labor unrest even more explosively; indeed, "Across a band of Central Europe, chaos seemed to be stalking the land and emerging both in ancient capitals and rural villages" (Seipp 4). If critics felt that American authorities had botched the demobilization[4] (similar charges were also leveled against the British government), then the war's losers had no one to blame, for the Imperial German Army practiced self-demobilization (ibid. 129). As for Austro-Hungary, its dispirited army simply collapsed with the empire for which it had fought. Prisoners-of-war were also a major factor in the chaotic environment of postwar Europe. The Russian army took around 2.5 million Austro-Hungarian soldiers captive and two hundred thousand more Germans.[5] The Russian Imperial Army could not even think of demobilization on an institutional level, exiting the Great War with the signature of the Brest-Litovsk Treaty in March 1918 only to turn around and fight a losing Civil War against the Red Army for the next two years.[6] Poles, their land partitioned among three powers for almost a century and a quarter by the end of the Great War, fought with both the Allies[7] and the Central Powers.[8]

War and the Picaresque: *Heimkehrer* without a Home

The Great War and its aftermath satisfied perfectly the conditions of the picaresque, and the demobilized soldier[9] became an exemplar of the modernist picaresque (anti)hero. This might seem counterintuitive, as the socially marginal rogue would appear to present the very antithesis of martial order[10] and of the battlefield heroics it was intended to promulgate. But by the time of the Great War, the *pícaro* is no longer necessarily a rogue, nor is the military necessarily a bastion of order. Perhaps the most lasting cultural legacy of the first total war was to unsettle permanently the idea of the soldier as hero.[11] Drawing more on the *pícaro*'s customary haplessness than on his original venality, the picaresque form underscored the rootless scamp as a perfect prey for conscription.[12] Demobilization only heightened this sense of shiftlessness, which was doubly true for the defeated. If picaresque heroes are socially marginal, then so were the soldiers returning to stifling cities where, as American historian Frederic Logan Paxson observed of his contemporaries, they scarcely knew "whether they were returning as heroes or as so many pests" (11–12). Their life stories had turned episodic of necessity: so many battle engagements, advances, retreats, and sequences of movements not subject to their own control or agency. The demobbed soldier was a literal *polit*, a remnant or survivor of a conflict that had killed or maimed many if not most of his immediate comrades.

The German term for a demobilized soldier was *Heimkehrer*, which implied—too sanguinely—that there were homes to which the soldiers might return. In fact, the continent, especially Mitteleuropa, had been so radically altered as to abolish any notion of home. Returnees might encounter the destruction of individual households and villages, a loss of home on an immediate, personal level, or else they might share in a national sense of dislocation as the map of Europe was redrawn and national identities seemed to shift overnight. Poland emerged to a short-lived independence, while the Austro-Hungarian Empire collapsed. Ethnic identities proved more durable than national ones, and no population felt the cataclysm more forcefully than the Jews:

The dismemberment of the old empire, and the redrawing of the map of Eastern Europe to create new homelands based on ethnicity, worked to the detri-
ment of Jews most of all, since there was no territory they could point to as
ancestrally their own. The old supranational imperial state had suited them; the
postwar settlement was a calamity. The first years of the new, stripped-down,
barely viable Austrian state, with food shortages followed by levels of inflation
that wiped out the savings of the middle class and violence on the streets between paramilitary forces of left and right, only intensified their unease.[13]

For its Jews, the collapse of empire coincided with the collapse, abandonment, or simply the attrition of the *shtetl* and the way of life that it represented. To paraphrase a chronicler of Spain's involvement in World War I,
the Jews did not (all) enter the war, but the war entered the Jews.[14] The
homelessness, displacement, and trauma that figured in the interwar fictions of many nations[15] were undeniably acute for the Jews of Eastern Europe. Jewish veterans found themselves in a double bind: unable to go back
home but equally thwarted in any attempt to integrate into a secularized
urban existence, that, no matter how cosmopolitan, was still susceptible to
the scourge of anti-Semitism. As Seth Wolitz explains of this Jewish "lost
generation," "Their dissociation from Jewish society did not open up another society for them in the city, and in their double alienation they find a
connection and shared language only among themselves" (xxxviii).[16] They
were either literally or figuratively refugees, almost to a man. The robustly
modernist literature that grew up between the wars probed the anxieties of
that *fugitas*.

Like the first one, this second part of my book subdivides into two chapters; the first links demobilization to the modernist picaresque and the
sputtering end of Haskalah, and then reads Israel Joshua Singer's novel[17]
Shtol un ayzn (*Steel and Iron*, 1927) as an illustrative *counterpoint* to my
main argument. Singer's story is a conventional realist *Bildungsroman*, taking place during the war and triggered by the spontaneous desertion of its
protagonist from the Imperial Russian Army. *Steel and Iron* takes its cue
from Zola, Mann, and Gorky and thus offers a narratological point of contrast with the modernist picaresque. It begins with a decisive moment in the
protagonist's life and follows his transformation from obedient soldier to
iconoclastic leader of men. Written in Yiddish and set mostly in Warsaw,
Singer's early novel may be imagined as the vertex to an isosceles triangle

for which the congruent bases' angles in terms of setting, theme, and tone are Joseph Roth's German-language *Hotel Savoy* (1924) and Yisroel Rabon's Yiddish-language *Di gas* (*The Street*, 1928). The second chapter of this section proposes these two picaresque novellas, which bear each other an uncannily strong affinity, as the modernist refutation of nearly everything that Singer's novel represents, including the plot structure, the character of the hero, and the construal of time and event.

Roth's and Rabon's novellas are of roughly equal length, both set in Łodz shortly after the cessation of World War I hostilities and recounted in the first person by conscripts for the Austro-Hungarian Empire.[18] Neither protagonist comes from Łodz; both have washed up there incidentally, in transit to somewhere else. These protagonists, Roth's Gabriel Dan and Rabon's unnamed soldier, exemplify the modernist picaresque. Both books are narrated episodically, covering an arbitrary span of time in their protagonists' lives. They begin without fanfare and end without closure, with little urgency driving the plot forward. There is much activity and movement, but little of the character development that was the staple of the *Bildungsroman* and other forms of the novel of progress. In each case, the protagonist's motility bespeaks passivity—being borne along a current—rather than the purpose and agency of the *Bildungsheld*, whose movement aims to (re-) shape his world. Roth's Gabriel Dan looks westward, while Singer's Benjamin Lerner looks eastward; the most isolated among these characters, Rabon's soldier looks downward, ultimately seeking his livelihood in the mineshafts of Silesia.

What binds these books together, such that they should be juxtaposed here? In depicting the travails of demobilized Jewish soldiers,[19] they share a chronotope in the broad sense discussed in the introductory chapter; moreover, they form part of the same cultural narrative, to use James Phelan's term:[20]

> By a cultural narrative, I mean one that has a sufficiently wide circulation so that we can legitimately say that its author, rather than being a clearly identified individual, is a larger collective entity, perhaps a whole society or at least some significant subgroup of society. Cultural narratives typically become formulas that underlie specific narratives whose authors we can identify, and these narratives can vary across a spectrum from totally conforming to the formula to totally inverting it. (8)

The works examined here all take part in the cultural narrative of the demobilized soldier, and more specifically, the demobilized Jewish soldier after the Great War. While they qualify as "specific narratives whose authors we can identify," these books take on a trebled force through their consideration together. Because of their thematic bleakness, they have typically been read as anatomies of anomie and alienation. The sense of rupture shared by all three protagonists is profound and inarguable. However, the energies of these novels bend away from the dearth or impossibility of human connection and toward the craving for it. Describing Roth's nonfictional account of life in Provence, *Die weißen Städte* (1925), Jon Hughes[21] pinpoints that author's "desire to find continuity, wholeness, and community in a world from which they had apparently vanished" (3). Hughes goes on to invoke a resonant phrase of Peter Gay's: "The resultant sense of absence, of loss, resulted in what Gay has termed a 'hunger for wholeness,' a desire for the unity and identity-forming bonds once provided by an identifiable community" (ibid.). The erosion of that identifiable community and its salutary bonds is a feature of modernity; in the decade before the Great War, Sholem Aleichem was able to harness the explosive comic energy generated by the collision between that notional community (in *shtetl* form) and lived Jewish experience. But in the wake of the war, even the notion of such social structures was decidedly a relic of the past.

Mobilization, Demobilization, and the Post-Haskalah

The terms "mobilization" and "demobilization" were not unknown before the Great War, but they entered the American English vernacular only with that conflict (Paxson 7). They referred to military operations—and the civilian structures that would undergird them—on a much vaster scale than previous wars had required. With rapid urbanization at the turn of the twentieth century, the scale of life was becoming altogether larger and less manageable. In his transnational account of European demobilization that takes Manchester and Munich as its test cases,[22] Adam Seipp defines demobilization as "a set of processes that bridge the chasm between "wartime" and "postwar," effectively extending the lived experience of societies at war beyond the conclusion of hostilities and the diplomatic agreements that periodize warfare in the historical consciousness" (6). In a modern industrial war, demobilization has four aspects: physical, economic, bureaucratic, and cultural (8). Because the Great War had been total, governmental efforts on the cultural front to reverse a course of bellicosity would have to be far-reaching: "Demobilization was a vast set of socio-cultural processes that derived from the unprecedented penetration of wartime into the everyday lives of ordinary Europeans and the governments at all levels that tried to survey, cajole, coerce, or compromise with them over more than four years of war" (ibid.). Seipp's recognition that demobilization is a deeper, more complex process than simply a standing down of men and materiel sets us on a course to examine the reverberations of the terms "mobilization" and "demobilization" far beyond their immediate martial context.

The term "mobilization" had two common usages during the first decades of the twentieth century: gearing up for war and engaging in a labor strike or other action of labor militancy. Of course there is a third meaning of the term that is just as relevant to our consideration of the modern Jewish picaresque. Mobilization was also the aim of the romantic nationalist movements that swept through Central and Eastern Europe at the turn of the twentieth century, borne on currents that had bathed Western Europe over a century before. Note the use of the term "mobilization" in writing about parallel movements across Central and Eastern Europe:[23]

> The formative force with the greatest sociopolitical effect was romantic nationalism. The birth of nations and the recognition of an "imagined community" (Anderson 1983) in the West at the end of the eighteenth century had a tremendous impact in Central and Eastern Europe, sparking imaginations even before political nations were born. National identity, conceived in Western terms, provided a primary impetus for mass **mobilization**. At the beginning, as Miroslav Hroch convincingly points out, this **mobilization** was an intellectual phenomenon inspired by a handful of poets, writers, historians, linguists, and artists (Hroch 1985). The international trend of romanticism arrived in Central and Eastern Europe at the turn of the century and initiated a renewal of national literature, music, theater, and painting that both reflected and created deep, passionate national feelings. (5; my emphasis)

Among the Jews of this region, this romantic renewal movement took the form of Haskalah and the distributaries into which it flowed. This is not the venue in which to review exhaustively the history of the Haskalah, a deep and broad account of which has been rendered by others.[24] Our aim is to note here the movement's recourse to images of mobility and mobilization, both from within its own textual tradition and in the secondary literature describing it. The task of the movement's proponents, the maskilim, whose efforts had begun in mid-eighteenth-century Germany, was to first rouse the people, as if from slumber (as the poet Y.L. Gordon urged in 1866 "Awake, My People"), and then to spur them to action.[25]

In all of its iterations and variations, the Haskalah was conceived as a transformational movement[26] by its participants, and the term "mobilization" comprehends both the motility and the militancy that they considered indispensable. The deepest textual underpinnings of the Haskalah, its Biblical "prooftext" as it were, embraces motility as the means of disseminating enlightenment:

> And they that are wise (maskilim) shall shine as the brightness of the firmament; and they that turn the many to righteousness as the stars for ever and ever.
> But thou, O Daniel, shut up the words, and seal the book, even to the time of the end; many shall run to and fro, and knowledge shall be increased.
> —Daniel 12:3–4

Above all, the terms *maskilim* and *Haskalah* are cast in the *hif'il*, or causative, verbal conjugation pattern. It is not a movement of the wise or of wisdom or light per se, but the movement of *making* wise, of *en*lightenment; a certain degree of proselytism, or in the face of opposition, struggle, is woven into its very nature. Carrying out this conversion necessarily requires running "to and fro" in order to spread knowledge. But the maskilim were to be more engagée than mere messengers. Shmuel Feiner, writing of the eighteenth-century Haskalah, describes how the movement co-opted the lives of prominent historical personalities of the past, such as Maimonides, Abarbanel, and Mendelssohn, in order "to project their vision of the future into the past":

> These historical figures were depicted as modern maskilim in every sense, men who could endow eighteenth-century maskilim with legitimization and a distinguished lineage. The exemplary historical figure was depicted as a **militant** personality, advancing against the stream, obstinately struggling for the sake of the truth, and standing firm in the face of the refusal of "ignorant fools" to accept the light of the Haskalah. (Feiner, *Haskalah and History* 342; my emphasis)

This observation of Feiner's demonstrates how readily the martial sense of mobilization enters into the discussion of Haskalah and accords with his general characterization of the movement as a revolution (*mahapekhat hane'orut*).

There is wide agreement among historians that although the "high" German Haskala was short-lived (coming to a close by 1800, as marked especially by the closing of the newspaper *Hame'asef* in 1797), it nevertheless "left deep, ineradicable impressions" (Feiner, *Jewish Enlightenment* 370) and "permeated nearly all the ideological movements that appeared in the following two hundred years" (ibid. 371). The Haskalah anticipated and ushered in modern, liberal values and engaged modernist concerns: "The modernist doctrine of the Haskalah encompassed values such as religious tolerance, contempt for superstition, the self-consciousness of living in a modern era, an optimistic view of the course of human history, and faith in man's power to shape his life by means of his reason" (Feiner JE 372). These humanistic theses were illustrated in the emerging canon of Yiddish literature, especially drama and fiction. From the writers' perspective, a "republic of letters" was forming,[27] and readers could now perceive themselves as part of its consuming public.[28] Not only values but social and intellectual movements could be traced to the high Haskalah or considered part of a long Haskalah, in a sense parallel to "the long eighteenth century."[29] Toward the end of the nineteenth century, an elite intellectual movement had transformed into a mass cultural one. Haskalah moved eastward with the Jews over the course of the 1800s, and the movement ramified into moderate and radical branches. These intellectual currents coincided with the spread of nationalism throughout Central and Eastern Europe in the nineteenth century, as well as the rise of Marxism. Haskalah ideals of positivism extended in many directions, including Zionism and Bundism, even as Yiddish literature helped to foster a partial rapprochement with Hasidism. The commonality among all these maskilic branchings was a master narrative of progress,[30] of continually improving the condition of the Jews and the state of the world, as well as a willingness to brook varying degrees and forms of social control in order to propagate perceived Jewish advancement.[31] This optimism was underwritten by the freedoms and educational opportunities newly available to Jews during the reign of Alexander II but just as swiftly revoked in the wake of the pogroms of 1881–82. The impulse to improve the Jewish lot by improving the Jews only took on renewed force after it was clear that an "enlightened" Russia would not solve the Jewish problem in Europe. Micha Yosef Berdiczewski,[32] writing in 1897, concluded, "The days of the Haskalah are behind us . . . we must bear in mind that we are all na-

tionalists and that all the forces that have acted upon us are equally sacred."
Political and economic movements (Bundism, Zionism, diasporism, agricultural utopianism) effloresced, together with cultural ones.

Dan Miron has synthesized these historical facts from the perspective of
developments in modern Jewish literature. In his essay about passivity (thematic and narratological) in the work of Isaac Bashevis Singer,[33] he presents
a brief but essential account of the influence of maskilic ideology on Jewish
literary culture. Jews had exempted themselves from history for centuries,
he argues, but in leaving behind the religio-legal traditions that authorized
this posture of passivity, cultural leaders sought to create a corpus that
would *activate* the nation as humanists:

> Modern Jewish culture demanded that the people of Israel apprehend life
> through the lens of humanism, and by this willful act of comprehension break
> through to the heart of historical becoming. It hoped for the awakening of a
> national will ("Awake my people, how long will you slumber?"), recommended
> activity, vigor, readiness to struggle and effort to change. Yiddish literature en-
> dorsed these recommendations with the best of its talents, all of its earthy vivac-
> ity and all of the immediacy of its contact with the Jewish masses. When Yid-
> dish literature sprang from the ideological soil of the Enlightenment (Haskalah)
> in the nineteenth century, or when it reflected, at the turn of the century, the
> birth of modern Jewish nationalism, or when it played a central role, later in the
> twentieth century, in the burgeoning Jewish socialist movements, its call to the
> Jewish people was a call for change and awakening. (9)

The commitment to "activity, vigor, readiness to struggle and effort to
change" dominates modern Jewish literature virtually unchallenged *until
the twentieth century* and then must compete with a different kind of narrative altogether. This maskilic storyline is compactly instantiated in I.J. Singer's demobbed soldier novel but is dramatically undermined in Roth's and
Rabon's novellas. As I maintain in the introduction to this study, Miron's
micro-history constitutes the kernel of a much larger argument than the
one he makes. Rather than treating Bashevis as a special case (partially anticipated by Sholem Aleichem), I argue that an axial line runs from Sholem
Aleichem, through a particular terrain of twentieth-century Yiddish fiction, to Bashevis and beyond. Without a doubt, this axis passes through the
picaresque narratives of the demobilized soldier under consideration here.
In the twentieth century, Yiddish literature must reckon with the failure of

humanism and its schemes for human perfectibility. The maskilim envisioned an orderly movement[34] of the people from a benighted past into an enlightened future, an organized marching of the foot soldiers of *Kulturkampf*. But the modern world brought forth a different kind of motion altogether. Instead of orderly mobility, there was chaotic clinamen: the unpredictable and peripatetic zinging of the atom.[35] If Haskalah was about mobilization, then the picaresque strain within Yiddish literature represented a demobilization, or standing down. Demobilization is not only a matter of historical fact, the *Sitz im Leben* of these novels, but it is also an essential *figure* for the modernist picaresque. The exhausted cessation of motion, the craving for rest, and the exasperating deferral of that rest, all define the trajectories of the interwar fictions we shall consider. Wartime might have called for "soldiering on," but what about when the war had ended or at least these particular actors had withdrawn from the hostilities? They are de-mobilized not in a spirit of triumphant completion but of exhaustion and attrition. For Roth and Rabon, if not for Singer, perhaps it was finally time to live and let live.

Steel and Iron: A Study in Maskilic Manhood

Israel Joshua Singer's *Steel and Iron* (*Shtol un ayzn*) furnishes us with a sort of negative proof for a study of the *polit*, by considering a fiction that takes note of the picaresque—only to reject it. The naturalistic conditions of the picaresque novel are powerfully present in this 1927 novella:

> In the dingy, grimy alleys that snaked along the waterfront they settled in dank garrets and cellars where they existed without heat, water, light, or sanitary facilities. The adults were driven to work in the forests, where they died like flies from hunger, consumption, and the harsh conditions. The children swarmed through the city streets, begging, stealing, subsisting on the undigested grains of oats that they salvaged from horse manure, scrounging off the soldiers, wallowing in the gutters, and for a crust of bread allowing degenerates to abuse their bodies. (185–86)

Any one of these swarming, nameless, abject children might, like Lazarillo de Tormes, narrate the harrowing vicissitudes of his or her childhood—in this case a Jewish childhood in wartime Poland rather than a Catholic one in Golden Age Spain. Yet they are mentioned late in Singer's narrative and hardly constitute his central concern. Not only does the novella display an awareness of *conditions* conducive to picaresque narration (after all, the grime and suffering might fuel many other narrative forms equally well), but elsewhere it furnishes a condensed though finely etched miniature of a picaresque sequence of *events*:

> He was square and muscular, with dark, narrow eyes, a thick crewcut, and a blue anchor tattooed on his arm. He looked like a prototype of the proletariat displayed on revolutionary posters. He had already worked in coal mines in Germany, peddled beads in Argentinian villages, shined shoes in Odessa, waited on table in Paris, worked on the docks in Antwerp, sewn caps in London, been an itinerant goldsmith in Poland, washed dishes in New York waterfront bars, and been a stoker on ships sailing to the Far East and Africa. He could speak dozens of languages in the jargons of the street, the sea, and the jail; for wherever his restless spirit carried him he immediately got into trouble and served time. He was a born rebel with a fierce, undying hatred of all law and authority. (258)

The character whose scintillating biography is so tantalizingly abridged[36] surfaces about ten pages before the novel's end for the specific narrative purpose of helping the protagonist escape from a German-run prison. Identified by the narrator only as "Squarejaw,"[37] this figure never receives a proper name. After masterminding an escape for himself and the grateful protagonist through the sewer tunnels, he mysteriously slips out of the narrative. One moment, the two escapees are apprehended by bayonet-wielding Russian soldiers; the next, they are released, and Squarejaw is never mentioned again. Singer's narrator takes no leave of him at all. As a hardened man of experience with revolutionary tendencies, Squarejaw parallels the role of Zwonimir in Joseph Roth's novella, and to a lesser extent, the wrestler Jason in Rabon's work. Yet while those secondary characters will pose a challenge to the narratorial dominance of each book's main protagonist, Squarejaw poses no such challenge. The narratorial gaze remains tightly riveted on Benjamin Lerner.

More than anything, Lerner—whose vocation as a student of life is inscribed in his very name—craves action, movement. Indeed, what sets his story in motion is the traffic jam that renders it impossible for him, "wearing the full fieldkit of an Imperial Russian infantryman" (3), to move freely across Warsaw to the military depot where he is due in an hour's time. "Swallowed up in the maze of horses and vehicles," he is "totally immobilized" (5; *farshtekt gevorn* in the original [Y8–9]). Detention renders him desperate; flouting military regulations, he hails a droshky only to be apprehended by a predictably censorious officer who denounces him as a deserter (among other choice epithets). Lerner refuses to accept blame for the infraction, expecting the worst sort of retribution. When the MP only asks for his name and orders him to report to his commanding officer, Lerner slackens into a course of urban wandering that will lead to the desertion already imputed to him.

Taking stock of wartime Warsaw as his wanderings begin, Lerner grows exasperated at the omnipresent immobility: "Something seemed to wrench inside of him. The fact that the street was unchanged, that the theater was still standing where it always had, that the town hall was as tall and erect as ever, that a fireman still kept watch from its tower, and that its clock still told the correct time after he had lived through so much hell at the front irked and insulted him beyond all proportion" (12). Whatever has wrenched within him, the rest of the city continues its quotidian existence. The normalcy of the city all around Lerner belies the hell he has witnessed at the front:

> Rotting there day after day in mud, filth, and blood, he had assumed that the world had been torn from its moorings, that the people had undergone some phenomenal change. As often as he'd tried to picture his home and close ones then, he had been stymied. Even earlier that day when he had been hurrying to make formation he had not seen anything around him. Nothing had existed beyond the fact that he was late. But now he grew sharply aware of the streets and the buildings. Everything was just as it had always been, as if the world hadn't turned upside down since his departure. (12)

Constancy is tantamount to stasis for Lerner, and after the cataclysm that he and his comrades have endured, stasis comes as a blow. The violence of war should have engendered motion if not outright revolution—but the shock has only, Lerner perceives, affected the actual combatants. Moreover, Lerner himself is totally unsettled by the lifestyle of the strolling *flaneur*, in which it becomes possible to notice these "pedestrian" details.

At his core an "action hero,"[38] the protagonist spends the rest of the book pursuing the mobility, action, and adventure for which he yearns. Since this early novel by Singer is relatively little known and out of print, it is useful here to summarize the broad contours of its plot. The first four chapters include Lerner's desertion; a visit to his bourgeois uncle's and simultaneous reunion with his cousin Gnendl, with whom he also has a long-standing if anodyne romance; and a great deal of urban wandering. This section ends with the German invasion of Warsaw and the retreat of the Russians. During chapters 5–10, Lerner works in near-slavery conditions at rebuilding a bridge for the Germans that the Russians have detonated; while laboring alongside a diverse cross-section of Warsaw's poor, he foments a workers' revolt. In chapter 11, the narratorial point of view changes to Gnendl, her unsuitable suitor Yekel Karlover, and her ejection from her parents' house upon refusing Karlover's advances. Chapters 12–15 involve Lerner and Gnendl working with the philanthropically minded contractor Aaron Lvovich to resettle and productivize a group of Jewish war refugees on an estate in Russia now under German jurisdiction. In the final chapter, Lerner is incarcerated (betrayed by one of the refugee beneficiaries of his altruism), escapes, and joins the Bolshevik fighters. Restored at last to military action in the book's final scene, after a long interval in civvies, Lerner's final utterance is the word "*Foroys!*" (Y 346) ("Forward!" 267)—shouted while waving a rifle and leading a Bolshevik charge on the Winter Palace during the October Revolution of 1917. With a protagonist who elects to *re*mobilize after a tour at the front, Singer's novel stands in marked contrast to a body of other interwar fiction that explores the psychology and sociology of demobilization.[39] At a time when other literary protagonists seek rest, Lerner is a "vigorous and energetic man" who "craved activity, any kind of activity" (56). While others struggle for the merest subsistence, Lerner has energy to observe that, "All around him men were fulfilling their destinies" and to wonder, loftily, "what was his?" (62). He is willing and even eager to fight on, but only for a cause he finds compelling.

Lerner's character is a study in maskilic manhood, a century and more after the end of the original German Haskalah.[40] One aspect that gives the book a rather dated feel is its anxiety to insist upon and yet to qualify and contain his masculinity at every turn. Several minor characters represent alternative visions of manhood, all of which are measured against Benjamin. Among the most derided are the Hares, a brotherhood-of-necessity of eleven other deserters and bohemians who are sitting out the war in a sixth-floor walkup artist's studio.[41] They rejoice at Lerner's arrival (a twelfth Hare!), but the bonhomie is not mutual, for "Lerner could not stand them and came only when he had nowhere else to go" (54). The omniscient narrator is even more withering in his assessment of the band's hollow iconoclasm: "They drank down the raw wartime whiskey in one gulp, proud of their masculinity, their free spirit, and their contempt for the Establishment" (54). If Sholem Aleichem were still alive and writing in Europe, these certified nihilists would surely populate his monologues and short stories. Their masculinity is sham: Lerner is at once more vigorous and active than the cowering Hares and more refined than they in his tastes and sensibilities.

This combination is typical of maskilic gender ideals, as Paula Hyman sketches them:

> Even as they began to acculturate at the beginning of the nineteenth century, Jewish men identified selectively with a more cerebral form of masculinity— Enlightenment rationality and the *Kultur* of the *Bildungsbürgertum*. During the course of the century acculturation did lead, however, to Jews' internalization of the gender norms of the larger society. According to those norms, the male was depicted as strong and powerful but also rational, responsible for economic and political life. (213)[42]

The narrator indicates Lerner's identification with refined, cerebral masculinity by endowing him with a passion for reading (one that Rabon's protagonist shares) and lavishing attention on the reading materials themselves: "Lerner sat in the midst of all the turmoil and read everything that came his way—books crookedly printed on tissue paper and bound in burlap, dense sociological studies, primitive manifestoes, obtuse theoretical tracts, and raw revolutionary ballads that wallowed in gore and naivete" (177). Yet this lexigraphic identification proves selective indeed. The serenity of the library cannot finally compete with the alluring tumult of the street:

> Occasionally he read in the public library, but the silent hall, the imperturbable readers, the padding librarians, and the musty delitescence in the midst of all the turmoil and excitement depressed and annoyed him. He would rush outside and lose himself in the noise and the crowds as if this small act of commitment would somehow affirm his standing in the human race. Out in the street he felt involved, fulfilled." (51–52)

Comfortably inhabiting the library, but then leaving the library for a life of action on the street: this is an efficient cultural shorthand for the radical maskil of the late or post-Haskalah. With his intellectual bona fides, Lerner is Jewish enough, but with their limited sway over him, he is manly enough.

Not only does Lerner's enthusiasm for reading signal his "finer nature," but so does his noticeably delicate appetite. As if to suggest that he is slightly more finely constituted than those around him, Lerner cannot stomach certain food or gastronomic situations. Despite his hunger, Lerner loses his appetite at the sight of his uncle portentously tugging his beard (23). Later, he cannot bring himself to eat the "slop" the German overseers serve to the men working on the bridge, so in an act that combines aesthetic scrupulosity with indignant protest, he empties his ration onto the ground (74). Lerner's "nobler" nature is evident even to the anemic, Christ-like, and learned Hasid Jehiel Mayer, who toils ineffectually on the bridge until a falling girder crushes his legs. Mayer, who is a veritable caricature of the mild, long-suffering Jew, nonetheless tries to make common cause with this secularized yet undeniably superior specimen of humanity: "Ostracized by everyone, he made overtures to Lerner, in whom he detected a finer, a nobler nature. Once he went so far as to ask, 'You seem to me a cultured man. Have I guessed correctly?'" (94). The Hasid has guessed more correctly than Lerner gives him to know, for according to his boorish uncle, Lerner is descended from the Ryzhin Rabbi; to have *yikhes* (distinguished ancestry) and yet not to draw one's sense of self from lineage—that is a true maskilic Adonis!

Lerner's deeds (organizing the bridge workers, resettling the refugees) are fueled by a keen sense of *noblesse oblige*, although the narrative never clarifies whether that *noblesse* rests entirely on remote ancestry or on more recent familial attainments. While manifestly "better than" his fellows, Lerner must cultivate an air of equality in order to be effective as their leader. Success entails either being superior without knowing it or convincingly affecting not to know it. Consider a passage in which Lerner complains to his revolutionist mentor Schzigel, known at the bridge by the nickname Sheepskin:

> Lerner complained to Sheepskin, "They're nothing but scum of the earth, the lowest cruds I ever did see."
>
> "All masses are scum," Sheepskin agreed. "You just keep it up. But ditch the derby; that don't help any."
>
> The next day Lerner showed up in a plain woolen cap and Sheepskin smiled approvingly. "That's more like it. Now get rid of the other derby ... the one inside your skull." (109)

The derby inside Lerner's skull refers, of course, to the attitudinal change required of him in order to win the allegiance of the workers to the communist cause. One might readily imagine the next scenes rendered cinematically like the sentimental, set-to-music training montages typical of 1980s movies:

> Lerner persisted. He made overtures to the men, he started to talk their language, to play cards, to tell stories. They listened to his experiences at the front. Wiser, better educated, handy, and rugged, he quickly became a favorite in the barrack. . . . His intelligence awed them. Somehow he always managed to find the right word. He could knock off a letter before a man could properly scratch his head, and they were astounded. "God damn it, that's just what I wanted to say! God bless you, pal!"
>
> Slowly, so gradually that he himself wasn't aware of it, Lerner felt a change come over him. He lost his contempt and began to look at his co-workers as human beings with feelings, doubts, and frustrations. (109–10)

Passages like this one attest to Lerner's successful *Bildung*. While educating others, he grows into a capable adult and fosters a meaningful place for himself in the new world order that a successful revolution will promulgate. Most revealingly, the transformations that he wrings are manifestly a function of Lerner's will and persistence. No sooner does he mount a charm offensive than he is hailed as a right good fellow and embraced by his "peers." Yet Lerner has been given a special, sympathetic dispensation by the narrator; where the narration is earnest about Lerner's efforts (which could be so easily mocked in their naive idealism), he is wry about a similar dedication to communist organizing on the part of a secondary character. Dr. Grigoriy Davidovich, the medical man in the German work camp that is rebuilding the bridge, is a portrait of the Jew uncritically enamored of Marxism. Idealistic enough in his youth to marry the communist daughter of a Russian village priest, Davidovich is now disillusioned by the peasants and workers he has devoted a lifetime to healing, serving, and radicalizing. Singlehandedly staffing an under-supplied infirmary with rampant typhus has made him morose: "Ever since coming to the bridge he had functioned in a kind of semi-comatose state. The years he had spent gushing with love for all living things, the years of self-sacrifice and blind devotion weighed on him now like a malignant hump on his back" (121). Davidovich's failure is the flip side of Lerner's success at mobilization: "But the harder he tried to become one of them, the more they resented him. For all his sermons about love and fraternity they were unspeakably brutal to one another" (127). Delivering "sermons" from on high, the narrator implies through the juxtaposition, is precisely what the effective maskilic hero must not do. Yet Davidovich is not the only would-be hero in the novel who indulges in this sort of condescension. Aaron Lvovich is a prosperous Jew who once entertained Lerner's military unit on his estate, only to be eventually cut off from his vast holdings in Russia by finding himself on the wrong side of the German lines. Just as Sheepskin was Lerner's mentor in fomenting revolution, so too Lvovich acts as his mentor in productivizing a group of two hundred Jewish refugees, relocated to a dilapidated Russian estate now under German control. He too vents a misanthropic frustration at the obtuseness of his charges and so rehearses the claims of the embittered, unthanked maskil:

> Aaron Lvovich tried to judge objectively what was happening. His only motive, he told himself, was to rescue these unfortunate people from the squalor and hopelessness of their existence. He yearned to remove them from conditions that forced them to steal, beg, smuggle, and prostitute, and transform them into proud, self-sustaining members of society. And for these unselfish ambitions his reward had been abuse, recrimination, and a relentless and illogical hatred. (188)

And a page later: "He fairly shook from frustration. He had sought their trust and had gained their fear" (189). For all that the narrator takes a romantic view of Lerner's revolutionary efforts among the bridge workers, he eschews such sentimentalism in depicting the refugees. They are greedy and coarse, louche and lewd. The best among them are ignorant and bumbling, the worst are calculating opportunists who land Lerner in a German jail for his trouble. Yet Lerner is spared having to excoriate them because Lvovich does it for him in passages like the one above. Lvovich himself illustrates how the best besets and undermines the good. Once the Bolshevik revolution breaks out, he is so determined to "shape the destiny of millions" (237) that he abandons the settlement at Zaborowa and leaves the burden of leadership to Benjamin and his cousin. Here Singer seems to favor local and incremental progress over sweeping revolution.

There is a curious deficiency in Benjamin Lerner's maskilic masculinity where Gnendl is concerned. Part of the "Jews' internalization of the gender norms of the larger society," in Paula Hyman's formulation, includes zealously defending the honor of Jewish women and assuming the romantic role of pursuer. Although Lerner defends Gnendl from the jocular jeers of the Hares and the leer of their unsavory landlord, he proves unable to help spare her (because he has been carted off to prison) a humiliating gynecological exam at the hands of a German medic and soldiers, and a possible rape on that occasion.[43] Moreover, Lerner does little to pursue her. She initiates a search for him, finding him at the Hares' hideout. Lerner does nothing to discourage the interest in Gnendl shown by Lvovich, whose gaze upon her "was at the same time paternal and masculine" (191). Months after the bridge insurrection, during which time Lerner and Schzigel have become fugitives for shooting a German guard in the course of their escape, Lerner tracks Gnendl to the home of Miss Malgosha,[44] an odd duck of a Christophilic Jew who has taken her in. When the eccentric lady of the house offers them a few days alone together, Lerner refuses and chivalrously exclaims that he will sleep on the floor. Why the exaggerated chastity? A full-blown passionate romance would eventually resolve itself into bourgeois domesticity, and the fervor of revolution and public service must predominate over the pull of the merely domestic.[45]

Like the demobilized soldier stories of Rabon and Roth, Singer's novel refuses to conclude "properly." In its last pages, time speeds up precipitously and months' worth of events are elided and telescoped into a sentence or two: "Together with the thousands of soldiers, deserters, and civilians who crowded the depots smoking, arguing, and milling around aimlessly, he rode through Russia, mostly on top of the railroad cars" (263). Lerner's fellow men might be the aimless multitudes that populate the novellas of Rabon and Roth; Singer's protagonist walks among them but is not one of them. They mill; he moves. The penultimate page of the book has him wandering among the *demos*, completing his education on the street:

> Lerner was everywhere, roaming from palace to palace, from speaker's stand to speaker's stand, from barrack to barrack. He listened, watched, read, and let himself be carried along by the stream of people toward the Institute where bread and arms were being distributed. He took one of each—a loaf of bread in his right hand, a rifle in his left. (266)

He flirts with the abdication of all agency ("let himself be carried"), but finally he seizes the initiative to sustain himself (bread) and fight for his ideals (rifle). Like his nameless counterpart in Rabon's Łodz, Lerner becomes a

denizen of the street: "The street was his home, the speakers' stands his table, the proclamations his nourishment, the turmoil his entertainment"
(263). But in Singer's novel being on the street is a matter of choice. Lerner
has options that Rabon's demobbed soldier does not. "When he could no
longer control his hunger," the narrator relates, "he would go to some cheap
tavern" (51). He has family, however coarse, a woman who loves him, and a
friend, Lvovich, who happens to be wealthy. He has enough social upholstery to strive for heroism.

Warsaw is less than two hours from Łodz on today's trains, but in the
1920s the two cities—at least as they figure in these fictions—might as well
have been separated by two millennia. For the distance between Singer's
Shtol un ayzn and Rabon's *Di gas* is precisely the two thousand-year-old
difference between a dictum in *Pirke Avot* and its waggish Yiddish update.
The original mishna enjoins, "*Bim'kom she'eyn ish hishtadel lihyot ish*" (In a
place where there is no man,[46] strive to be a man). In folkloric rhyme, the
Yiddish cheekily asserts, "*Bimkom she'eyn ish, iz hering oykh a fish!*" (Where
there is no man, herring is also a fish!). Benjamin Lerner strives mightily to
be a man, to be a fully empowered agent of enlightened change. He strives
as a soldier, he strives as a labor organizer, he strives as an agricultural manager on the estate, and he strives finally as a revolutionary. Rabon's protagonist, on the other hand, has no השתדלות (*hishtadles*)—striving—within
him. Whether by temperament or as a result of the Great War or some inef-
fable combination of both, he is a man gone slack if not quite a slacker.
Where Lerner actively seeks out the fulfillment of his destiny, the veteran in
Łodz struggles merely to survive and to remain minimally human. But herring is also a fish, and Rabon's novella is also a fiction. Its modernism lies
both in its embrace of radical contingency as a core aspect of the human
condition and in its consistently interior focus. *Shtol un ayzn* is a relatively
short novel (346 pages in the Yiddish) about a big, thick world of event,
character, and experience.[47] Singer can only gesture at much of what there
is to describe. The narrative condenses and compresses experience, using
representative characters and instances to sketch a reality that far exceeds
what it can name directly. *Di gas*, on the other hand, is a thorough description of the consciousness of one individual in a pinched, parched world.

CHAPTER 4

SPILLAGE AND SHARDS
The *Polit* between the Wars

> Readers expecting a narrative of "events" and excitement need to
> be weaned onto another, more "nonchalant," style, one that takes
> its time, makes no beelines, is always ready to turn away from a
> given direction in order to explore something other. Such a style,
> always ready to interrupt itself, is inevitably episodic . . . and,
> veering easily (i.e. *without* a sense of discontinuity) from topic to
> topic, following associative drifts or the promptings of memory, it
> is digressive: it is organized, that is, by relationships of resemblance
> and contiguity, metaphor and metonymy rather than the formal
> unity required by argument or the narrative of event.
>
> —Ross Chambers, *Loiterature* (31)

In the introductory chapter, we considered the contours of the modernist
Bildungsroman and its critique of conventional plots of progress. Jed Esty
carefully documents the passage from a world understood as a consortium
(or contest) of nation-states to a world-system constituted by empires and
other postnational global structures. In so doing, he recurs to the key term
container, which is the function he assigns to the nation-state in relation to
the potentially messy or overflowing complex of cultural aspirations and
expressions of its denizens:[1] "If the nation was the proper cultural container
for the bildungsroman's allegory of development, then modern imperialism
was a culture-diluting practice that violated 'national-historical time' and
set capitalism loose across the globe in ways that would come to disturb—
indeed still do disturb—our dreams of inevitable, and yet measured, human
progress" (6). His analysis goes on to modify the term *container* with the
terms "national," "political," "cultural," and "spatial."

But it was not just the altered—the modernist—*Bildungsroman* that registered the rupture of national containers and the challenge that breach posed to narratives of progress and development. Indeed, the phenomenon is even more striking in the twentieth-century picaresque genre. Telling the stories of Jewish demobilized soldiers after the Great War, the picaresque novellas under consideration in this chapter limn a modern *shevirat kelim*, or breaking of the vessels that contained nation, polity, culture, and language. With his urban hydraulics, Joseph Roth documents the ensuing spillage and flood. Somewhat more dryly, Israel Rabon moves his characters through a landscape of fragmentation. It is tempting to designate this breakage as belated, since in this case the rupture does not betoken the collapse of the singular nation-state but rather that of the quintessentially multiethnic empire that had succeeded it.[2] But of all her citizens, Austro-Hungary's Jews were the most nostalgic, wistful, and out of sync with the new dispensation. As J.M. Coetzee observed of Franz Joseph's Jewish subjects,[3] "The old supranational imperial state had suited them; the postwar settlement was a calamity." When Roth registers the calamity as a breaking of the vessels, these include not only the meta-container of the hotel building, which is ultimately destroyed, but also the more fragile vessel of the Kantian individual—the object of so much nineteenth-century literary desire and attention, who is dissolved in and through the narrative.

Both Roth's and Rabon's novellas typify the modernist Jewish picaresque, and the genre-defining *polit* as protagonist and narrator. While both works feature first-person episodic narration, hallmarks of the classical picaresque, both are also indisputably modernist. Indeed, the years between the world wars were when the modernist picaresque reached its fullest expression, and these texts are saturated with a specifically Jewish consciousness of cataclysm and rupture. It may be debated whether the modernist picaresque "canon" extends all the way back to encompass Sholem Rabinovitsh, all the way forward to include Isaac Bashevis Singer, or all the way outward to incorporate Isaac Babel—but these interwar novellas are the core texts from which the argument of this volume might be said to emanate. These demobilized soldier protagonists are literal *pleytim*—remnants—of a war that shattered every meaningful container and reordered every scale of values. Neither *Bildung* nor *Haskalah* is available to them. Their lives, at least during the brief time span depicted in each of these fictions, consist of a series of episodes: adventures and misadventures, and each ends somberly if inconclusively.

Before turning squarely to *Hotel Savoy*, consider briefly a pivotal scene in a kindred text, published just three years after Roth's, Kafka's *Der Verschollene* (later entitled *Amerika*[4]): this modernist *anti-Bildungsroman*, replete with its own picaresque elements, reacts against the long and heavy form of the novel of education. It is a novel of light—and lightness—through and through. Yet Karl's triumphant disembarkation in New York is nonetheless marred by a sense of loss:

> "Oh God, I've quite forgotten all about my suitcase!" "Where is it?" "Up on deck, an acquaintance is keeping an eye on it for me. What was his name now?" And from a secret pocket that his mother had sewn into the lining of his jacket for the crossing, he pulled a calling-card: "Butterbaum, Franz Butterbaum." "Is the suitcase important to you?" "Of course." "Well then, so why did you give it to a stranger?" (4)

Certainly Karl's suitcase is important to him; it is his world in miniature. There is the fact of the suitcase itself—a small zone demarcated from the rest of the world as his own, and then there is the question of its contents. Karl's suitcase holds, in addition to food and clothing from home, a picture of his parents. The scene cited above is the first of several anxious references to the whereabouts of his luggage; his suitcase will come to stand in for "something he's lost."[5] Of course the ur-loss for Karl, dishonorably banished as he is, is his home and family; this sense of loss expresses itself in the novel's working title. A suitcase is a compressed home, whose toiletries, wardrobe, and snacks might be said to recapitulate in miniature the bathroom, bedroom closet, and kitchen respectively. Baggage renders concrete the distinction between inside and outside, mine and yours, and dispossession threatens the dissolution of these boundaries. The specter of such chaos on a mass scale impelled Uncle Sam to at least one very concrete form of solicitude on behalf of his valiant nephews as the Great War was ending, the transformation of the Lost Baggage Bureau into the formidable Baggage Service of the A.E.F. "The function of the new Service thereafter was to manage the transportation of all troop baggage during the exodus from France and to locate, collect, and if possible restore to its ownership, all baggage lost by the soldiers of the expedition" (Crowell and Wilson, *Demobilization* 75). The restoration of their lost baggage was among the small but meaningful services that a triumphant army could offer its shell-shocked men. Encompassing both practical and symbolic dimensions, the recovery and preservation of soldiers' personal effects—their portable homes writ small—was crucial to morale. A well-functioning nation not only constituted a container as Esty suggests but restored the containers of individuals. The opposite of such solicitude dampens the spirit in corresponding fashion, which is precisely the situation that obtains in Joseph Roth's *Hotel Savoy*.

The Poetics of Dissolution:[6] Joseph Roth's *Hotel Savoy*

Let us imagine the grand edifice of hospitality as Roth's protagonist and narrator Gabriel Dan first sees it, looming up from the street in Łodz, a reification in stone, glass, and polished wood of civilized Europe. Gabriel lacks any luggage, which means that in some sense he is safe from the predations of the hotel's bellboy-cum-owner, Ignatz Kaleguropulos. For the proprietor's expedient is to seize the baggage of impecunious guests and to place it under a patent lock of his own devising. He holds the trunks as collateral until guests either settle their bills or—as is the fate of one guest— die trying. Whether Kaleguropulos's extension of credit is a form of charity or an act of aggression is debatable;[7] Gabriel puts up indefinitely at the hotel, carrying nothing to which he might be denied access. In this respect, he is essentially similar to Rabon's discharged soldier: neither man carries with him the bourgeois trappings of a portable home. Gabriel Dan's range of experience is unmistakably picaresque, as he recounts, "I am on my way back from three years as a prisoner of war, having lived in a Siberian camp and having wandered through Russian towns and villages as workman, casual labourer, night watchman, porter and baker's assistant" (9). The experiences that constitute these two novellas are arrestingly, even uncannily similar.[8] But the similarities remain superficial because a deeper difference separates the two demobilized Jewish *pícaros*: Gabriel Dan is secure in the knowledge that he will sleep each night in the Hotel Savoy, while the existence of Rabon's veteran is defined by his vagrancy. Perhaps better educated, Dan is the more "writerly" narrator,[9] in part because of his consciousness of himself as a character, abstracted from the experiencing self: "I am thankful once again to strip off an old life, as I so often have during these years. I look back upon a soldier, a murderer, a man almost murdered, a man resurrected, a prisoner, a wanderer" (9).[10] "An old life," introduced by the indefinite article, is a layer of which one might divest himself like so much soiled clothing, or like a costume unsuitable for the next scene. That life appears to

leave no residue, none of what Bakhtin conceives of as the *trace* of time
(FTC 91). He recollects in relative repose the travails of a grammatical—if
not a fully psychological—third person. Yet Rabon's unnamed soldier recalls in detail what it is the prerogative of the slightly more advantaged man
to forget. Rabon's novel opens with a scene of cruel unrecognition, as a former comrade fails to remember his acquaintance from the front. Gabriel
Dan can afford to forget just a little of his experience, as he catalogues his
attire (which is also his wardrobe *in toto*): "I am wearing a Russian blouse
which someone gave me, breeches which I inherited from a dead comrade,
and a pair of still wearable boots the origins of which I cannot myself remember" (9). Thus the two men move through the same city but view it
from different angles. They share the sense of exhaustion that has washed
them both up for what turns out in each case to be a brief interlude in Łodz.
Gabriel Dan might at one point opt to resume his Vienna-bound travels,
but he rationalizes his inertia with a logic that could just as well be voiced
by his Yiddish-speaking counterpart: "It was a really amusing town full of
all kinds of wonderful people; there was no one like them in all the world. . . .
Certainly it was better to stay on" (56).

A Creature of the Hive

Like Rabon's protagonist, Roth's is an observer, a witness to the lives and
stories unfolding around him. This acute witnessing is a typical trait of the
modernist *pícaro*: sequences of action are refracted through the psychologically rich self-awareness of a first-person protagonist narrator. His affinity
is to the hero of the premodern Greek romance, who in Bakhtin's account
maintains a unique perspective as participant-observer in life's dramas:

> What is preserved of the metamorphosis-into-ass is precisely this specific
> placement of the hero as a "third person" in relation to private everyday life,
> permitting him to spy and eavesdrop. Such is the positioning of the rogue and
> the adventurer, who do not participate internally in everyday life, who do not
> occupy in it any definite fixed place, yet who at the same time pass through that
> life and are forced to study its workings, all its secret cogs and wheels. (Bakhtin
> FTC 124)

The *polit* protagonists under consideration are quintessentially men just
"passing through" life, or at least Łodz. While Gabriel is a sympathetic and

warm-hearted character, there is no one else in the novella to whom he draws so close that he cannot coolly appraise motives or analyze modi operandi. He is literally the third person in many, though not all, of the book's conversations and interactions. He expresses the novella's first indispensable premise this way: "This Hotel Savoy was like the world." In context, he is making a statement about class consciousness and the cramped coexistence of wealth and poverty. He elaborates, "Brilliant light shone out from it and splendour glittered from its seven storeys, but poverty made its home in its high places, and those who lived on high were in the depths, buried in airy graves, and the graves were in layers above the comfortable rooms of the well nourished guests sitting down below, untroubled by the flimsy coffins overhead" (33). The hotel is a very particular vision of the world, however, and one that emphasizes divisions, the containment they bring about, and the hierarchies into which the contained may be organized. "As architectural units," Bettina Matthias observes, "hotels reflect the late nineteenth century's changing approach to space and its social functions, and to the notions of public and private, anonymity and intimacy, function and ornamentation, and seeing and being seen . . ." (4). Hotels are semipublic, semiprivate spaces offering a partitioned arena for intimacy and privacy. In its partitions, the hotel rather resembles the suitcase. Gabriel Dan thrives on this compartmentalized existence; the Savoy precisely captures the extent of his fellow-feeling. Characterizing himself as "a true egoist," Gabriel explains his alienation as a deficiency of comradeship:

> I am alone. My heart beats only for myself. The strikers mean nothing to me. I have nothing in common with the mob, nor with individuals. I am a cold person. In the war I did not feel I was part of my company. We all lay in the same mud and waited for the same death. But I could think only about my own life and death. I would step over corpses and it often saddened me that I could feel no pain. (65)

He has failed (at least he conceives of his lack of solidarity as a failing) as soldier and worker—precisely in two arenas of "mobilization." His instinctual tendency is toward a demobilized, if not an immobile, existence. In Richard Sennett's classic definition, a city is "a human settlement in which strangers are likely to meet."[11] Dan is ambivalent about encountering strangers. On one hand, he makes the dancer Stasia's acquaintance and is then quickly introduced to her social circle of poor performers and dreamers dwelling on the seventh floor, but on the other, he follows an elegant woman in gray all the way to a chocolatier while taking pains *not* to meet her. He tolerates the proximity to so many other human beings, but he also relies implicitly on the hotel's solid if thin walls. Clinging to his individual identity yet forced to grapple with the proximity of so many others in the trenches as well as in peacetime, he has become a creature of the hive.

Gabriel Dan witnesses unfolding events in real time and is suffused in turn by various emotions—hatred, affection, nostalgia—with respect to the hotel that figures the world. Enchanted at first with his room after long years at the front, his allotment of space seems distinct and personal to Dan, like a bourgeois home: "My rooms seemed friendly, as if I had lived there for a long time. The bell was familiar, and the doorhandle, the light switch, the green lampshade, the clothes cupboard and the washbasin. Everything was homely, like a room in which one has spent one's childhood. Everything was consoling and warm, like returning again to someone beloved" (12). These inanimate objects are invested with warmth insofar as they seem to ratify the protagonist's aspirations to an individual identity, to be a person with his own space. Later in the book, when Gabriel toys with the idea of resuming his journey toward Vienna, he reverses course and notes, "I returned to my room as to a long lost home" (61), but of course his hotel room is no such thing. He craves the feeling of "return" so strongly that he is willing to ascribe it to the most pedestrian, un-home-like surroundings. Over the course of his stay, as he learns the ins and outs of the place, Dan manifests a more critical attitude toward its rapacity: "Now I could feel mounting in me my hatred of the Hotel Savoy where one would live and another die, where Ignatz took trunks in pawn and girls had to strip naked before factory owners and house agents. Ignatz was like a living precept of this place, Death and a lift-boy" (52). As a modernist text replete with psychological interiority but unfolding within a very constrained spatial scope, perhaps some lability of feeling stands in here for the lability of experience we encounter in the Golden Age picaresque.

Despite his self-description as a "cold person," Gabriel Dan has a knack for gathering people and events unto himself. There is often little direct characterization of him; but for the information yielded by the contrast with others, he might remain an inscrutable *homme gris*. His temperament registers indirectly, in sharp contradistinction to that of his long-lost war buddy Zwonimir Pansin. Pansin is a man apart, signaled rhetorically by

Dan's (and Roth's) anaphoric refusal, upon introducing him, to tamp down the man's exuberance under the blanket of an ordinary pronoun:

> Zwonimir makes independent excursions inside the hotel, goes into empty rooms, leaves notes with greetings and knows everyone within three days. (71)

> Zwonimir greets everyone loudly and heartily. (ibid.)

> Zwonimir has already been in the hotel's basement, underground, where the kitchen is. He knows the cook, a Swiss, whose name is only Meyer but who makes good puddings. Zwonimir is given free tastings. (ibid.)

Zwonimir, for whom the hotel's walls are flimsy and easily traversed, makes himself at home in the hotel—and thus the world—in a way that is unimaginable for Gabriel Dan. If the Savoy offers Gabriel a perfect opportunity to live among others while preserving boundaries that he would not dream of crossing, then such boundaries entirely fail to register with the personable Croat. His movements, his words, and his affections flow unchecked. Although he is a self-proclaimed revolutionist who sides with the workers "out there," and although he will die in the context of labor militancy if not in an act of actual heroism, Zwonimir Pansin seems to be sanguine about the realities of life within the Savoy. He is untroubled by the concerns about social justice that churn within Gabriel: "'A splendid hotel,' says Zwonimir, and cannot sense the mystery of this house in which strangers live, eat and starve alongside one another, only separated by paper thin walls and ceilings. He finds it natural that the girls should pawn their trunks and end up naked in the clutches of Frau Jetti Kupfer" (72). Gabriel Dan's socialist consciousness is inextricable from a proto-feminist consciousness that winces at exploitation in its many guises. The contemplative Gabriel is nearly consumed by "the mystery of this house" and cannot readily make sense of a benevolent Other who neither acquiesces to the mystery nor resists it. To his Jewish friend, Zwonimir Pansin's behavior is both unsettling and wonderful. Zwonimir is a sort of *ur-goy*, a difference that includes not only a perplexing if benign indifference to class consciousness but also an unselfconscious decency: "He is a healthy person. I envy him. In our part of the world, in the Leopoldstadt, there were no such healthy fellows. He enjoys the vulgar things of life. He has no respect for women. He knows no books, reads no newspaper. He does not know what goes on in the world. But he is my loyal friend. He shares his money with me and would share his life with me" (72). Where Dan is cerebral (writerly if not bookish), Zwonimir is somatic, robustly embodied, living cushioned within a sphere that radiates outward from his own senses. He might "not know what goes on in the world" described in newspapers, but he closely observes and swiftly begins to actuate what goes on in the world of the Savoy.

Liquefaction, Dissolution, and Flow

Before the Hotel Savoy burns, it melts.[12] The very emblem of solidity, this edifice of stone and of the mind recalls M.M. Bakhtin's notion of the chronotope, the intersection of space and time made flesh. The hotel's *chronos* is the time of a newly collapsed empire; its *topos* is 1) its position at the margin of that empire (at "the doorway to Europe"), and 2) its stacking of life stories belonging to members of nearly all classes, one upon the other. Indeed, Gabriel Dan suspects the fluid ease with which Ignatz moves up and down among these lives. The hotel is a liminal space, designed for a temporary stay. It is what Marc Augé terms a *non-place*,[13] citing "anonymous hotel rooms" as a variety thereof. Zygmunt Bauman fills out the description thus:

> The temporary residents of non-places are likely to vary, each variety having its own habits and expectations; the trick is to make all that irrelevant for the duration of their stay. Whatever their other differences, they should follow the same patterns of behaviour hints: and clues triggering the uniform pattern of conduct should be legible to them all, regardless of the languages they prefer or are used to deploy in their daily endeavours. Whatever needs to be done and is done in "non-places", everyone there should *feel* as if *chez soi*, while no one should *behave* as if truly at home. (102)

The "non-place" of the hotel typifies the state of the empire, at the site and moment of its disaggregation. Among our picaresque protagonists, Gabriel Dan is the only character who stays in a hotel, saving money on his way to the clear spatial telos of Vienna. His travels through space, should they ultimately continue, must also constitute an attempt to travel in time—albeit one doomed to fail. This thwarting of Gabriel Dan in relation to time—he cannot move "forward" in his life due to exhaustion and inertia, nor can he move backward to a more comfortingly structured time—strands him as a modernist heir to Bakhtin's Greek adventure-hero, who is similarly thrown back upon space when stymied by time:

> How indeed can a human being be portrayed in the "adventure-time" that we have outlined above, where things occur simultaneously by chance and also fail to occur simultaneously by chance, where events have no consequences, where the initiative belongs everywhere exclusively to chance? It goes without saying that in this type of time, an individual can be nothing other than completely passive, completely unchanging. As we have said earlier, to such an individual things can merely happen. He himself is deprived of any initiative. . . . In essence, all the character's actions in Greek romance are reduced to enforced movement through space (escape, persecution, quests); that is, to a change in spatial location. (FTC 105)

Gabriel Dan is a reluctant *polit*, a solid man in a liquefying world. He yearns quietly for the nineteenth-century of stolid Franz Joseph and solid edifices. A world without walls breeds a dank, fungal danger to the spirit: "Homesickness grows in the open air. It grows and grows when no walls hem it in" (105). Gabriel doesn't give himself over to adventures in the manner of Lazarillo or Tom Jones; he remains too conscious a narrator for that. "Adventures"—outlandish, colorful experiences and interactions—impinge upon him from without. In his narrative, the picaresque is a milieu rather than a description of narratorial temperament. Łodz is the affirmation of the present; Vienna is his past and ostensible future.

Fish in the Rain

It is not just the chronotope of the hotel that erodes throughout *Hotel Savoy*, but also a Kantian notion of individual personhood being dissolved. So how does a solid man, and a highly conscious one at that, experience the crumbling of the hive, the dissolution of borders and boundaries? Gabriel Dan registers the action of his environment upon himself in narrow terms. He reflects a good deal on what he calls his "egoism," a persistent sense of being apart from other people. He describes himself to Zwonimir as an egoist and claims that he therefore cannot care about making the revolution. Yet demobilization promises to bond him to his erstwhile comrades in a way that the war itself never could: "They never used to be my brothers, not in battle, when, driven by some incomprehensible will, we would kill un-known men, nor at the base, where we would all move legs and arms in unison at the command of some bad-tempered man. But today I am not alone in the world. I am part of the homecoming soldiers" (115). During his Łodz interlude, Dan chronicles the dissolution of boundaries between him-self and others. He describes several days' work with thirteen other men, loading hopsacks full of grain onto railroad cars for one Ch. Lustig. During the exertion, he reports, "We work hard and we sweat. We smell our own sweat, our bodies all thrust together, we have blistered hands and feel our power and our pain together" (74). Whereas the Allied powers were not a sufficient enemy to bind him to his peers, Gabriel maintains,

> the hopsacks were our common enemy. Ch. Lustig has welded us together in sweat. We notice anxiously that the hopsacks are coming to an end, and soon our work will cease with them. Our parting feels painful to us, as if we should have to be sliced apart.
>
> And I am no longer an egoist. (75)

Not only does Gabriel voice this rather painful sense of adhesion with its negative formulation (no longer an egoist), but he also indicates a height-ened sense of camaraderie in the affirmative: "I live in community with the inhabitants of the Hotel Savoy" (65). Civilian life holds out the possibility of obliterating altogether the partitions between Gabriel's consciousness and that of other people:

> For a long time I was lonely in the midst of thousands. Now there are a thou-sand things which I can share: a glimpse of a dilapidated gable, a swallow's nest in a cupboard of the Hotel Savoy, the irritating beer-yellow eye of the old lift-boy, the bitterness of the seventh floor, the mystery of a Greek name, of a sud-denly living grammatical concept, the melancholy recollection an awkward Aorist tense, the constrictions of my parental house, the laughably ponderous Phoebus Bohlaug and "little Alexander's" life saved by his transfer to the army service corps. (24)

But surely this is going too far. These are experiences, too numerous and nuanced to be shared even by close friends, let alone casual acquaintances. At best, they might be communicated to a romantic partner over the weeks and months of a developing relationship. As we shall discuss below, no such relationship flourishes. Do these "redemptive" passages imply that Gabriel has been "transformed" into a different (better) sort of man, a communitarian in place of an individualist? No, he is less a man transformed than one adjusted, one who has found an external situation corresponding to his internal state.

The conventional *Bildungsheld* moves as a world-shaper, his movement a function of his agency and of the power that he exerts upon his surroundings. By contrast, the *polit*'s movement is the passive transport of one borne along a torrent. Both of the tropes that dominate the second half of *Hotel Savoy* bear witness to these hydraulic dynamics. One is rain, and the other is fish: the world rendered liquid, and the creatures that thrive best in those fluid environs. The rain reveals the city in its martial aspect: "On rainy days like this the town assumes its true appearance. Rain is its uniform. It is a town of rain, a comfortless town. The wooden sidewalks become slippery, the duckboards squelch when one treads on them, like damp leaky soles" (88). The flow of rain becomes indistinguishable from the flood of returning soldiers:

> It blends in well with the rain that at this season the flood of soldiers coming home should surge with renewed force.
>
> They go on through the thin, slanting rain. Russia, mighty Russia, is shaking them out. There is no end to them. They have all travelled the same road in their grey clothes, the dust of the wandering years on their feet, on their faces. It is as if they belonged to the rain. They are as grey and as enduring
>
> They are an endless river of grey in this grey town. Their canteens rattle like the rain in the runnels. A great homesickness emanates from them, a longing which drives them onward, the overwhelming memory of home. (114)

The human tide not only melds together but melds into the rain itself, which is figured not as cleansing "the dust of the wandering years" but as muddying the town with "an endless river of grey." The distant beacon of "home" might be what beckons the soldiers onward, but it is a collectivized and abstracted idea, not the individual homes to which they might return as individuated men. Their collective consciousness—as comrades and now as demobilized soldiers—lays the groundwork for their overturning of the old bourgeois order. The weather is of a piece with the demobilization, which in turn will bring about revolution willy nilly: "When we sit in the hutments and talk to the solders coming home—outside, the slanting rain falls ceaselessly—we can sense the revolution. It is coming from the East and no army or newspaper can halt it" (116). Attendant on the rain are the dangers of elision, inundation. This flood bears not only revolution but an essential change in the nature of the human subject. The demobilization is turning men into fish.

The piscine metaphor conveys a lack of agency and suggests that the singular individual has given way to the collective, indistinct, mass ("They look as alike as fish" [76]). Moreover, fish are driven to spawn by an instinctual force greater than they can hope to comprehend. So, too, goes the demobilization: "Once again it is time for the returning soldiers. They come in groups, many at a time. They come in shoals, like certain fish at certain times of year. They flow westwards, these returning soldiers" (75). It is absurd, however, to imply that homecoming from war is seasonal or natural; demobilization on this scale is an unprecedented phenomenon, a far cry from the comforting recurrent cycles of the natural world. Their experiences may have been epic, but these returning soldiers are denied the satisfying narrative arc of the classic Odyssean homecoming:

> They know about foreign countries and strange lives and like me they have brushed against many lives. They are tramps. Are they happy to be tramping home? Would they not have been happier staying on in the big world rather than returning to the small home of wife, child and fireside?
>
> Perhaps it is not their intention to go home. They are being spilled westward like fish in their season. (76)

Gabriel manifests a sympathetic imagination in wondering about his erstwhile comrades' thoughts. Once again abstracting himself, he takes up the question of their desires and intentions. In so doing, he recognizes that he is not a singular hero, or a singular man of any sort. He imputes to them a familiarity with "strangeness" that equals his own. Dan, living in an age of mass production, cannot assume that his experience, his picaresque path, has been unique. Herein lies another key distinction between the Golden Age and modernist picaresques. In the older form of the genre, the narrator (who usually coincided with the protagonist) maintained a consciousness of the hero as a man apart. Gabriel Dan speaks not only for himself but for the fiction of his age: indeed, the novel can no longer return to "the small home of wife, child, and fireside" any more than individual soldiers can. The illusion of individuality that was part and parcel of *Bildung* and the nation-state with which it grew up is now conclusively disrupted and exposed as illusory; the containers are broken.

A more minor but nonetheless present form of hydraulic imagery has to do with the flood of secrets that flow at Gabriel Dan during his brief tenure as the industrialist Bloomfield's secretary. This episode of isolated professional success interrupting a generalized state of unemployment and idleness roughly parallels Rabon's narrator's stint as a cinema narrator. "Hidden doorways open at my command, people pay respectful attention to me. . . . And here stand I, ready to accept everything which floods my way. People offer themselves to me and their lives are unveiled before my eyes. I can neither help them nor harm them, but they are thankful to have found a listener who has to listen, and they pour out their sorrows and their secrets" (97). People's sorrows and secrets constitute a flood that Gabriel cannot even hope to stanch. He tries to serve as a receptacle for them but is fated to overflow just as surely as are the receptacles of nation, barracks, and hotel. Ultimately, Gabriel learns to tolerate if not to "go with" the flow. This resigned acceptance should not be mistaken for "growth" or a transformative process. There is no hope of optimization. The best one can do is to escape the conflagration. A man cannot become a *mensch* but only rather a fish. Roth's German-language Jewish novella instantiates, ironically enough, the Yiddish proverb, "*bimkom she'eyn ish, iz hering oykh a fish!*"

When Narration Is the Only Salvation: Yisroel Rabon's *Di gas*

Given the desolation that swiftly comes to predominate in Israel Rabon's lean novella *Di gas* (*The Street*, 1928), it is easy to forget that the work opens with an act of gratuitous kindness. One Mr. Jakob Vizner, Custom Tailor, a figure hitherto unknown to the unnamed first-person narrator, has written a letter informing him of his father's death. The landlord, Mr. Vizner goes on to write, has placed new tenants in his father's apartment, but since the son of the deceased was serving as a soldier at the front, the rent control laws entitle him to claim the apartment as his own. The thoughtful tailor has even enclosed a newspaper clipping showing that he has solicited legal advice to this effect on behalf of the absent son. "I racked my brain," says the newly demobilized soldier, "but could not remember any Jakob Vizner in our old apartment building. Clearly he was some newcomer to our neighborhood who was prompted by a decent sympathy to write." The Yiddish is "*fun groys gutskayt un rokhmones hot er mir geshribn.*" If we were to isolate this last phrase, "prompted by a decent sympathy to write," it could serve well as a kind of subtitle or catchphrase for the novella as a whole. Despite all its bleakness and torpor, *The Street* is very much a story about decent sympathies both interpersonal and narrative. As such, it underscores the humane aspects of the modern Jewish picaresque over and against its roguish forebears. The few writers and scholars[14] who have engaged the book critically have recognized it as a compressed masterpiece of high Yiddish modernism, but most of its critics have characterized Rabon's novella as, above all, a chronicle of alienation, social fragmentation, and interwar disaffection.[15] The most prominent of them positively insists, "The basic theme of *The Street* is the narrator's alienation" (xxix).[16] Indeed, he views two of the book's most distinctive features—its interruption of an otherwise realistic voice with surreal or fantastic episodes and its cast of bizarre secondary characters—as techniques to illustrate the protagonist's alienation.[17] While these themes are inarguably prominent in the work, I would argue that its energy thrusts in precisely the opposite direction: toward human connection and coherence. The fuel for that motion toward healing is the act of narration itself.

Now I should hardly wish to suggest, in using terms like "thrust," "energy," and "healing," that Rabon endorses any sort of programmatic approach to improving the Jewish or human condition. More maskilically inflected works, as we have seen, implicitly sigh and say, "Oy, if only the Jews would. . . ." Rabon, on the other hand, shares with Sholem Aleichem, Joseph Roth, Isaac Bashevis Singer, and others a willingness to let the Jews be as they are, without trying to reform them. Decent sympathies, acts of gratuitous kindness, are left to flourish as they might, haphazardly. Benjamin Lerner seeks to make his mark on a great world, while Rabon's veteran tries merely to survive in a small one. The company in which he finds himself is relatively unambitious and does not seek to change the world. These characters know no positive telos, being neither Bundists nor Zionists nor intellectuals, with the possible exception of Vogelnest (Wolitz 225). They are not trying to reshape Jewish culture or to productivize anyone. Indeed, the milieu is a working class one where laborers who have been too "productivized" are striking. Yet even if the narrator's and other characters' sphere of action is constrained, there are still distinctions of value to be made. Modernism, even at its highest and coolest, still asks with Aristotle, what tends toward human flourishing? What activities give pleasure? The simple answer that this novella offers is the act of narration.

While the book is not an autobiography in any strict sense, it is most certainly a life narrative, and the most sweeping theme it presents—the salvific power of storytelling—reflects the events of its author's own life. Yisroel Rabon, born with the surname Rubin in 1900, spent his earliest years with his parents and three siblings in the Polish village of Govorchov. His wagon driver father's untimely death left his mother in poverty and prompted the family's move to Balut, a poor district or suburb of Łodz. With relatively little oversight from his mother, who worked long days as a peddler of used goods, he became an autodidact. He received part of his education from books (he read voraciously in translation and mastered French as a teenager) and part from the Flora Theater, where his brother-in-law treated him to lots of what writer Yosef Okrutni characterized as "cheap melodramas." He began publishing poetry in his teens and spent his career alternating between poetry and prose. *The Street* was published in 1928 and his memoiristic *Bildungsroman*, entitled *Balut*, appeared in 1934. He published three books of poetry between 1928 and 1937, as well as short stories, essays, at least one children's story, and *shund* (trashy or pulp fiction) that appeared pseudonymously. He also worked as a journal editor intermittently throughout the twenties and thirties. The Germans occupied Łodz in September of 1939, whence he escaped to Vilna, only to be shot in Ponar two years later.[18]

The reader first encounters Rabon's deracinated, nameless Jewish protagonist newly released after four years of service in the Polish army.[19] Informed so considerately by Mr. Vizner of his father's death, he realizes that he can't go home again, because no home remains. Standing at the train ticket window in the regiment's travel office and eligible for a travel voucher to anywhere in Poland, there is really nowhere particular to go. But before him in line stands a Polish soldier who is ecstatic to be returning to his hometown of Łodz. "'To Łodz,' the tall lean Pole cried, and there was so much joy, so much human yearning in his voice that I felt its warmth streaming over me" (3). So when his own turn comes, the narrator stammers out the name of the same city. Two months later, then, in the waning days of summer, he finds himself subsisting in a war-traumatized city, his peregrinations dictated by the insistent need for food and shelter, and for bits and bobs of work that will afford him these other necessities. As fall and then winter come on, his quest is increasingly one for warmth, both physical and interpersonal. A hard-up *flaneur*,[20] he loafs and bumbles about the city, mastering the geography of its parks and train station, its churches and flophouses. He participates in conversations, witnesses conversations, begs for food and money, seeks and gains and loses employment. He falls in with a circus and works briefly there as a sandwich board advertiser, then at a cinema. He meets a whole series of grotesques, and he gathers them about himself as a community of storytellers. His movements through interwar Łodz may be charted as a series of encounters with more and less successful storytellers,[21] within the larger matrix of his telling his own story. Interspersed among these events are episodes of dreams, fantasies, and recollections from the war, which are recounted in a more absurd, violent, or pathetic register than the rest of the rather naturalistic prose.

In depicting a harsh and wintry metropolis, *The Street* chronicles many instances of cruelty. The first episode of the novel proper (the train ticket to Łodz was part of a prologue) dramatizes the casual cruelty of unrecognition. The narrator espies and approaches an old comrade-in-arms whom he once saved from starvation at the front by sharing half a chicken. Now evidently well fed, the man fails to even recognize his erstwhile benefactor. (He can afford to forget this old act of kindness, as Gabriel Dan can forget the provenance of his boots.) Far more acute cruelty follows, when the narrator returns to his abject lodgings in a basement space with a mad, old Polish shoemaker, a virulent xenophobe and anti-Semite. He arrives in time to witness the shoemaker's participation in a horrifying children's game of make-believe gone awry and to prevent—through violent intervention— his landlord from actually hanging a little Schwabian boy as part of the dystopian fantasy. In view of this kind of bleakness, and the narrator's lack of a family or circle of friends to buttress him, the critical focus on alienation is understandable.[22]

The motley crew of fellow wanderers and sufferers whose stories the narrator ultimately elicits—these include Jason, a wrestler with a traveling circus; Vogelnest, a suicidal poet; and an unnamed "man from Komarno" who has toured remote provinces of China as a "professional Jew" for the benefit of a small Christian sect there—are all displaced Jews like him. Yet their shared Jewishness furnishes neither material comfort nor spiritual consolation, nor even—usually—conversational fodder for developing friendships. *Yiddishkeyt* is a shared affliction that need hardly be named among fellow sufferers, and organized, institutional Jewish life figures not at all. Chone Shmeruk notes that despite its autumnal setting, the book never references the High Holidays or other Jewish liturgical time (244),[23] and Seth Wolitz focuses on the crisis of language and identity faced by the generation of Jews that came of age in Poland between the wars, suspecting its own superfluity to the dawning order (219). Unpacking their quandary at some length, Wolitz argues that these young, urbanizing Jews fell into despair because following the Great War, they perceived neither a usable past in the *shtetl* nor a meaningful future for themselves as part of the Polish polity (220). But the traditional existence crystallized in the image of the *shtetl* had ceased to be viable for these young Jews even before the war; the wrestler Jason, for example, had manifestly broken from traditional Jewishness already. The predicament of these characters *as Jews* only intensifies but does not fundamentally alter their predicament as modern city-dwellers living near the turn of the twentieth century.

Among theorists and critics who discuss the literary representation of the modern and modernist city, there is dissension about nearly every aspect of the new urbanism and its distinctiveness from the rural and urban lifestyles that existed before. They bear witness to the collapse of the knowable community, to import Raymond Williams's[24] phrase from the English countryside to the Galician city. Where Walter Benjamin saw the city's hallmark as requiring its inhabitants' adjustment to a series of ceaseless shocks, Franco Moretti discerned nearly the opposite tendency: an urban reality that "mitigates extremes and extends the range of intermediate possibilities."[25] Critiquing the theoretical orthodoxy of identifying the modern city with "loneliness, isolation, fragmentation, and alienation," Hana Wirth-Nesher exposes the regressive quality of such a reflexive equation as "a romantic insistence on the fall from rural harmony into the discord of the metropolis" (17).[26] The sheer size of the new city engenders some trade-offs, introducing a degree of anonymity that inhibits the exercise of empathy even as it allows for the exercise of freedom.[27] The street of the novella's title—perforce ironic[28]—is the locus of this new anonymity, for better and for worse. "I felt better in the street" (33), proclaims the narrator. The traditional Jewish street formed its own chronotope, a site of boisterous economic and social activity, with temporal rhythms governed by market days, Sabbaths, and holidays; the deracinated urban street replaces a communal extension of private space with a newly blank canvas for unfulfilled vagrancy at best and menacing social unrest at worst. In the city of Łodz, there is no automatic or even discernible Jewish collective. Although the narrator might feel better on the street, he nonetheless refers to being "locked in the street" (21), which inverts the customary notion of outdoor freedom and indoor confinement. "The communal legitimacy of the street is negated," as

Wolitz observes (221). The satisfying, joyful bustle of the traditional *yidishe gas,* then, is predicated on having a private, personal space into which to withdraw, no matter how humble. A life denuded of the privacy of home is a life rendered grotesque. This grotesquerie might inevitably attend the Jewish occupancy of the *shtot* (large city) as opposed to the diminutive (and Judaized) *shtetl.*[29]

Beyond the particularly Jewish realm, Rabon's modernist picaresque novella points to an important distinction between the chronotope of "the street" and that of "the road." Bakhtin associates the rise of the picaresque with the chronotope of the road, associated with flux and adventure. The open road is the conduit to some desirable destination and itself promises all kinds of edifying, amusing experiences along the way. The street, more uniformly paved, suggests a very different set of associations. Rather than the via to an idealized elsewhere, it is a static presence outside the window—another urban topos akin to apartment houses, train stations, government buildings, parks, streetcars, and so on. It is defined not in relation to a place elsewhere but in relation to the interior spaces that surround it. The street is, consummately, outside: outside of all warmth, inclusion, and security. While the road is also outside and entails exposure, it affords both the pleasures and dangers of relative solitude. The city street, by contrast, is the site of density, concentrating and connecting persons and opportunities in multifarious commerce. But Rabon's street is a lonely one, peopled by unapproachable strangers. The protagonist's sustained vagrancy marks, above all, his failure to find or make home. Whereas he aspires to some safe and happy stasis, the street remains the locus of his forced motility.

Rabon must have been keenly aware of working in a "minor" literature, for he modeled many of his book's events, as well as its style of narration, on Knut Hamsun's spare masterpiece *Hunger,* published in 1890. While few critics would regard the Norwegian canon as a "major" one per se, this particular novella penetrated widely and deeply into the European consciousness. Hamsun's novel follows the trials of an unnamed writer plying his trade and trying to survive the autumn and early winter in Kristiania (Oslo). Although the protagonist of *Hunger* has a somewhat darker, more cynical outlook than Rabon's hard-luck soldier, the essential nature of their experience, as well as the tropes used to portray that experience, are quite similar. Isaac Bashevis Singer translated Hamsun's novel into Yiddish in the same year that *The Street* appeared, but Rabon was a self-trained polyglot, and he likely read the book years before in German or French translation. Thus it is not surprising that Hamsun's writer and Rabon's soldier undergo several of the same misadventures, if with different emphases: hard-won bits of money given away in perversely proud acts of charity; the pursuit of encouraging though ultimately unattainable women; the witnessing of and intervention in adults' cruelty to children in the guise of a game; and the apprehension of incipient madness. Ultimately, both narrators leave their respective cities. Rabon's soldier heads to a mining job in Katowice with a friend made in the local flophouse, and Hamsun's writer signs onto a Leeds-bound ship as a deck-hand: neither city can support men like these. The cities themselves are important characters, and the *topoi* of modernist urban alienation abound: closed windows and window dressings, clocks, municipal parks, policemen. Yet Rabon's narrator does find companionship and even friendship, rarely spending time alone during the book's second half. He solidifies relationships by hearing out other people's stories, whether in a restaurant with Jason or around the fire at the municipal beggars' house.

Hamsun and then Rabon alight on a disjointed, random narrative as the form that best accommodates and illustrates their characters' urban mess. The sequence of events is determined arbitrarily, a verbal representation of the central fact of both books: aimless wandering. Another interesting similarity, alluded to briefly above, is that both protagonists act—almost consistently—against the dictates of rational or enlightened self-interest. They do not husband their few resources carefully enough; when money comes to them, they are likely to give it away in the satisfaction of some internal drama. Rabon's character does this rather tenderly (settling on a polite and therefore humane schoolgirl his last coins), while Hamsun's more resentful writer parts with much needed money as an act of aggression. When an author in a "minor" tradition so closely echoes a "major" work,[30] the inevitable juxtaposition draws attention to the differences. While Hamsun's book cannot be considered "normative" in any sense, it does afford an earlier baseline of the modern, urban picaresque against which we might stand the *polit*. A discrepancy between the Norwegian and the Yiddish versions of this type of protagonist throws into relief one of the main differences between the *polit* and other modernist *pícaros*: whereas Hamsun's writer is bitter and misanthropic at his core, Rabon's demobilized soldier craves meaningful human connection and interpersonal warmth. Here, at least, the *polit* proves a *mensch*.

Against a backdrop of generalized cruelty, coldness, and indifference, the book's several episodes of gratuitous kindness gleam as treasures for narrator and reader alike. These instances of sympathetic decency run throughout the book, from the neighbor who writes the letter unprompted, to the school girl who taps deep wells of gratitude within the narrator and calls forth his most joyful if foolish generosity just by thanking him for restoring to her a dropped object. There is the middle-aged woman with a basket whom the hungry, scruffy narrator accosts in the hopes of rendering her some service and earning some money. While she at first takes him in his unwashed state as a thief, she quickly realizes that he's simply down on his luck. While he waits in the courtyard, she assembles a bundle of food for him and lends him money, which he later repays. She also tries to buoy his spirits, insisting, "So you see. One doesn't get lost. If God wills it, one finds a job and lives like everyone else in the world." The manager of the Circus Vangoli offers the narrator an honest if menial job, which then leads to significantly better, if short-lived, work in a cinema. Jason, the prosperous wrestler, offers the narrator more hospitality, food, and drink than he feels he can accept, and the depressed poet Vogelnest offers him—in touchingly plain terms—his friendship. He tags along briefly with the circus performers in their wagon as they take leave of Łodz, and while there, he enacts a scene of almost comically bourgeois domesticity, as the men play cards and the women cook over spirit stoves. In this scene, more than anything, the narrator and his friends from the circus manifest a longing for connection, normalcy, and home—as perceived by a petit bourgeois consciousness.[31]

In addition to these heartfelt sympathetic encounters, there are funny, ironic instances of sympathy as well. Peter Dunn, in his work on the classical Spanish picaresque,[32] reminds us that the picaresque is an ironized quest plot, and as such includes comedic nodes. These are present in *The Street* if one knows where to look. The narrator sees comedy of a mild sort one morning when he looks up to a nearby balcony and sees two Jewish *altekakers* commiserating in *daytshmerish* (overly Germanized Yiddish, often used to comic effect) about their respective morning coughs.[33] Even the coughing reflex, governed as it is by mirror neurons, might be construed as a very literal somatic instance of sympathy—*feeling with* the other.

The treasuring up of these tender moments argues for the book's (and the noticing narrator's) forbearance against the forces of alienation. Just as great a threat to the narrator's well-being as (meteorological) cold or (interpersonal) coldness, however, are the forces of fragmentation and incoherence. While the narrator's default mode is to report naturalistically on his movements from scene to scene in the metropolis, the chronological narrative flow is interrupted several times. These interruptions portend a kind of chaos that the narrator can scarcely hold at bay, and it is worth training our attention briefly on some of them. One is a traumatic memory of a boyhood injury to the narrator's hand, which forced his mother to journey with him to the regional capital to seek medical attention that the family could ill afford. Stuck in the big city without return fare or money for a meal, he remembers the sight of his mother putting out her hand on the street to beg.[34] A second interruptive episode is a Hoffmanesque, uncanny fantasy in which the narrator is baked into a loaf of bread. A third is the wartime memory of staving off hypothermia by hacking his way into the bowels of an expiring but still warm horse, and subsequently waking to find his own body frozen into a bloody cruciform. These episodes, each disturbing in its own right, are some of the "many things in *The Street* which cannot be safely anchored in the reality described in this book" (Shmeruk xxviii)—a "hard" reality[35] of Łodz in the 1920s. These intrusive or interruptive episodes, which Shmeruk characterizes as a "complicated web of hallucinations and possible hallucinations of a grotesque nature" (xxviii), destabilize the narration sufficiently in his eyes as to blur the line between reported "factual" and imagined experience, and between the "narrator's own" experiences and those recounted to him by his outlandish interlocutors. Without diminishing the oddity of the narrator's bread dream or the extremity of his taking refuge inside the horse's corpse, it is still straightforwardly simple—and fruitful—to distinguish between material presented as dream, memory, or other people's stories. When these various kinds of episodes are treated distinctly, it becomes possible to discern in them a sophisticated hidden structure, an "adventure novel." In terms that resonate with Bakhtin's characterization of the picaresque, the novella's events are encoded as a spiral of return or revisitation of previous scenes that gives expression to the narrator's ever more constricting, and finally strangling, prospects (Wolitz 222).

But there is one activity and source of energy that pushes out against this constrictive funnel: in recounting each of these episodes, the narrator contains its toxicity. In his landmark essay, "The Metropolis and Mental Life,"[36] the sociologist Georg Simmel posits a modern, metropolitan existence whose hallmark is an "intensification of emotional life due to the swift and continuous shift of external and internal stimuli" (103). This rapid-fire neural stimulation gives rise to a calculative, rational (as opposed to emotional) way of being in the world, and eventually to the "adaptive phenomenon" of the "blasé outlook" (106) that typifies urban consciousness. However, Rabon's demobilized soldier does not develop the sensibility predicted by Simmel's model. The rapid-fire stimuli that threaten his equanimity are not those afforded by the ever-shifting panorama of the street, so much as they are the thoughts, traumatic memories, and fears that flicker through his own mind. The danger that he perceives is incoherence and disparateness, aspects of the modern condition exacerbated by the violence he has witnessed and perpetrated during the war. All the postwar fragments of consciousness are in need of gathering up, a task for which the only suitable tool is narration. Thus does he string together the episodes of his own story, larded liberally with the nuggets of other characters' stories as they become known to him. It is highly significant that after working at a string of menial jobs, he achieves his greatest success and satisfaction as the *narrator* at a silent movie house. In that capacity, he takes the disparate visual images that glance across the screen and combines them into a meaningful story to which his working class audiences can relate or one that transports them beyond their workaday concerns.

The ranks of the audience are swollen by a textile workers' strike, the novella's true *Sitz im leben*. Łodz began to industrialize rapidly between 1815 and 1825, with its promotion by decree of the tsar in 1820 from a village of population 767 to a "factory city," charged with producing textiles for much of the Russian Empire.[37] Łodz developed later and faster than others in central Europe so that the city became "an unquestionable symbol for hasty urbanization, rabid capitalism, and cosmopolitanism," according to Delphine Bechtel. German, Bohemian, and Silesian immigrants poured into the city to staff its textile factories, and "the town attracted newcomers like a magnet, and grew like a mushroom, on sand, swamp, and peat bog" (Bechtel 80). For much of the nineteenth century, the "Manchester of Poland" was the country's second largest city, and between 1823 and 1873 the population doubled every ten years. The period from 1870 to 1890 saw another spurt of industrialization, this time involving many Jewish workers and factory owners. Growing up alongside this industrial activity, of course, was a robust labor movement. The first large strike occurred in 1892. Nicknamed "Antechamber to Hell," even before the Great War, the city was known for its cultural heterogeneity and concomitant threat to the ethnic and national identities of its denizens.[38] Its leading industrialists were more concerned about the bottom line than about any kind of ideological, philosophical, or ethnic commitment; their combination of economic liberalism and loyally conservative politics inspired the stereotype of the go-along-to-get-along *lodzermensch* (Chu 118).

The First World War ravaged the city, which proceeded to lose about 40 percent of its inhabitants to the draft, to disease, and to repatriation of German workers who had flocked to the textile mills decades earlier. In 1931, Łodz's Jewish population reached its peak of over two hundred thousand, fully a third of the city's inhabitants.[39] As Bechtel describes it,

> Łodz was thus both revolutionary and modern, as well as miserably backward. Although it was the first city in Poland and Russia to boast a steam-powered factory (in 1839), and opened the first electric tramway in the Polish Kingdom (1898), the city still had open-air sewers and lacked running water as late as the 1920s. In addition, industrial plants were located in the heart of the city, next to fallow land with manufacturing refuse heaps, pollution, continuous traffic, and restless agitation. The situation was a miracle for progressives and liberal theorists, but proved to be a nightmare for conservative landowners hostile to the city in general. (81)

The cognitive dissonance that Bechtel describes between ultra-modernity (factory and tramway) and backwardness (open sewers) might correspond to the intimate psychic reality of this veteran of the Great War who grew up in a provincial Jewish setting. Perhaps this is precisely the chasm that the narrator attempts to bridge in linking one event to another through the simple but potent act of narration.

Working in the cinema is his apotheosis. To a roiling audience of discontented workers, the narrator—hired as a *redner* (literally, "speaker") by the cinema's manager—weaves elaborate stories whereby the events of the French revolution onscreen recapitulate their own workers' revolution and they storm the cubicle of a recalcitrant projectionist as surely as they have witnessed the actors onscreen storm the Bastille. The narrator is aware of the magic wrought by his words. When narrating an Eddie Polo film, the 007 of the twenties, he says dreamily, "I wanted to forget where I was, to intoxicate myself with lovely language" (126). Intoxication, with its implication of disinhibition and its lexical overtones of toxicity, is an apposite image indeed. At its inception, the medium of film gripped viewers in a way that was unique in their experience: "Of all the new technologies which came to the fore during the 1920s," Jon Hughes reminds us, "none has proved so important and influential as film. The cinema screen, in

Hofmannsthal's words the 'Ersatz für die Träume' of the urban masses, bore witness to the camera's uncanny ability to 'dissect', reproduce, and manipulate the human image. For many the result was a crisis of identity, a feeling of a loss of control, and of the self as a shifting, ill-defined concept" (4). If film unsettled a stable identity, then it also held out the promise of new revelations that might enrich that identity on a higher plane of consciousness. For "the camera introduces us to unconscious optics as does psychoanalysis to unconscious impulses," observes Walter Benjamin (237).[40] As might an analysand, Rabon's narrator asserts a unified sense of self by folding powerful cinematic images into a narrative. Perhaps it is an aspirational pursuit for him: he is better able to arrive at narratorial cohesion within the cinema than in the recounting of his own story.

Though he is completely unassuming and wears his verbal artistry lightly—and certainly betrays none of the angst or arrogance of Knut Hamsun's aspiring writer-protagonist—there are intimations that latent within the narrator is a writer. In a very unsentimental text, the narrator permits himself an unusual lyrical reverie on the romance of the print alphabet after noticing a young woman reading on a park bench:

> And I felt again the yearning to read a book. I began to imagine the ordinary letters of the alphabet as enclosed in light and as having human characteristics. The letter aleph resembled an angry stepfather who sits in his daddy chair and never moves from his place; *gimel*, like a badly looked after tubercular; *zayin*, like a boy wearing a cap with visors on both sides; and *lamed*, like a good lamb with a neck that is too thin and long. (47)[41]

In this way, he resembles not only Hamsun's protagonist but also Singer's Benjamin Lerner. But typically, the books diverge on this subtle point. Lerner is ready to disregard the homespun nature of his reading materials, the better to process their content, whereas Rabon's narrator is actually fascinated with the alphabetic medium.

Working as cinematic narrator, making coherence out of disparate images, the narrator seems to have hit his groove. He has formed some tentative friendships with performers from the circus; maybe there is hope. But the strike winds down, and the cinema owner informs him that employing a narrator is not really helping the bottom line. He is let go. By now it is the dead of winter, and sleeping outside is no longer possible. He receives a pass to the municipal Beggars' House[42] and there describes a cast of even more wretched grotesques[43] than the strange folks associated with the circus. Ultimately, the book concludes with his joining the mysterious "man from Komarno" in traveling to Katowice to seek work in the mines there. But before we reach the Joycean last line, "The snow covered the earth and us,"[44] a peculiar thing happens to the narration.

At various points throughout the book, the protagonist-narrator shows himself ready to relinquish the work of telling his own story. Over a good twelve pages, Jason the wrestler recounts his dashing, improbable biography, with its outrageous love affairs, wartime heroics, near-death experiences, and describes his sideline as a highly paid, altruistic gigolo. As if playing a zero-sum game, our narrator disappears while Jason speaks. Usually chronicling his movements about the city minutely, the day following the night spent as Jason's hotel guest goes unreported until five p.m. It is as if the narrator has gotten temporarily lost in another's story. He takes back the reins in time to describe his dismissal from the cinema, his last call on Vogelnest before the poet's suicide, his final visit with the circus crew before they leave town, his arrival at the beggar's house, and so on. But once the man from Komarno starts telling *his* improbable biography, it is as if the narrator truly cedes the floor. The man from Komarno's story stretches over whole chapters and leaves the narrator, as it were, powerless to speak. What is ultimately so sad about the book's ending isn't that the snow is general over Katowice, or that the narrator finally has to leave Łodz to find work in the Silesian mines, but rather that he abdicates the healing, order-making work of narration to others. It feels like a kind of slackening or giving up. In the bleakest, coldest circumstances, the narrator has succeeded in drawing so much warmth and human emotion to himself. But the cinema job has ended, the circus has moved on, Vogelnest has committed suicide. All that human connection proves fleeting and revocable. And narrator's narrator though he may be, the fully demobilized soldier simply has no words.

Bad Romance

One of the most important shared elements among these fictions of demobilization is the inability of each protagonist to succeed romantically, or to be more specific, the failure of each to pursue the woman to whom he feels drawn. This is the clearest indication that we are not dealing with the conventional *Bildung* genre.[45] Other theorists of the turn to modernism have also noted the displacement of the traditional marriage plot. Without unions between men and women, there is no replication, no social integration. The heroes remain men alone, ionized particles unable to adhere to the opposing particles that would stabilize and ground them. Interestingly, this refusal of the marriage plot figures not only in the thoroughly picaresque fictions considered in this chapter, but also in Singer's wistful *Bildungsroman*. Lerner leaves Gnendel in a most unheroic position at her gynelogical exam, and after he is taken from her, she never figures in his known thoughts again. Regarding *The Street*, Chone Shmeruk considers the protagonist's fleeting interactions with Clara (Vogelnest's wife) and Luba (the mysterious, ethereal Beloved), and Jason's tragic romance with Ela and concludes, "In this inability to consummate a love relationship, even of a simple individual couple, one can see an expression of the same fateful and total alienation which is to be found in the book" (xxxv). Although I follow a different line of interpretation for the novel as a whole, Shmeruk is right to note this peculiarity.

Roth's narrator is, true to form, the most self-aware about his lack of romantic success. Although, as he acknowledges, "A great store of loneliness has grown in me, six years of solitude" (110), he is unable to push his relationship with Stasia beyond friendship. It is the man's place to initiate and pursue, he muses: "I realise now that women are aware of everything that goes on in us, but nonetheless wait for the spoken word" (111). Indeed, to fail at those tasks is to behave "as if *I* were the girl and Stasia the man" (112). That is to say, initiative, activity, and world-shaping are the province and duty of the man. Gabriel is left to rue the lapse, but there is no suggestion that he will learn from the experience and correct it in the future because that is not how the *polit* operates. There is no learning curve, no redemptive arc, and no sense of a wide-open future in which to apply lessons gleaned from one's past. Ross Chambers proposes[46] that the narrative relationship (between narrator-narratee) is an essentially erotic one in that the act of narration is a metaphor for seduction. If that is so, then these "failed" or irregular narrations are of a piece with the failed seductions or unconsummated erotic trajectories of their main characters. If the *polit* as demobilized soldier has borne out the rhyming maxim (. . . *iz hering oykh a fish!*) and become the proverbial fish, then he is a cold fish indeed.

PART 3

The *Polit* as Soviet Citizen

THE *POLIT* UNDER TSARS AND STRIPES[1]

"... to speak means to be forever on the road."

—Osip Mandelshtam

At this rather advanced stage of our acquaintance with the *polit*, let us review some of his distinguishing traits. He is quintessentially mobile, albeit with varying degrees of energy and agency, which do not always align. Motl's level of energy, for example, vastly outstrips his agency over the family's peregrinations, while Rabon's soldier moves diffidently, conserving energy and content to be borne along by circumstances largely beyond his control. Moreover, the *polit* often lives in some kind of alternate temporality, differing from linear, developmental time as well as from Bakhtin's national-historic time. His heterochrony may involve immaturity that ranges into pedomorphism or else a sense of being suspended in time[2] in the wake of cataclysmic events, such as the Great War. Either through his own self-expression or through the author's positioning of his character, the *polit* lives a life against sentimentalism. This antisentimentalism often involves an ironic humor that expresses a sense of playfulness about human experience captured in the aphorism, "you might as well laugh!" The *polit*'s struggle is for survival rather than completion or optimization. Thus far, the Yiddish picaresque.

But what about the trait that has classically been regarded as constitutive of the European picaresque: delinquency, roguishness, and even criminality?[3] This continuum exists within the modern Jewish picaresque,[4] but its contours emerge more fully when we move beyond the Yiddish-speaking Pale of Settlement and look to Jewish literature written in Russian. Of course Sholem Aleichem contributes greatly to the idea of the swindle as a picaresque move, but as befits a deterritorialized language that lacked the conventional trappings of power, his swindlers work by stealth. The card-sharps' deception is discovered only after their exit; that the trick *dreydl* bore a *gimel* on every side is realized only in adulthood; the true vocation of the man encountered in the train compartment (whether procurer or card-sharp) is recognized only after his departure. Evil is apprehended slyly, from a safe distance, but outright confrontation is rare. Add an army and borders to the equation, and everything changes. This chapter will examine two Russian-language fictions by Jewish authors that treat Jewish themes; in both of these, roguish, delinquent, and even violent behavior glints at the front-and-center of the picaresque sensibility. Although written early in the Soviet period, neither work could be published until after the fall of Communism.[5] The first book we shall consider is Ilya Ehrenburg's early and most explicitly Jewish novel ("the most unusual book of his career,"[6] according to Ehrenburg's biographer) *The Stormy Life of Laz Roitshvantz*[7] (1928). Then we will examine Isaac Babel's *Odessa Stories*, a series of linked fictions mythopoeically representing the last days of pre-Soviet Odessa Jewry. This latter book is less obviously picaresque, but like many of Sholem Aleichem's stories, it enables us to test some of the boundaries of the genre and observe how a definable sensibility overspills the conventional generic container. Ehrenburg and Babel were friends in a time of cataclysm, each in his own way coming to grips with the transformations in Russian life wrought by Soviet rule. Both writers instinctively understood that their epoch called for new approaches to storytelling—or for the refurbishing and modernization of older ones. Eschewing both nineteenth-century modes of linear story-telling and the conventions of social realism, each engaged in forms of *partial* narration that took full advantage of a picaresque poetics. The Ehren-burg of *Laz Roitshvantz* (and *Julio Jurenito*[8]) fully embraced the logic of displacing metonymy, while Babel pieced together a riven world through composite narration.

"To die on an empty stomach is uninteresting": Picaresque Events

Laz Roitshvantz's name attests to his impeccable credentials, both as *pícaro* and as Soviet citizen. The red in his surname, as he vainly attempts to explain to a non-Yiddish speaking interrogator from the Commisariat of Economic Affairs, is no recent dye job. And his first name, Leyzer in Yiddish, furnishes a direct genealogical link to the ur-*pícaro*, Lazarillo de Tormes, right down to the tender diminutive for long-suffering Lazarus. The character even hazards such a genealogy for himself, when he tells the story of a poor Jew ordered to run thrice around the perimeter of Rome for the pleasure of the Pope, only to be relieved after his first lap by Jesus himself. Invoking a personal connection to that tormented runner, Laz says, "'Let's say his name was Leiser. I rather think he must have been my grand-dad's grand-dad, for our line of outstanding Roitshvantzes started with such a distressing apparition" (149). In claiming this lineage, Laz at once reinforces his linkage to a long chain of Jewish suffering[9] but also to a venerable franchise of resourcefulness and resilience; after all, Laz's mythic progenitor survived the day.

Ehrenburg offers his own paragraph-long account of this most "unusual book," in the safe retrospect of his memoir *People, Life, Years*.[10] Before summarizing the plot, he takes pains to distance himself from the sources of his Jewish material, emphasizing that he comes to it second-hand and only as an adult:

In Montparnasse during the late twenties I met a Jewish writer from Poland, Warszawski, and some of his friends. They told me many amusing stories about the superstitions and the cunning of the old type small-town Jew. I read a collection of Hasidic legends which I found pleasingly poetic. It gave me the idea of writing a satirical novel. Its hero is a Gomel tailor, Lazik Roitshvanets, a poor fellow whom fate tosses from one country to another. I described our NEP men and provincial dogmatists, Polish cavalry captains, German petit bourgeois, French aesthetes and English hypocrites. Finally, in despair, Lazik decides to go to Palestine, but the so-called Promised Land turns out to be like any other: the rich have a good life, the poor a wretched one. Lasik tries to organize a "Return-to-the-Homeland Association," on the grounds that he was not born under a palm tree but in his beloved Gomel. He is killed by Jewish fanatics. Western critics called my hero "the Jewish Schweik." (This book is not included in my collected works, not because I think badly of it or repudiate it, but because, after the Nazi atrocities, I think it premature to republish some of its comical passages) (Pinkus 44)

It is terribly ironic that Oyzer Varshavsky should be the purveyor of "charming" stories and superstitions, for his own novel *Shmuglars* (*Smugglers*)[11] exemplifies in Yiddish fiction a hyper-realist naturalism that treated the Polish *shtetl* in the time of the Great War without an ounce of nostalgia or even pity. Ehrenburg also accounts for Laz's omission from his collected works, tactfully if incredibly sidestepping the possibility of Soviet suppression.

As the author notes, *The Stormy Life of Laz Roitshvantz* adheres so strictly to the picaresque form and so precisely exemplifies a Central European form of absurdist humor that it has been called "the Jewish Schweik." However, Ehrenburg's novel makes a significant departure from its Czech cousin: while the protagonist engages in dozens of occupations over the course of the novel and enters multiple sectors of the Soviet and European economies, the one career he conspicuously eschews is that of the military man. He is not a demobilized soldier; instead, he is a newly and somewhat breezily mobilized communist, one impervious to ideology and looking not so much for a just society as for that evening's meal. We might think of it as a quest for social justice on a very personal level. Presumably, given his short stature, no army in the world would accept him anyway. Although Babel notes the presence of Jewish "midgets" in the Red Army in his story "Afonka Bida," Roitshvantz was never destined to be one of them. But like the good soldier Schweik, Ehrenburg's little man has an inability to fall in with the demands of his circumstances and therefore a penchant for being misunderstood and punished.

This is not to say that he lacks opportunities to make good. After serving the brief jail term in his hometown that touches off the narrative, a lovelorn and discouraged Laz fails as a party candidate in Kiev, before making for provincial Tula where he might have entered the Soviet economy, had there been any live specimens of the rabbits he was assigned to breed. Ever the benevolent schemer, he tries his hand as a literary man in Moscow, a wonder rabbi in Frankfurt, a film star in Berlin, an avant-garde artist in Paris, and a missionary in London, before boarding a Palestine-bound ship in Liverpool. The only place he remotely fits into the nascent economy of the Holy Land is as a beggar. The transition between locations and occupations is marked more often than not with a stint in jail, a well-deserved drubbing at the hands of some outraged mark, or both.

A lifetime's worth of experience, including watershed events such as first love, marriage, and death are all condensed into a two-year period. If the bending or squeezing of time is one of the hallmarks of the picaresque, then *Laz Roitshvantz* exhibits the heterochrony of compression. During the span of time represented, Laz ages at an accelerated pace; his unusually small stature gestures at once backward to childhood and forward to a shrunken old age. Indeed, in the faux-scientific assessment of the Koenigsberg apothecary Herr Dr. Dreckendorf (whom Laz rechristens Dreckenkopf), our hero is possessed of the "Stature of a degenerate, just over four foot. Maximum." His staccato notes continue, "Easily pass as an eight-year-old. Premature senility" (126). Laz is simultaneously neotene and gerontomorph (prematurely aged)—anything but the middle-aged man in the prime of life that his chronological age would suggest. By the time he lies on death's doorstep in the Holy Land, the narrator observes, "in these years of wanderings he had indeed grown old. He had begun to stoop. People took him for forty. He was always ailing—phlegmy, throaty, complaining of pains in the chest, pains in the loins" (239). This compression of Laz's aging process (to say nothing of the horror of being taken for forty!) corresponds to one of the nonmimetic or "primitive" aspects of the novel: the flattened temporality of over two thousand years of Jewish history. Just as signs of Laz's childhood and old age manifest as a jumble, so too is Jewish time jumbled in his consciousness. He moves frictionlessly among Biblical stories, Talmudic anecdotes, Hasidic stories, and European-Jewish folkloric material.

The novel is narrated by accretion. A narrator whose presence is most evident while establishing Laz's identity at the very beginning ("There was a Laz too in Odessa, where I once happened to lecture on French literature,") gradually recedes into omniscient invisibility, while the protagonist racks up a collection of incidents, anecdotes, and useful jargon. Recounting just the final two years of the character's life, the novel records Laz's suffering through twenty incarcerations in six countries. In fact, it is difficult to trace this history minutely because of vague sentences, such as, "From time to time he was arrested and beaten up, then let out again" (219). Twenty is a nice, round number, though, and it is the one to which he lays claim when tallying up the stations of the cross he bears. These imprisonments provide the markers by which to measure this stormy life, especially since each one entails an apologia addressed to the warden or to a fellow inmate, and it usually takes the form of a Jewish story.

In the manner of the classic picaresque, the book lends itself to making lists: of locations, incarcerations, Jewish stories, occupations, and conversations. The progress of this particular rake might be traced in terms of these agglutinative categories. For this analysis, it will be most useful to attend to the incarcerations, accompanied as they are by stories and exempla ranging across all periods of Jewish history. These "nuggets" of Jewish content cannot be ignored, and indeed many critics of the novel have addressed their significance. Efraim Sicher sets the prevailing tone with his observation that "the Yiddishisms and Hasidic stories are largely stylized or invented. Lazik adapts Talmudic pilpul (academic, hair-splitting argument) to Marxist dialectics, showing up the absurdity of communist demagoguery" (201). While it is true that the Hasidic texts are stylized with respect to their origins, we shall see that they are deployed in a bracingly specific and detailed way in regard to Laz's immediate circumstances. Ehrenburg's English-language biographer, Joshua Rubenstein, also implicitly questions the authenticity or legitimacy of the author's resort to Hasidic material, noting, "Except for a handful of Hasidic tales, Lasik has nothing to do with traditional Jewish life in the myriad shtetls throughout Poland and the Ukraine, communities Ehrenburg could only vaguely know from visits to his grandfather in Kiev. The novel is not about the life that Lasik and Ehrenburg's family left behind; it is about a Jew who rejects this traditional life and tries vainly to find a place for himself in the broader secular world" (99). While Laz's character is surely part of the broad shift from shtetl religion to urban secularity, these summary dismissals not only overlook Ehrenburg's personal investment in writing about the Hasidim (as he did in his travelogue "Visa of Time," published in 1931 though describing the early 1920s) but they also miss an opportunity to contextualize his work in terms of the uses to which Hasidic materials were being put in order to address Jewish modernity. The strong "folkloric" element of Ehrenburg's novel ought to be considered alongside the ethnographic projects that had come into vogue with the turn of the century. Y.L. Peretz discovered in Hasidut a vocabulary for anticlerical and even antinomian populism,[12] while S. An-sky (Shloyme Zaynvl Rapoport) vividly rendered Jewish modernity with folkloric stylizations drawn from his ethnographic fieldwork.[13] Folkloric elements can be used to impart an outsized resonance to pedestrian details, such as questions of origins. The *pícaro* is customarily of lowly birth; rumors of illegitimacy dog the childhoods of Lazarillo de Tormes and El Buscón. Laz is technically legitimate but nonetheless socially marginal as the product of a "cholera wedding" (*shvartse khasene*),[14] a union between orphans brokered by the community's elders in an attempt to stem the tide of an epidemic. Thus, Laz is—as he reminds all who will listen—a creature literally born of misfortune.

Sicher characterizes Laz as a figure with "nothing left in which to believe," a state of skepticism that leads to either willful or careless misinterpretation of Jewish textual and folkloric materials: "Ehrenburg's Christian mystical views show through his readings, or rather misreadings, of Jewish texts such as the Talmud and Hasidic stories" (201). Let us consider, however, the possibility that Ehrenburg is far more careful in the use of these materials than he has received credit for being. Perhaps an analogous interpretive case is the status of Tevye the dairyman's malapropisms and misquotations. While at first those were regarded by critics as evidence of Tevye's untutored carelessness, they were eventually recognized as highly intentional on the part of Rabinovitsh and often clever reworkings on the part of Tevye "himself."[15] In this novel, Ehrenburg proves neither hostile to nor distant from *yiddishkeyt*. As with Tevye's digressions and perorations, there is always a logical thread connecting the nugget to the situation at hand.[16] In fact, Laz's nuggets proceed by a textual maneuver very deeply rooted in classical Jewish sources, and one which is readily adapted to a picaresque poetics: the logic of parable (*mashal*) and explanation or immediate experiential referent (*nimshal*). Usually addressing himself to a person in a position of power (occupational superior, jailer, potential patron), Laz again and again offers an obscure exemplum that points a moral. He usually hastens to declare the epimythium himself, not leaving to chance his intended interpretation. These Jewish nuggets become the "beads" or units of picaresque experience, as will be evident upon considering the following summary of the Jewish material.

Ehrenburg's Discursive Picaresque

The Stormy Life of Laz Roitshvantz hews very closely to the conventions of its genre, but the element that sets this novel apart as truly modernist is that its picaresque structures operate not only on the level of event but on that of discourse. Laz's constant recourse and essential posture is imposture, and his speech habits give voice to his survivalist malleability: "In order to earn a crust of bread and a slice of sausage he learns to mimic any official language and beguile his listeners with a mouthful of verbiage to convince them he loyally 'belongs'" (Sicher 201). Thus does he hope to win the sympathy and even the affection of all he encounters. Laz's character embodies the Bakhtinian trifecta of clown-fool-rogue, with the major emphasis on the rogue, even as the other categories remain near at hand. These are the wandering, rootless figures deemed "life's maskers,"[17] but who might more accurately be denominated "life's *unmaskers*" (Emerson and Morson, 352) for the way that their masquerade reveals the social truths that usually re-

Chapter	*Mashal*	*Nimshal*
3	two Jews find a *tales*; peroration on Talmudic thought; description of cholera wedding (*shvartse khasene*)	Laz's problematic tendency to think too much
6	Story of Kotsker rebbe hearing a forbidden womanly voice (*kol isha*) in a clock's chiming even amidst his ascetic isolation	Imprisonment or even death cannot keep Laz from his love for Fanny Hershanovich, even if it be declared and reciprocated only in his own fantasy
8	Talmudic case regarding the status of the egg hatched on the Sabbath (*betzah shenoldah beshabat*)	Rendering fine, if meaningless, distinctions: despicably bourgeois fox-trot vs. acceptably socialist waltz
9	Sturgeon is *treyf*; cleaning before Passover	Banned (anti-Soviet) books are *treyf* and must be purged like *khometz*
11	*dayenu*	"I've had enough!"
13	Tsadik of Berditchev defends exploiter Meisel but ends colloquy with God that would have brought the Messiah, out of consideration for the washerman Hersch	The importance of not selling people out[a]
14	Hadrian beheaded Jews for not bowing and then for bowing	Damned if you do, damned if you don't—apropos of rabbit breeding
16	Cites sale of *khometz, eruv* as problem-solving legal loopholes	Urges the publication of conventional *shund* with allegorized socialist interpretations
21	God spares Alexander the Great's realm only for the sake of small cattle and despite the cruelty of his justice system	Poland is barbaric and is spared only for the sake of its innocents
26	Jesus takes Leyzer's place in running thrice around Rome for the Pope's amusement	True divinity appears in humble form. To anti-Semitic cellmate Kotz: how do you know I'm not Jesus?
30	Joshua's succession to Moses; Moses and Pharoah	Just as Moses was reluctant to die, so is Laz
36	Why should God have been jealous of Baal if the idol is powerless?	To Scotland Yard detective who has arrested Laz as a communist agitator: "'If those poor Soviet folk haven't got anything but sheer stupidity, why get so worked up?'"
37	Mystical speculation on the "song" of all things including the sea—> self-satisfied King David and a skeptical toad	"'What I'd like to know is: in what way are your trumpetings better than my anonymous croak?'"
39	Tells fellow beggars about Zadik of Rovno, who defends his sinning flock by saying he doesn't yearn for a paradise only for the perfect. "How can anyone rise who has never fallen?"	Russia is the imperfect paradise, "But men there are at least in search of something. No doubt they are making mistakes."
40	The Besht and the boy with the tin whistle	The meaning of Laz's irreverent, impoverished life. "On his dead features was the smile of a child. Just like that had smiled little Yuska, when they allowed him to blow his tin whistle" (269).

[a]Rubenstein glosses this parable as follows: "The revolution, the civil war, the unending executions—all were carried out in the name of mankind's future happiness. But if the Rebe could not allow an old Jew to die to insure the coming of the Messiah, then who could ever have the right to order the sacrifice of another human being?" (99).

main suppressed or implicit. The irony of Laz's attempts at imposture is that they always end up underscoring his unbridgeable alterity, his outsider status in relation to each in-group that he tries to infiltrate. Bakhtin formulates this refractory otherness as a boon: "Essential to these figures is a distinctive feature that is as well a privilege—the right to be 'other' in this world, the right not to make common cause with any single one of the existing categories that life makes available; none of these categories quite suits them, they see the underside and falseness of every situation" (DiN 159). Failing more than refusing to fit in to any one of the novel's many subcultures and microcosms, Laz ultimately finds life itself unavailable, bringing to mind the old saw "you could live if they let you." Yet every lie that he tells along the way to his death is redeemed by the deplorability of those to whom he lies. In fact, it is the rogue's own "gay deception" that exposes the greed, venality, cupidity, self-righteousness, and cruelty of those who would deny or torment him. In the premodern novel, reflecting a more figured, externalized, carnivalesque world, "The rogue continually dons and discards masks so as to expose the falsity of those who presume their roles and institutions are natural" (Morson and Emerson, 352).[18] In the fully modern world, in which the carnival is sublimated, those literal masks are abstracted into rhetorical ones equally well suited for questioning the naturalness of institutions and institutional thought.

The Bakhtinian category of novelistic speech called "gay deception" dovetails with the antisentimentalism of the *polit*. Every fib of Laz's tends toward the sympathetic aim of speaking truth to power. As Bakhtin posits, "Falsehood is illuminated by ironic consciousness and in the mouth of the happy rogue parodies itself" (DiN 402). Casual and mischievous lying becomes the discursive means of disrupting more pernicious and deeply entrenched lies: "This kind of speech presumes that all 'pathos' is a 'lie,' and that no language of any class, group, or profession contains a 'straightforward truth'. . . . The rogue parodies and reprocesses discourses of falsity so as to reveal what is false about them and to rob them of their harmful power" (Emerson and Morson, 359–60). It is virtuous to lie to the liars. Consider Laz's blithely multiplying, nonexistent rabbits, or, to stay with the rabbit motif, recall the leporine specimen intended for a Parisian painter's still life that Laz so artfully seasons, cooks, and devours. The deception remains gay because Laz's crimes are virtually victimless. He steals food only from those who enjoy relative plenty, and his false brand of religion[19] deceives only those for whom Jewish rituals are but outmoded superstition in any event.

Even if his "gay deception" may be tallied as a social good, Laz's perpetual need to ingratiate himself underscores the insufficiency of being, simply, the hungry stranger, the Jewish tailor that he actually is. Yet at the same time, we must ask, how simple is he? Laz seems to be an instinctual linguistic chameleon, mixing his own peculiar idiolect with a series of ideological, occupational, and other identity-defining sociolects. One by one, he parodies various discourses and speech registers (NEP lingo, Soviet realist fiction) that "seek to impose order on an essentially heterogeneous and messy world" (Emerson and Morson 30)—what Bakhtin calls centripetal language—thus acting as a centrifugal linguistic force. In an elegant essay,[20] Michael Holquist plumbs the ethical implications of the contest between order-making and order-disrupting linguistic activities and how these relate to multilingualism, which happens to be such a pervasive feature of Jewish modernist fiction:

> The struggle between languages that Bakhtin posits as the fundamental condition for the emergence of the novel is most productively perceived not as horizontal combat between centrifugal and centripetal forces, but as the vertical tension between high languages that claim authority precisely because they are unitary, and low languages that are so because they revel in the multi-languedness of their characteristic forms. (66)

In Jewish literature generally, as well as in this novel specifically, the choice among languages is always marked by a hierarchical power differential. This is true not only of the language of composition but of the language choices that so often appear on the plane of representation. Dumped, upon his release from a Polish prison, into neighboring Königsberg, Laz hears German as poorly spoken Yiddish. Of course the humor of this mistake is that his evaluation of the two languages is at odds with the relative value assigned them by the rest of the world. In Tel Aviv, Laz is so remote from the national project of renewing spoken Hebrew that he thinks his coreligionists are praying in the street. The Gomel *landsman* he encounters in that holy city is abused for selling Yiddish newspapers, and Laz himself is dressed down for professing his quixotic affections to a bevy of dancing girls in shameful *jargón*: "'Impudent little twerp! How dare you sully this elevated atmosphere with your slavish Yiddish jargon? They sing to us in the sacred tongue of the Shulamite, and you come bounding in and soil our noble ears with your Gomel filth. You must be declared a Bolshevik!'" (251). The elevated atmosphere so sullied is a cabaret. The enforced hegemony of Hebrew reinforces Ehrenburg's satiric point about Mandatory Palestine as a "normal,"[21] territorially based nation: its vaunted statehood inheres in the sovereign ability to discipline and punish. The suppression of Yiddish is of a piece with Mandatory jails, where the boards are just as hard as in other jails the world over.

In Ehrenburg's novel, language politics assert themselves not only in the choice among national idioms but also in the various registers of speech within Laz's Russian. Soviet political reality imposed a new set of requirements on speech and language, in the service of a totalizing and totalitarian vision. Ehrenburg mocks this newspeak to great effect during Laz's brief sojourn in Moscow's literary circles, lampooning Soviet, proletarian realist prose:

> 98th Instalment. The hum of the soap was like iron honeybees. With a valiant toss of his head Senka Puvak cried: "That's done it, my lads, the situation's saved." Dunya smiled at his side, and gazed with pride at the driving belts, while the red star rose and fell on her bosom, swollen with healthy enthusiasm. The soap bubbled. "We'll supply the whole Union," declared Senka. He turned his eye to the star on the girl's breast: "Well, Dunya," he cried, "shall we be going? Ours is the path of the young class to the sun. Let us forget the dirty amusements of those who once owned this factory. Let me crush you to my bosom with my arms of labour." And Dunya, abandoning herself to the pulse of a new life, a faint blush on her cheeks, whispered: "Look, we have beaten the pre-war norm. Hum on, oh soap, hum on! If it's a boy, we shall call him simply Soap-Hum." (81)

Enthusiasm for government-mandated industrial productivity merges with the gendered conventions of cheap romance (heaving bosoms, blushing cheeks, crushingly masculine arms) into one risible burlesque of the national romantic fiction or even the *Bildungsroman*, whose "original magic," as Jed Esty observes, was "to harmonize, as it were, production and self-production" (74). The Soviet sociolect that promised to harmonize self-production with soap production (and human reproduction) was monoglossic, conforming to Bakhtin's definition of a speech genre that can never fully suppress others but that tries to legitimate itself at their expense (Bruhn and Lundquist 29). Laz suggests appending piously communist introductions to trashy romances (the genre known as *shund* in Yiddish) because no one is buying the humming soap—the fictional offerings that *do* pass ideological muster. Laz's own peculiar idiolect, about which more later, incorporates a plurality of speech genres and so is heteroglossic and centrifugal. The heteroglot is not suppressed altogether, but devalued, as hybrid (or "mongrel") Yiddish is in relation to "pure" Russian or Hebrew. As Bruhn and Lundquist explain, "monoglossia does not have the power to rule out heteroglossia, but it can divide the indefinite field of speech genres in stabile [sic] axiological hierarchies and condemn the *non grata* elements to the outskirts of language" (ibid.). Michael Holquist teases out the ethical implications in this tension between official and unofficial speech: "the history of the novel can be read off as a story of struggle between different centrifugal and centripetal forces at different points in history. . . . The struggle is not only necessary, it is ethical. It is not just a conflict, but a set of revolutions, in which the absolutist claims of an authoritarian language is [sic] overturned by the demonstration of language's multiplicity in parodying genres" (Bruhn and Lundquist 66). There could be no more apt description of *The Stormy Life of Laz Roitshvantz*.

Attentive readers of both Ehrenburg and Bakhtin have recognized the immediate political stakes of this historical struggle in-and-through language. Holquist correlates the common thread of collapsing hierarchies in the work of Bakhtin and Erich Auerbach to their need to counter the myths, respectively, of Soviet Russian and Nazi German as privileged languages representing whole, unified polities. Emerson and Morson consider the possibility that gay deception was a phenomenon that Bakhtin apprehended personally and all too well, noting, "Although Bakhtin's praise of answering lies with deception may be understandable in the Soviet context, it may also seem like a sentimental response to falsehood" (360). We do well to set this criticism against Sicher's assessment that Laz was a mouthpiece for *his* creator: "Lazik may have cheated the system, but he does not think himself guilty of deceiving anyone. Yet he is punished everywhere for what he has not done. This might also be said of Ehrenburg's own supposed treachery"[22] (202).

Mashal, Metonymy, and the Picaresque

By examining the distinctive elements of Laz's idiolect, we stand to learn a great deal more about the workings of speech genres. He comes of age as a Soviet citizen having been educated in the "wrong" language (and thought) system. He strives repeatedly to use *meshalim* (parables or extended analogies) to bridge the gap between his upbringing and the absurd adult world in which he finds himself. This trope of substitution relies on the figurative logic of metonymy: this for that. The bank of images, stories, situations, rules, and inspiration on which Laz draws is of course the sweepingly diachronic Jewish tradition, as distilled for the Jewish masses. One might posit that Ehrenburg pits one form of monoglossia, rabbinic language, against another, the regnant Soviet monoglossia.[23] However, this would represent a misapprehension of the Jewish mythic tradition to which the Gomel tailor is heir. After all, several of the analogic stories charted above are hagiographic tales of Hasidic masters, a discourse that represents antinomian strains in Jewish thought and culture. Laz's mythic Jewish vocabulary is itself heteroglot; the whole of his speech is best captured by the term *polyglossia*, as Bruhn and Lundquist define it:

> Polyglossia is historically linked to trade alliances, imperialism, emigration, and other economic and cultural exchanges[24] leading to the meeting of different national languages. . . . A language can only overcome its self-complacent and narrow view of the world by mirroring itself in another language—ordinary heteroglossia cannot solve this problem. Polyglossia, then, is connected to the centrifugal powers of language, it strengthens the sense of linguistic stratification and it prepares the linguistic soil for the possibility of acknowledging that different speech genres are also different outlooks on the world. This is the situation that the term *dialogized heteroglossia* is meant to capture. (30)

Indeed, Laz brings Jewish and Soviet discourses into dialogue with one another even as he enacts a low-caste version of emigration and various "other economic and cultural exchanges." His pointed *meshalim* impose a kind of mirroring of one world view in another.

Laz's idiolect is quite funny, and the humor often works by "twisting" or bending the logic of metonymy. "Metonymy involves a comparison between two conditions or elements that have a pre-established connection in the empirical world. . . . [A]s Jakobson argues, it embodies the governing principle of prosaic, non-poetic language: that language should reflect and articulate the perceived condition of the external world" (37).[25] In other words, metonymy is supposed to be "straight," whereas Laz excels at seeing and reflecting a world askew. As he sends up the rhetoric of so many occupations, vocations, locations, and cultural milieux, he steadfastly avoids the abstractions and categorical thinking in which unpalatable facts are customarily cloaked. As with his *meshalim*, everything has a concrete referent, and the reader watches him invoke those referents to draw connections between present and past experiences. Ehrenburg builds his comedy upon the sedimentation and increasingly baroque recombination of various allusions. Thus is the circumlocution "Pole of Mosaic Law," itself pompous and pretentious, spoonerized to "Moses of Polish Law," then further transposed to "Moses of German Law" (121). The novel is generous to its readers in that we are offered the tools to understand these increasingly complex references—but his interlocutors in new situations could not possibly be expected to do so. Various motifs thus become, effectively, inside jokes between Laz/Ehrenburg and the reader. Of course there is an element of unreality here in that none of the humorous connections seem to predate the period of narration. This diminution of mimesis contributes to what Bakhtin might call a "primitive" sense of temporality in the novel: there is little effort to account for a time before the novel's action begins, other than to gesture vaguely at a distantly remembered and barely relevant childhood.

Laz is especially given to euphemisms that work by metonymy. Certain terms are invoked so often and in such stilted fashion that they become funny: "functions" for all matters pertaining to sex, and "confession" for all matters relating to Jewishness. Herr Rosenbaum, the portrait of an assimilated German Jew preposterous in his efforts to "pass," disclaims any vestigial or inherited knowledge of Yiddish, insisting, "'I only understand you because I live near the frontier.... But please do not assume I am a Jew; I am a real German. I admit that I belong to the Mosaic Confession, but that is my private business'" (121). Terms such as "confession" are manipulated, spliced and reconfigured to the point of unrecognizability. Because of its taboo nature to begin with, sex is a topic ripe for the displacements of metonymy. Ehrenburg mocks in turn various discourses of human sexuality: romanticism, revolutionary sexual candor and functionalism, prostitution, perversion, and hedonism. Nothing can shake Laz's own romantic yearning after Fanny Hershanowitz, the modern and freeloving daughter of a traditional cantor, whose boyfriend Schatzman has fulfilled just one of the three conditions that her father (by his own ironic estimation, a "retrograde religious functionary," 39) regards as necessary for contracting a marriage—the other two being a marriage contract and wedding ceremony. Laz's own sentimental blather is every bit as ridiculous as the many varieties of language he will go on to lampoon: "Regardless of his diminutive stature and piping voice, Laz was jealous by nature. Hearing the name Schatzman, he set about hammering still more fiercely on the door and howling: 'Open this door, I tell you, if the iron door of the prison opened for me, this ridiculous ramshackle thing is not going to stay closed. Fanny cannot hold converse with Schatzman, for Fanny's soul is swanlike, and Schatzman is as stupid as a turkey-cock'" (39). After buying some orchid perfume for Fanny that is confiscated during his first incarceration, those exotic flowers (Laz ponders their edibility at various points) become inextricably linked with thoughts of the intended recipient. Being reeducated as a good communist in a bid to join the Party also means being reeducated about sex and relationships, which now must be undertaken with maximum efficiency as the means to an end. In the hyper-functionalist, albeit by the time of the novel, outdated, view of his instructor, Trivas, "sex is the naked instrument of population increase, and, leaving aside for the moment the capitalism of Malthus and like obstacles, we can regard this so-called love as the standard labour process of two self-employed persons both engaged in craft production. The shorter the process, the more time the proletariat has left for the trade unions and co-operation" (51–52). In plain, twenty-first century English, then, the message to Laz is, "Get it on, and get on with it!" Laz's one-night marriage, a sham intended by his bride to appropriate for herself his more desirable room in their communal apartment, is never consummated. Thus is the naked economic armature of marriage exposed and ridiculed. Economics similarly governs Laz's interactions with the Parisian coquette Margot, who is known to all but Laz as a prostitute. Insisting on her fee first, she then hurries him to bed, which quickly sobers a champagne- and romance-addled Laz. "Either you are Venus escaped or you are a hundred per cent Marxist maiden who has attended Comrade Trivas's lectures. Why call me into bed while I treasure pink premises? I long just to flutter with you and twitter and discourse upon love, to sing you lullabies and to lift you shoulder-high, my gentle fairy-tale, I long to die because this is not life, but paradise. And here you go offering me naked functions" (207). Laz is ridiculous, but his point is not: the bourgeois commodification of sex is every bit as stark and impoverished as the functionalist Soviet approach.

"You see, I got into a historical maelstrom . . ."

An additional element that distinguishes *The Stormy Life of Laz Roitshvantz* as a *modernist* picaresque is the protagonist's consciousness of his own condition. He exhibits a consistency of character typical of the picaresque, which is first expressed in his pride about the longstanding "red" in his family name. In the dancing instructor now known as Paul Violon, Laz discerns Osip Katz, and the barber who goes by *Georges* is good old Sima Zucker. But until he reaches Paris and restyles himself briefly as a patronymically bleached *Chvance*, Laz delights in his crimson-tinged surname. Over the course of the narrative, the protagonist comes to conceive of himself as a man with an excess of story. Asked by the Polish gendarmery captain who suspects him of spying for Russia why he entered Poland, Laz responds, "If you had a bit of time to spare, of course, I could start right from the beginning. It all began with a deaf and dumb woman named Phart" (108). Interestingly, he does not commence with the *shvartse khasene* that gave rise to his being, but rather with the more recent event—a baseless denunciation—that set the novel's plot in motion. Relatively close to the beginning of his adventures, Laz already understands his story to be a long, labored one, even when launched *in medias res* with the turpitude of Miss Phart. By the end of his travels, he has enough distance from the events that have befallen him to reflect to a Gomel *landsman* also kicking about Tel Aviv, "'You see, I got into a historical maelstrom'" (247).

Most picaresque fictions represent a somewhat arbitrary temporal span of the protagonist's life and end inconclusively. However Laz's ultimate demise, from hunger and weakness of body and spirit brought on by the multiple incarcerations and beatings he has endured, affords an unusual opportunity to apprehend the death of the *pícaro*. To the guard at Rachel's Tomb, inured to his beggarly suffering, Laz delivers himself of one last soliloquy:

> "You can shout as much as you like," he said. "But I am not going, have I not told you that I am dying? While I still stood a chance of living, people were always bullying me: 'You impudent rascal, Roitshvantz, how dare you live here?' and they tried to tear me limb from limb. Then I did go, because I still wanted to live. But now it is a matter of complete indifference to me, and if you want to tear me in pieces, tear away! Yet really, what a shocking thing, Lazar Roitshvantz daring to die in such a fine place! But you will just have to get reconciled to that fact. Even when I was in full life I never seemed able to choose a suitable location for myself. No, the wind simply had its way, and I boarded a cruel train. Likewise now. I crept on as long as I could and when I couldn't creep any longer—well, I just crept in here." (262–63)

Laz resigns all agency, proclaiming himself one borne along by the wind. There is pathos in this resignation, in his sense that—because of its biblical grandeur—the gritty desert locale of Rachel's Tomb is "such a fine place," and in his own consciousness of being a clown-fool-rogue or "non-serious person." "I am sure serious people die very differently," Laz speculates. "They count up how many books they have written, they recall how they made great revolutions, or when they sold this or that and what price the goods fetched" (264). Fittingly, Laz's *kheshbn-hanefesh*, or spiritual self-accounting, entails telling one last story, which he labels, pathetically, as such. He recounts the Hasidic tale of the boy whose inappropriate blowing of a whistle on Yom Kippur nevertheless opens the gates of heaven for the prayers of the Besht,[26] and styles his own lack of couth as performing a similarly salutary social function. A rather mawkish, sentimental ending is finally forestalled by the final sentences: "Sleep on in peace, poor Roitshvantz! No more shall you dream of great injustice, or a modest slice of smoked sausage" (269). With a zeugma too mild to be funny, Ehrenburg yokes together Laz's quotidian strivings with more expansive—and elusive—dreams of justice. To whatever extent the central character has instantiated the type of the Eternal Jew, the author proclaims with his death the end of that myth.

Ehrenburg's Heirs

It must be noted that the jocular, conning, border-crossing picaresque spirit that Laz shares with Hasek's Schweik not only had other Soviet avatars (notably Ilf and Petrov's Ostap Bender) but has also endured—or been reawakened—in post-Soviet times. Although a thorough treatment is beyond the scope of this study, readers' attention should be called to the work of two Soviet-born, Jewish émigré authors writing in German[27]: Vladimir Kaminer and Vladimir Vertlib. The former, born in Moscow in 1967, lives and works in Berlin as both a writer and a DJ, while the latter, born in Leningrad in 1966, spent stints in Austria, Israel, and the United States before finally settling near Salzburg. Both figures are culturally cosmopolitan and protean, enacting subtle and ironic negotiation about national identity and cultural affiliation, and both have employed the picaresque to express their visions of restlessness, mobility, and cultural polymorphism. Kaminer's *Militärmusik* (2001) is an autobiographical novel tracing a bohemian course through the author's youth—including scenes from the KGB-dodging underground music world, a hippie forest encampment in Latvia, and dilatory military service—until the moment of his emigration to Berlin. The protagonist's Jewishness is a cultural marker, but he is several generations removed from even the kind of elementary Jewish folklore and legal knowledge that Laz Roitshvantz takes for granted. Vertlib's oeuvre shows a more consistent engagement with questions of Jewish identity, a central concern not only in the picaresque *Zwischenstationen* (*Intermediate Stations*, 1999, chronicling his international odyssey) but also in *Das besondere Gedächtnis der Rosa Masur* (*The Special Memory of Rosa Masur*, 2001), modeled on the author's grandmother, and in *Letzter Wunsch* (*Last Wish*, 2003), which probes the fraught question of who-is-a-Jew in postwar Austria. Both novelists are thoroughgoing postmodernists whose work is pervaded by a sense of irony about the significance of their Jewish heritage and Soviet Russian origins in an age of New European multiculturalism and political correctness.

From *milkhiks* to *fleyshiks*

Cafés, according to Shachar Pinsker,[28] not only "illuminate key aspects of modernity and modernism in general" but are particularly important to understanding Jewish modernism as it took shape in Eastern Europe and then moved with Jewish émigrés both westward to New York and eastward to Tel Aviv. In Paris, Laz Roitshvantz frequents the *Rotonde* with its competing schools of painters. Yet he is always in search of a substantial meal: to wit, meat. Untethered from the dictates of Jewish dietary laws, he delights in his first taste of rabbit, in butter-fried cutlets, and always, in a good sausage. Had Laz made it south to Odessa, though, he might have adjourned from his quest for *fleysh* long enough to enjoy a bowl of the iced cream that had become a fashionable treat just a few years before, during the days of Menakhem Mendl. The estimable *luftmensch* of Kasrilevke, as he relates to his suspicious wife, makes a habit of savoring this delicacy at the Café Fanconi while cutting nonexistent deals on the bourse. Had he conducted his business just a few years later in the same establishment, Menakhem Mendl might have rubbed shoulders with Benya Krik or with Boyarsky, suit manufacturer and would-be suitor to aging Krik sister Dvoira. It would surely have been Boyarsky's treat, since he indexes his wealth to his prospective in-laws by nonchalantly confiding the hefty sum he throws away daily at Fanconi's.

In Pinsker's account, the food served is perhaps the *least* important aspect of the café, given its elevated function as a *thirdspace* or threshold zone where cultural identity is established and then contested. But let us bring the focus back to the menu, which holds an out-sized significance as it pertains to questions of temperament. It is no accident that easygoing, gullible, eager-to-please Menakhem Mendl favors a creamy confection.[29] Ruth Wisse observes that the term *milkhiker* (as in *Tevye der . . .*) is a neologism that speaks to that beleaguered patriarch's disposition and way of being in the world as much as it does his adopted vocation. Rachel Rubin extends this point to claim that Sholem Aleichem populates his world with two opposing temperamental types—milkmen (Tevye, Motl Komzoyl) and butchers (Leyzer Wolf, Pedohtsur). Here is where Babel differs. "Unlike Sholem Aleichem, Babel privileges the fleshy, active world. The vibrancy of his gangsters is elevated at the expense of bookish introspection" (Rubin 37). An aspect of Babel's project, then, is to move Jewish literature from *milkhik* to *fleyshik*; we might imagine a twinkly-yet-saucer-eyed Sholem Aleichem comforting himself with the thought that at least things are being done in the right order.

The robustly muscular, *fleyshik* aspects of Babel's fiction allow us to push further into the criminal, roguish provinces of the picaresque literary complex. Babel did not write a singular, thoroughly picaresque work[30] like *The Stormy Life of Laz Roitshvantz*. Instead, he dispersed aspects of picaresque action and character throughout his various works, notably the criminality of the gangsters in the *Odessa Stories* and the mobility of alter ego Lyutov in *Red Cavalry*. His oeuvre is infused throughout with a picaresque spirit of insouciance and a marked lack of teleological or programmatic thinking. His narrative structures further reinforce this stance against striving. Eschewing the conventional novel in favor of stories, plays, and journalistic sketches, Babel instead embraces the centrifugal poetics placed under the heading of "partials" in the introduction to this study. My analysis will concentrate on the *Odessa Stories*, a set of linked short stories (more below on how to classify the genre) that might appear, at first blush, not to fit the picaresque type at all. Taking place within the confines of the Moldavanka, a heavily criminal, mercantile and Jewish quarter of Odessa, they don't feature the kind of mobility that comes with riding the rails or even with the mounted Cossack regiment that Lyutov joins. Moreover, biographical heterochrony is mostly absent; the characters follow a course of normative, linear development punctuated by life-cycle events like marriage and childbirth. In fact, the climactic story even hinges upon an Oedipal display of force in which the Krik brothers displace their father as sole sovereign of his business and household. But I will argue that the pervasive, energizing principle of *Verkehr* (traffic or exchange[31]) substitutes for geographical mobility and affords instead a kind of microcosmic kinesis worth ten railroads and a couple of steamer ships to boot. This variant of mobility, combined with the roguishness of the protagonist, and the episodic, nonlinear composition of the stories, secure for this work a place alongside other exemplars of the modernist Jewish picaresque.

Even the most prosaic account of turn-of-the-century Odessa must acknowledge a city of unusual heterogeneity, energy, and growth.[32] By virtue of its geography, Odessa developed as a port that became home to a teeming mixture of Russians, Ukrainians, Jews, Greeks, Moldavians, Poles, Germans, Turks, Karaites, Bulgarians, Armenians, French, and Italians. Where Jews were concerned, the expansion was explosive: from 246 souls at the city's founding in 1795, to 152,634 by 1904 (Rubin 19). High culture and low were both robustly represented. The city harbored the "Odessa Sages," who would come to be regarded as the trailblazers of the new Hebrew literature and the *klasikers* of the Yiddish.[33] At the same time, memoirist Konstantin Paustovsky estimates that in Babel's day, about two thousand professional criminals plied their trade in the Moldavanka (Rubin 21). Perhaps these extremes are best represented by juxtaposing two Yiddish maxims about the city. Taking any hedonistic pleasure was known as living *vi got in ades* (like God in Odessa), while at the same time, the city was imagined as a latter-day Sodom and Gomorrah so corrupt that "Seven miles around Odessa burn the fires of hell" (Zipperstein 1).

Yet Babel saw and rendered an Odessa that reached far beyond the prosaic, into the realm of myth. His Moldavanka is a place out of ordinary time, akin to Rabinovitsh's Kasrilevke or Bashevis's Frampol and Tishevits. Historical specificity and self-conscious irony certainly separate these environs from the atopic towns and forests of Rabbi Nakhman of Bratslav's tales, but even so, there is something recognizable that runs from one to the other— perhaps the conspicuous lyricism in depicting the landscape.[34] Even plausibly "historical" events (Froim Grach's execution, say) are represented mythopoeically, like the Nazi invasions of Bashevis's *ur-shtetlekh*. Babel's Moldavanka is a fabled *topos*, belonging to a primitive chronotope that antedates the modern nation-state; it even comes complete with a king. Many critics have observed that this mythic presentation of Odessa was intensified and heightened by the author's apprehension of imminent loss. The narrator "is guided by nostalgia; he weaves the stories into legends because, unlike the inhabitants of this world, he is very much aware that all this is just about to vanish ultimately and irrevocably" (Hetenyi 183).[35] The sketches of Benya, his relatives, and his associates are wishful reconstructions, attempting to insert into the twentieth century the resourceful, gay deceiver Hershele Ostropolyer of Yiddish folklore and of Babel's own story "Shabbos Nakhamu."

Babel's Centrifugal Narration

What to call these grouped stories, with their linked but also disconnected snatches and glimpses of life in an Odessa on the cusp of Revolution? If the picaresque is not the right *generic* designation for them, then what is? Like the Tevye stories, they are published piecemeal, beginning in 1921 (with "The King" and "Justice in Parentheses") and continuing into the 1930s.[36] Unlike the *Tevye* cycle, not all of the material could appear during the author's lifetime.[37] Also unlike Tevye's, these tales are not told chronologically and lack a clear compositional order: "The King" begins at the wedding of Dvoira, while the final story, "Sunset," is set during earlier, fruitless attempts to make a match for her. The anachronisms emphasize the fragmentary quality of the narration. Half-filled lacunae between plots encourage the reader to fill in missing events and connections, but this is not always possible. After all, there are two etiological tales of Benya's marriage—to two different women, with neither making provision for the other's having occurred (neither is presented as a "second marriage" and no divorce is broached). "Etiological" might seem like a curious term to employ in the context of marital unions, but both stories emphasize how the current state of affairs came to be over and above any subjective experience of romance. One of these tales is a "mere" digression (a category we shall complicate later). Sometimes the stories complete each other, or complete the reader's "knowledge" of events. The fixer and manager Zudechkis pledges to tell two stories in turn; after concluding the first, in "Justice in Parentheses," he stops short of the promised tale about Lyubka the Cossack. But the incident to which he alludes is recounted later by an unidentified omniscient narrator. So while Zudechkis fails to deliver, Babel does not.

However else one might divide or class these tales, it is essential to recognize that they are riven in two, with a yawning gulf between the "before" and "after" of the Revolution. Their fitful or otherwise less-than-smooth connectedness seems to suggest a generic designation of these tales as "fragmented" or "interlocking" narratives. They might be imagined as one larger story, the telling of which has been doled out to various mutually acquainted narrators, over time. Always hospitable to "partials," the corpus of Yiddish letters had begun to experiment with fragmented narration during its classical phase. In his analysis[38] of Y.L. Peretz's *Bilder fun a provints-rayze* (*Memoirs of a Journey through the Tomashev Region*), Marc Caplan matches that work's fractured poetics to "the fragmentation of traditional Jewish life under the weight of modernity" (79). But Peretz is no simple forerunner to Babel; indeed, there is a doubly instructive contrast to be drawn between their respective sets of linked stories. The key distinction correlates narrative structure to the very essence of the picaresque sensibility, while also helping us to differentiate the picaresque from travel literature. Peretz's *Bilder* began as an ethnographic and statistical study commissioned by the apostate Jan Bloch, who nevertheless retained enough Jewish fellow-feeling (or universalistic, humanistic *mentshlekhkeyt*) to desire a "scientific" refutation of Polish anti-Semitism, one grounded in data collected from the field. Peretz assembled the requisite data but transfigured it into a belletristic threnody for swiftly declining Jewish folkways and for the partly historical, partly mythical site of their transmission: the *shtetl*. In short sketches, shot through with meta-awareness of his own status as participant-observer and outsider-insider, Peretz created a "structure of proliferating peripheries" (Caplan 72) that could represent a community "pitched . . . between two temporalities" (ibid.). Much of this sounds like Babel's *shtetl*, as represented not only in *Red Cavalry* ("Gedali," "Berestechko") but in sundry other stories as well (such as "Old Shloyme"). But although Babel registered the deterioration and ruin[39] of old folkways with a stark clarity that seems, at times, emotionally detached and at others, to register great sorrow, he nonetheless placed this unavoidable narrative of decline into a different conceptual and emotional framework than Peretz. It wasn't simply a matter of Babel's being willing to break eggs in order to make the omelet of Revolution.

Peretz's meta-narrative, subtly informing his assumptions, is one of wholeness broken. Structurally and discursively, the *Bilder* sketches reflect a violent sense of rupture: hence, "Peretz shatters the narrative perspective *and* the narrative as such into fragments of genre, convention, and anecdote" (Caplan 77). Peretz's approach owes, I would argue, to his deeply maskilic sensibility. As Abramovitsh had done with Benjamin in his (far more comical) travelogue of nearly five decades earlier, Peretz hopes to anatomize Jewish social pathology, the better to heal a broken folk. Through the writing of the *Bilder,* he attempts to collect the scraps ethnographically and glue them back together again—or at least to gesture at the impossibility to doing so. It is ultimately a frustrating, futile task, as Caplan observes: "Instead of communicating between the traditional shtetl and urban modernity, he can only see his own reflection among characters that are, like him, trapped between spaces, statuses, and temporalities" (77).

In Babel's fiction, by way of contrast, the striving, regenerative spirit of Haskalah is truly absent. What ails the Jews is not susceptible to healing or to repair; the centrifugal forces bearing down on both *shtetl* and urbanized Jewry alike are too overwhelming to repel, especially by the 1930s, when the last of the tales were composed. "What use would that man have been to the society we are building?" the cold-blooded, newly arrived Cheka bureau chief asks a more sentimental and locally rooted colleague, regarding the legendary (and now casually executed) Jewish gangster Froim Grach. The junior colleague is forced to concede, "I suppose no use at all" (174). This fatalism is surely dispiriting, but in Babel's hands it leads to a form of picaresque liberation and ushers in, once again, the spirit of "never better!" and the concomitant realization that with doom certain, you might as well laugh. Thus does he jubilate in the Odessa sunshine and Madeira even as Soviet storm clouds gather at the far edge of the sky. Despite a life's experience encompassing many horrors, Babel, as Robert Alter insists, "remained ultimately an enthusiast, an enthralled observer of life's spectacle" (148).

There is a palpable change in mood from the stories written in the 1920s to those composed in the 1930s, a difference that serves to emphasize the tales' heterogeneity. Like Peretz, Babel is engaged in a project of gluing disparate things together—with the important difference that he is crafting a collage from colorful scraps, not attempting to piece together a broken social whole. Babel is a compositor, which is why it is worth positing the *Odessa Stories* (and *Red Cavalry* as well) in light of the *composite novel*. This generic designation is not as widely known as it deserves to be, but Maggie Dunn and Ann Morris[40] propose the following straightforward definition: "The composite novel is a literary work composed of shorter texts that— though individually complete and autonomous—are interrelated in a coherent whole according to one or more organizing principles" (2). Those principles might include setting, single protagonist, collective protagonist, pattern, and an emphasis on storytelling; most of these criteria are present in Babel's *Odessa Stories*. The term composite novel emphasizes the *unity* of a text with disparate parts even while acknowledging its seamed construction; it also suits the modernist spirit of textual "partials" by quietly reminding us that integral, linear, totalizing narratives are not necessarily normative. Acknowledging that these stories were written across a decade of transformative political change that divides later from the earlier material, I emphasize *composite* over *novel*. Nevertheless, in recognizing these tales' unity-within-disunity, we heed Babel's insistence that a text in parts need not represent a broken whole.

From *Verkehr* to *kilayim*

The *Odessa Stories* prompt us to contemplate varieties of mobility other than geographic, spatial, or even the spatio-temporal that typifies *The Travels of Benjamin III*. The teeming and vital slums of the Moldavanka recall to us Mark Anderson's emphasis on *Verkehr*—that is, traffic—in all its senses, including exchange, commerce, or intercourse. Fittingly enough, the principal gangster families (Krik and Grach, according to their gangster sobriquets), with their dynastic and even imperial consciousness, work as carters. They transport commodities between the train station and ships at port that have borne them from or will bear them to distant points around the globe.[41] The members of these relatively prosperous families, as well as their various hangers-on, serve as agents of circulation: for money, taste, sex,[42] and countless other commodities. Babel also turns them into agents of circulation, "able to move among worlds in a way that others cannot, thereby bridging many realms: legal with illegal, Jewish with non-Jewish, ghetto with mainstream" (Rubin 23). To this list, we might add, high-class and low-class. As surely as Lyutov's riding with the Cossacks would yoke together Russianness with Jewishness, these gangsters braid together improbabilities. When Benya Krik arrives at a funeral (only necessitated in the first place by the impulsivity of one of his gang) in his ostentatious car with its horn blaring Pagliacci,[43] Babel celebrates his city's "sheer multifariousness" (Alter 143).

The most explicit instances of *Verkehr* are the three catalogues of imports that appear among the various stories. One lists the delicacies served at Dvoira Krik's wedding, a second inventories the gastronomic exotica for sale at Kaplun's store, and the third enumerates the contraband items that have made their way from the ports of the world to the courtyard of Lyubka the Cossack's inn. These passages are illuminating, and it is worth examining each in turn. In the first story of the collection, "The King," an omniscient, unidentified, and rather wry narrator underscores the mechanics of circulation by asking rhetorically, "But do the foamy waves of the Odessan Sea throw roasted chickens onto the shore?" (136). The obviously negative answer launches him into the catalogue of what Dvoira's wedding guests enjoyed. It is delivered with anything but neutrality:

> On this blue night, this starry night, the best of our contraband, everything for which our region is celebrated far and wide, plied its seductive, destructive craft. Wine from afar heated stomachs, sweetly numbed legs, dulled brains, and summoned belches as resonant as the call of battle horns. The black cook from the *Plutarch*, which had pulled in three days before from Port Said, had smuggled in big-bellied bottles of Jamaican rum, oily Madeira, cigars from the plantations of Pierpont Morgan, and oranges from the groves of Jerusalem. This is what the foamy waves of the Odessan Sea throw onto the shore, and this is what Odessan beggars sometimes get at Jewish weddings. (136–37)

This brief passage telescopes a great deal of information about the mores of Babel's Jewish Odessa. The most affluent members of the community uphold certain customs: marrying off a daughter (in a fairly arranged manner, at that), holding a traditional ceremony and feast, and inviting the local beggars to partake of the bounty. However, they also conduct their Jewish observance on their own terms, without allowing legalistic scruples to interfere with their hedonism. Whereas the rum, cigars, and still-exotic oranges[44] are religiously unimpeachable, the "wine from afar" and the "oily Madeira" are almost certainly not kosher.[45] When wine is said to be "unkosher," it is not because of the food sourcing and production issues that usually govern kosher status, but rather because of concerns about idolatry—-i.e., wine of non-Jewish origin having been poured out as a libation to foreign gods.[46] How appropriate, then, that this is the pleasure-loving Odessan celebrants' most conspicuous departure from the dictates of Jewish law!

Throughout his corpus of work, Babel observes with an unsparing eye the merging and mixing of what has heretofore been kept separate. Thus does the *Verkehr* theme take on a particularly Jewish cast that we may describe with reference to the biblical term *kilayim*. This concept refers to inappropriate mixtures and combinations—whose unsuitability is sometimes rationally explained, as in the prohibition of yoking together an ox and a donkey (their different grazing habits and stature make it uncomfortable for both to plow together), but at other times extravagantly arbitrary, as in the prohibition of wearing a garment that combines wool and linen. Babel takes great care to highlight all manner of things that do not go together, in matters great and small. While we might describe this tendency in value-neutral literary terms such as "heterogeneity" or invoke Bakhtin's notion of the "carnivalesque," I favor *kilayim* because of its taboo nature; Babel likely sought to convey a transgressive frisson with these combinations, and that certainly would have formed a part of how most of his contemporary Jewish readers understood them. The largest arc of *kilayim*, perhaps, is the conceit of the Jewish Cossack or even the Soviet Jew, but this motif replicates itself in fractal fashion down to the smallest details, such as the portraits of Lenin and Maimonides that spill out of the rucksack belonging to the dying son of Reb Motale Bratslavsky in "The Rabbi's Son." The procuress Pesya-Mindl rocks the baby of her employer, Lyubka Shneiweis, while reading *The Miracles and Heart of Baal-Shem*. Calling the wedding delicacies "seductive and destructive," the all-knowing narrator continues, with mock-censoriousness, "They got Jamaican rum at Dvoira Krik's wedding, and that's why the Jewish beggars got as drunk as unkosher pigs and began loudly banging their crutches." What could be more incongruous than pigs at a Jewish wedding?

Even when all the goods are of the legal variety, their concentration gives off an aura of seduction. Consider the imports at Kaplun's, "the best store on Privoznaya Square":

> Inside was the aroma of many seas and wonderful lives unknown to us. . . . On the counter were olives that had come from Greece, Marseilles butter, coffee beans, Lisbon Malaga, sardines from the firm of "Philippe and Canot," and cayenne pepper. Kaplun himself was sitting in his vest in the sun on a glassed-in porch eating a watermelon, a red watermelon with black seeds, slanting seeds like the eyes of sly Chinese girls. (164)

These exotic wares gesture synecdochally at "wonderful lives unknown to us"—unknown because they hold out the promise of foreign pleasures ranging far beyond the few representative foodstuffs. This passage, from "The Father," is embedded in a story about the driving, disruptive nature of female sexual desire, wherein Froim Grach must marry off a long-lost adult daughter who has returned to his household in the sway of all manner of immoderate appetites. Basya has set her sights on Kaplun's soft and dandified son, but that match is not to be. Kaplun men, the father's enjoyment of his watermelon seems to suggest, initiate their own pleasures with sly women less frank about their desires than Froim's Basya. The mildly transgressive simile "like the eyes of sly Chinese girls" also sharpens the paradox at the heart of Odessa's cosmopolitan traffic and exchange. Foreign goods are readily available but also conspicuously marked as such, ultimately reinforcing the deep distinction between home and strange, ours and theirs. The watermelon seeds are as close as bourgeois Kaplun will come to those slanted eyes.

If the luxury grocery store is a contact point for "wonderful lives unknown to us," then how much more so is the inn run by Lyubka ("the Cossack") Shneiweis! Every comfort that could be desired by a weary traveler is on offer, including not just the customary bed and board but also the company of young women procured by Pesya-Mindl. While Zudechkis is being held there forcibly for nonpayment of his tab, he witnesses the delivery of a new shipment of contraband from Port Said, via the ship's engineer, Mr. Trottyburn: "Out of his bale he took cigars and delicate silks, cocaine and metal jiggers, uncut tobacco from the state of Virginia, and black wine bought on the Island of Chios. Each item had a special price, and each figure was washed down with Bessarabian wine with its bouquet of sunshine and bedbugs." This is also how it was done in Odessa: from the fact that "each item had a special price," one infers a series of minute negotiations and good-natured haggling, all lubricated by the Bessarabian wine. The sunshine and bedbugs are another odd yoking, this time less zeugma than synesthesia,[47] perhaps. In and around Lyubka's establishment, human beings circulate as noticeably as gaudy and luxuriant goods: "Tatars were walking up Dalnitskaya Street, Tatars and Turks with their mullahs. They were returning from a pilgrimage to Mecca and going back to their homes on the Orenburg Steppes and in Transcaucasia. A steamship had brought them to Odessa, and they were going from the harbor to the inn of Lyubka Shneiweis, nicknamed Lyubka the Cossack. The Tatars wore striped, rigid robes, and they covered the streets with the bronze sweat of the deserts" (165). Every import that passes through the city carries a tangible residue of its origins or recent itinerary, whether it's the bedbugs or the bronze sweat of the Arabian deserts.

Linguistic and Discursive *kilayim*

Many critics have noted Babel's curious yoking together of incongruous elements. Viktor Shklovskii drolly points out that "his principal device is to speak in the same tone of voice of the stars above and of gonorrhea."[48] At the rhetorical level, these combinations often entail recourse to zeugma or oxymoron (such as "amicable Brownings" [135]). Babel's peculiar *kilayim* becomes the heteroglot element in his centrifugal discourse, roughly akin to Laz Roitshvantz's bizarre idiolect. Then there is the closely related question, also true of Ehrenburg's novel, of how the various national languages in play interact with one another. The *Odessa Stories* belong to a small group of fictions, especially critical in Jewish literature with its many polyglot characters, where most of the action is implicitly understood to be taking place in a different language than that of the work's composition.[49] Babel's Russian incorporates his characters' Yiddish in ways both explicit and implicit. Rachel Rubin observes that while, in general, "The threat of language contamination seems to be a common way of articulating and deflecting anxiety about other blendings—in particular, miscegenation" (20), Babel is able to make "the case for language blending as the way to achieve literary excellence" (21). He incorporates French phrases,[50] enriches the Russian language by translating into it quite literally the Yiddish term *luftmensch*, and employs phrases that are common to Russian and Yiddish, such as Gedali's observation about the Revolution that he doesn't know what to eat it with— i.e., how to deal with it. Thus does Babel enact a program of linguistic *Verkehr*: language circulation, interpenetration, and hybridity. These ambulatory and heteroglossic elements are discursive analogues to the mobility (lateral and vertical, geographic and social) that typifies the picaresque genre as traditionally understood. Just as Ehrenburg's Laz embeds nuggets at the level of event and story, so does Babel embed nuggets of Yiddish language in his Russian. "We receive Benya's words in Russian," Rubin points out, "but they destabilize that language, inflected as they are with Yiddish idiom, hyperbole, and sardonic tone" (35). This hybridity has temporal overtones, according to Sicher: "Stylization of Yiddish speech resurrects a bygone age, and linguistic interference resists the destruction of History. Like Bialik in Hebrew, Babel naturalizes Yiddish in his Russian prose, playing on words and realizing idiom in anthropomorphisms, creating amusing resonance and ironic subtexts" (85). The conscious incorporation of a language associated with marginality and obsolescence into the privileged, majoritarian language of the projected future[51] was itself an act of aesthetic and political bravery on Babel's part, and one that smacked of the jaunty spirit of the *polit*.

Benya Krik: A Reign of *Styyyle*

Mendl Krik is a successful carter, but his son Benya aspires to be so much more; the family business is merely a base for more daring and dangerous operations. Although Benya does not inherit his kingship in direct, hereditary fashion from his father, the son's reign cannot be fully consolidated until Krik pére has been dethroned. This Oedipal drama looms large enough for Babel not only to present it in the story "Sunset" but to revisit the material in an eight-act play of the same name (1926). In the short story version, after Benya and his brother Lyovka have beaten their father to the point of disfigurement and grudging acceptance of their power, the ascendant gangster begins to remake his roughhewn progenitor in his own, smoother image. The short story ends with Benya bespeaking a new suit for his father. The scene is shot through with ironic doublespeak:

> "What kind of suit would you prefer?" Benchik asked Papa Krik. "Confess to Monsieur Boyarsky."
>
> "What you feel in your heart is good enough for your father," Papa Krik said, wiping away a tear, "that's the kind of suit you'll have him make."
>
> "Well, since Papa isn't a navy man," Benya interrupted his father, "a civilian would suit him better. First of all choose a suit for him for everyday use."
>
> Monsieur Boyarsky bent forward and cupped his ear.
>
> "What, pray, might you have in mind?"
>
> "This is what I have in mind. . . ." (195)

These lines take on added resonance for being the very last ones of the final Odessa story (at least in Constantine's English presentation). The trailing ellipses point toward an uncertain future, aspects of which have already been glimpsed in the demise of Froim Grach and the displacement of the old Jewish alms seekers from the Second Jewish Cemetery (although these events are likely subsequent to this story in chronological time). Of course Benya has *something* in mind; for a time, at least, his aesthetic sensibilities will carry the day and shape not only his own family's legacy but those of other families as well. The ordering of the suit, ostensibly a gesture of filial piety—clothing an aging parent—is in fact a further display of Benya's dominance,[52] down to his power to regulate Mendl's self-presentation through choice of clothing. Now that the physical fight has ended, father and son continue to thrust and parry with passive aggression, as when Mendl tacitly admits his subordination to his son's will: "'What you feel in your heart is good enough for your father,' Papa Krik said, wiping away a tear, 'that's the kind of suit you'll have him make.'" Benya lightly rebuffs this appeal to his conscience by pinning the conversation resolutely to the question of suiting cut.

Insofar as he departs from the profile of the traditional *pícaro*, Benya enjoys some ability to exert his will in the world lacking among other protagonists we've considered. First and foremost, he reigns as "king" through a sense of *styyyle* that is so outrageous, all-encompassing, and multifarious that it deserves a couple of extra "y's" in order to achieve the right lingering inflection. The manifestations of styyyle are sartorial, verbal, and automotive, as well as extending to other, less ostentatious arenas. Consider the following paragraphs, which are necessarily inseparable:

> "Monsieur Tartakovsky," Benya Krik said to him quietly. "For two days and nights I have been crying for the dear deceased as if he were my own brother. I know that you spit on my young tears. Shame on you, Monsieur Tartakovsky! What fireproof safe have you hidden your shame in? You had the heart to send a paltry hundred rubles to the mother of our dear deceased Josif. My hair, not to mention my brain, stood on end when I got word of this!"
>
> Here Benya paused. He was wearing a chocolate jacket, cream pants, and raspberry-red half boots. (151)

Here, surely, is Benya's gargantuan *chutzpah* on display—shaming the target of his gang's raid into paying out a handsome pension to the woman whose son was killed frivolously by Benya's own associate. The entrepreneurial young gangster manages to cast himself in the light of Robin Hood before the funeral is over. But just as prominent is the exhibition of Benya's styyyle. There is the mannered French "Monsieur," the voice of quiet command, the apposite but overblown metaphor of the fireproof safe. The second paragraph flows inexorably from the first, pausing to linger over Benya's person as sumptuous sartorial profiterole (or perhaps a chocolate sundae).[53] Babel is often quite attentive to clothing, especially as it touches on—literally—power (Cossack dress) and sexuality (women in various states of *disha-*

bille[54]). The incongruity of the occasion with Benya's dress recalls the trope of *kilayim*, one of the original biblical referents of which is the wearing of prohibited mixtures of wool and linen.

Benya's overt sentimentality would seem to cancel any claims he might have on the mantle of the picaresque (though that garment would be a bit frayed for his taste anyway). He not only claims to have cried in the passage above, but he is seen and reported to have cried twice in the course of bringing justice to Zudechkis—or vice versa. His eulogy at Muginshtein's lavish funeral, however incoherent it might be, drips with syrupy lachrymosity. But since his rhetoric is another manifestation of his styyyle—by turns mock-heroic, self-important, economical, and courtly—we might reasonably assume that Benya is well aware of its performative nature. This element of self-conscious performance undercuts the sentimentality, pitching his orations onto a detached meta-level. Moreover, the character's over-the-top rhetoric stands in pointed contrast to the author's spare narration. Robert Alter argues that Babel learned from Gustave Flaubert "how one might write about what was most disturbing in the world without pathos, without a hint of the histrionic, conveying a sense of things violently awry all the more powerfully through the stance of impassivity" (141). The more gruesome the violence and the more extravagant the mourning, the more unflappable the chronicling narrator can be.

Zudechkis: The Jester's Digressions

Given his royal magnetism, a focus on Benya the King is somewhat inevitable in discussing the *Odessa Stories*; however, the effects of Babel's composite narration are most fully felt when we shift our attention to a character of merely human proportions. The middleman Zudechkis figures in two tales: "Justice in Parentheses," which he narrates in the first person, and "Lyubka the Cossack," which is also narrated in the first person, but by an unidentified longtime habitué of the Moldavanka. In the first story, Zudechkis recounts his role in the botched theft of a cooperative store ironically named "Justice." The second is the improbable story of how Zudechkis became manager of Lyubka's inn. It is merely one of "many stories I can tell about Zudechkis" (155), according to the narrator. An ordinary Jew with a wife and seven children, this otherwise undistinguished figure serves to illustrate the circulation and exchange of what may be Odessa's most special commodity of all: stories. Narrator and narratee, subject and object, Zudechkis is at once the purveyor and the merchandise in the town's shadow-bourse of storytelling.

As a narrator, he immediately acknowledges a penchant for digression,[55] which he vows to resist: "But I must not send my tale down side streets, even if on these side streets chestnuts are ripening and acacias are in bloom. I'll start with Benya, and then go on to Lyubka Shneiweis. And that will be that. Then I can say I put the period where it belongs" (140). This proclamation gestures simultaneously at the pleasure afforded by digression (ripening chestnuts and blooming acacia) and its inappropriateness (failure to put the period where it belongs). In his trenchant analysis of the art of dilation, Ross Chambers[56] observes how "Delay and indirection—the phenomena of mediacy—become at once sources of pleasure and devices of provocation in a larger universe that seems committed to directness, speed, and immediacy (doing it fast, getting there right away)" (11). Zudechkis is a dispensable person, a relic of pre-Revolutionary inefficiencies and Jewish economic "parasitism" in particular, precisely because he is a broker. He gums up the workings of capitalism and introduces inefficiency into systems of exchange. Whether he is running as a go-between among gangsters to set up a heist or brokering the deal of a threshing machine to a landowner, he is the quintessential Jewish middleman. His very existence epitomizes "the phenomena of mediacy." When the act of narration is his to control, Zudechkis indulges a bit in "the relaxation of the vigilance, the abandonment of discipline" (Chambers 12) that digression represents. His manner of telling (*syuzhet*) is a provocation, just as Zudechkis's role within the tale's events (*fabula*) is to provoke a heist. Although Benya Krik is also a lush and extravagant speaker, he is capable of practicing a verbal economy at which Zudechkis can only marvel: "The King speaks little and speaks politely. This frightens people so much that they never question him. I left his courtyard and set off down Gospitalnaya Street, turned on Stepovaya, and then stopped to ponder Benya's words. I probed them by touch and by weight, bit down on them with my front teeth, and realized that they had not been the words that I needed" (142). The extended metaphor with which Zudechkis concludes suggests that Benya's words are fraudulent, like a false gem or metal that must be tested by the teeth.

While digression has historically been "considered neither a trope nor a legitimate rhetorical practice but an error, a wandering away from the subject at hand" (85), Chambers makes the case for this textual practice as "a key device in the hands of practitioners of oppositionality" (86). This would indeed cast put-upon Zudechkis in a rather different and more dignified light. In the story he tells about himself, Zudechkis is little more than a pitiful victim, a pathetic man who is only rescued from Benya's retributive beating by the intercession of his wife and children. But what if he were the jester to Benya's king? Narrators who flaunt their digressiveness play a "delicate game" according to Chambers, whereby they must not overstep or push the digression too far. "For this reason, digressive narrators are careful to perpetuate the ancient tradition of the court buffoon or fool, as the figure whose critical function was protected, as well as constrained, by the institution of royalty" (90). To call attention to one's digressions is to tease the audience and so elicit a response. This is the narrative correlative of Zudechkis's role (albeit failed) in teasing two different groups of gangsters into showing up at the cooperative store late one Friday night. In fact, Zudechkis flaunts his own fraudulence as a *narrator*, at least a mimetic one, by claiming access to events he could not possibly have witnessed. He was asleep in his bed during the theft, yet he renders the precise dialogue between friendly rival gangsters Kolya Shtift and Benya Krik. In this tale, at least, he hardly seems to merit the designation of a "practitioner of oppositionality."

However, therein lies the ability of composite narration to complicate our understanding of characters and events. Zudechkis concludes, "I have told you about Benya, and I will tell you about Lyubka Shneiweis. But let us stop here. Then I can say I put the period where it belongs" (145). In fact, though, the task of telling about his adventure with Lyubka falls to a narrator who accords Zudechkis more dignity than he arrogates to himself. Obviously well informed, this unidentified narrator reports of middleman-turned-manager, "He stayed at his post for fifteen years, and during that period I heard a great number of stories about him. And if I can manage, I will tell them one after another, because they are very interesting stories" (160). None of those stories are finally included in Babel's collection; most likely, they were never written. But this narrator is able to portray Zudechkis in a different light than in "Justice in Parenthesis." He is still the pathetic supplicant, stuck with another man's unpaid bill at Lyubka's inn, but here he takes command and acts competently in order to wean Lyubka's infant son and enable her to go about her business. We are able to see him as a figure in the round, and that is the payoff of Babel's composite narration.

Desiring Women

"'When we're young,' Benya muses to Froim Grach, one of his prospective fathers-in-law, 'we see girls like them's merchandise, but they're just straw that catches fire by itself.'" Thus does he acknowledge the delicacy and un-controllable danger lurking implicitly in female sexual desire. Given Babel's frank emphasis on such desire, it is natural to ask whether any of these stories give voice to a *pícara*. Female characters are focalized so tightly through lenses of male perception that they don't really become subjects unto themselves. Although the first tale opens at the wedding feast of Dvoira Krik, her name is not even mentioned until four pages into the story, and her own experience of the occasion is saved for a coda-like final paragraph that has her "edging her timid husband toward the door of their nuptial chamber, looking at him lustfully like a cat which, holding a mouse in its jaws, gently probes it with its teeth" (139). The digression that occupies that story's mid-section, describing how Benya fell in love with his wife Zilya Eichenbaum, heightens the contrast between Benya's desire for Zilya and Dvoira's undesired status, in being "married off" to a husband of no name and even less force of personality. Dvoira's sister in suffering (and eventual sister-in-law) is Froim Grach's daughter Basya, whose return to her father's household after nearly two decades in her grandparents' care registers mostly as a burden: she is more ripe for marriage than she is attrac-tive. The lack of feminine delicacy is compounded for both the Krik and the Grach daughters by their own fathers' rough occupations and reputations. This obstacle to their marriages threatens the social order. Golubchik the matchmaker reminds Froim of the implicit threat that, left unchanneled, his daughter's desire will run amok and lead to scandal: "'I see your child wants to roam in the pasture'" (163). If Dvoira, clutching her frightened bridegroom in her teeth, is feline, then Basya is bovine; she is depicted in the company of pregnant women who are "filled with all kinds of things, the way a cow's udder in a pasture fills with the rosy milk of spring" (163).

    When Froim does finally take matters into his own hands and approach the up-and-coming Benya about marrying his daughter, the young cad keeps him waiting outside a room at Lyubka's inn while he finishes a mara-thon session with the prostitute Katyusha. Perhaps one of the most affect-ing, evocative lines in Babel's entire oeuvre is this father's tacit acknowledg-ment of the value of the "goods" he has to offer on the marriage market: "Lyubka brought him a chair, and he sank into boundless waiting. He waited patiently, like a muzhik in a government office" (168). As with his parallel deal with Sender Eichbaum to marry his daughter Zilya, the marriage con-tract is a financial arrangement between men, having relatively little to do with the women in question. Unlike Peretz, Rabinovitsh, or other Jewish writers affected by a maskilic sensibility, Babel had nothing of the romantic. The business-like marrying off of daughters could continue unabated into a rapidly modernizing urban existence. Olga Litvak, who articulates the defining role of romanticism in the Haskalah, is perceptive about the gender implications of the political transformation under way: "the agony of the destruction of the Pale, and the radical emancipation of Soviet Jewry which followed, effectively displaced the process of enlightenment from the Jewish mind to the Jewish body. Babel saw in the genesis of the Soviet Jew, the birth of secular Jewish manhood, fully empowered by the state" (208).[57] But when figures like Basya and Dvoira continue to be stigmatized for their lustiness, it is abundantly clear that this newly empowered manhood still comes at the expense of Jewish womanhood and Jewish women.

"YOU MUST TO DARE!"
Afterlives of the *Polit*

This account has explored the workings of a particular sensibility in Jewish literary modernism, positing the picaresque as a minoritarian worldview in contradistinction to the synthesis of self and nation represented by the *Bildungsroman* among other major European forms. "Novels of education," as Jed Esty reminds us, "have always been entangled with the eschatologies of national myth" (54). The literary eschaton for the Yiddish-reading Jews of Europe arrived swiftly and decisively, redirecting the energies of whatever novels of education this culture continued to produce. The picaresque corpus we have thus far explored is shot through with exilic consciousness, with authors and characters alike acknowledging their precarious, deterritorialized, profoundly unredeemed status. As the majority of Ashkenazic Jews left Europe, this consciousness would shift—either to diaspora (as opposed to exile)[1] or to the project of nation-building in the Jewish homeland. These two great twentieth-century experiments in Jewish community building and rebuilding forced a renegotiation of the relationship between those mutually wary literary cousins, the *pícaro* and the *Bildungsheld*. However clumsily or elegantly, they would have to join forces, often fusing into one character. Authors in the Americas and in Israel intermingled elements of these two genres of education and so highlighted the antic episodes whereby a new Jewish subject was being formed. Leaving Europe usually necessitated leaving Yiddish behind,[2] either to acculturate to a new majority language, such as American English, or else to stretch the capacities of a renovated Hebrew.

We shall consider two exemplars of the fusion between picaresque and *Bildungsroman*, which will represent the American and Israeli Jewish trajectories. Saul Bellow's sprawling bid for the Great American Novel, *The Adventures of Augie March*, adopts even as it adapts the American idiom, infusing it with the Yiddish of Bellow's family roots and pushing its high and low registers alike to new limits. David Grossman's more tightly constructed *Yesh yeladim zigzag* (*The Zig Zag Kid*, 1994) lays an equally strong claim to the mantle of the picaresque, seizing upon that form as the means to probe the intersection of personal and national consciousness in postmodernity. Both novels renormalize the protagonist and help to reenter him into the kind of national time that Jed Esty characterizes as "shapely because it moves forward, but not forever and ever" (57). Bellow and Grossman alike embrace an ideal of progress and the possibility of development, but each author's positivism is chastened and complicated by a realistic apprehension of historical belatedness.

Augie, Marching: The Ponderous Picaresque

Augustus March is a fittingly named protagonist, given his flights of idealism couched in lofty rhetoric and his interminable march through new experiences by turns pedestrian and outrageous. The parade (or slog) is truly interminable because the novel, in typically picaresque fashion, eschews grand closure and ends abruptly with an expat Augie facing car troubles on his way to make a deal in postwar Belgium. Others have cogently chronicled the book's picaresque aspects, fitting its wending plot into the European and American generic tradition[3] and even comparing the questionable fidelity of Augie's actress wife Stella to the quiet arrangement whereby the archpriest guarantees Lazarillo's continuing prosperity (Gericke 81). Rather than rehearsing the case for Augie as *pícaro*, we shall focus on the trait that binds him most tightly to the tradition of the *polit*: his secularized stance against striving. Alter calls Augie "an inveterate displaced person" (123), which is the source of the discomfiture that launches him into the world to find a "worthy fate" and, not incidentally, to try to find or make a home for himself. Into his ambit traipses a steady stream of those who would harness Augie to their own programs or plans, furnishing some ready-made identity and purpose. He is steadfast in refusing these offers, demands, and importunities. This pattern culminates with the stark clarity of caricature, when he and Basteshaw alone survive the torpedoing of their merchant marine ship and are cast away together on a rescue skiff. In a long verbal duel that forms the novel's final set piece, Augie at last articulates a sort of Hippocratic ideal against well-intended interference in his own or anyone else's life.

> "I'm offering you a great course of life," he said. "Worth taking a risk for."
> "I already have a course of life."
> "Indeed?" he said.
> "Yes, and I'm dead against doing things to the entire human race. I don't want any more done to me, and I don't want to tamper with anyone else. No one will be a poet or saint because you fool with him." (509)

Basteshaw is the proverbial mad scientist, the mid-century bogeyman whose imagined depredations were eventually surpassed by realities brought to bear by both sides in the recent war. Augie rejects the totalism of his utopian scientific vision, refusing to attempt anything that seeks to affect the whole of humanity, even for the good. Utopianism, Augie posits, is dangerous at worst and ineffective at best, and grand, progressive schemes are bound to fail. Here is Augie's catalogue, in jazzy Bellovian prose, of such would-be do-gooders: "To tell the truth, I'm good and tired of all these big personalities, destiny molders, and heavy-water brains, Machiavellis and wizard evildoers, big-wheels and imposers-upon, absolutists" (524). Passivity, he concludes, is the only reasonable response to totalitarianism and hegemony. Thus demobilized, in a deeply personal way, Augie seeks to discern the "axial lines" that ought properly to govern his being:

> "I have a feeling," I said, "about the axial lines of life, with respect to which you must be straight or else your existence is merely clownery, hiding tragedy. I must have had a feeling since I was a kid about these axial lines which made me want to have my existence on them, and so I have said 'no' like a stubborn fellow to all my persuaders, just on the obstinacy of my memory of these lines, never entirely clear. But lately I have felt these thrilling lines again. When striving stops, there they are as a gift." (454)[4]

These axial lines already inhere in his person and require discovery rather than cultivation.

Augie's obstinacy and stubbornness in the face of would-be persuaders is a picaresque enough inclination toward self-preservation, but this impulse of refusal ultimately serves his vision of harmonious self-alignment with the unseen powers that govern the universe. "Augie is constantly falling into the company of self-appointed teachers, theoreticians, people who want to make experience conform to some ideal," observes Robert Alter. "But his own attitude toward the world is the picaresque attitude—empirical and pragmatic, attempting to deal directly with the facts of experience without any intervening preinterpretation" (123–24). It is not that Augie doesn't want to get there—to reach a self-actualized apotheosis; it is that he wants to get there on his own, making the record in his own way. This is what America makes possible for the Jews, Bellow seems to argue: to be at once a *pícaro* and a *Bildungsheld*. Augie will resist any appeal to remaking the world according to some mental image or perception, but he is finally open to the project of remaking himself, as long as it is on his own terms.

Late in the novel, his character reflects on this process of self-making, turning to metaphors of earthworks to emphasize the scale and intensity of the project:

> . . . all the while you thought you were going around idle terribly hard work was taking place. Hard, hard work, excavation and digging, mining, moling through tunnels, heaving, pushing, moving rock, working, working, working, working, working, panting, hauling, hoisting. And none of this work is seen from the outside. It's internally done. It happens because you are powerless and unable to get anywhere, to obtain justice or have requital, and therefore in yourself you labor, you wage and combat, settle scores, remember insults, fight, reply, deny, blab, denounce, triumph, outwit, overcome, vindicate, cry, persist, absolve, die and rise again. All by yourself! Where is everybody? Inside your breast and skin, the entire cast. (523)

This passage is as much about Bellow as it is about Augie, for what does it describe if not the process of writing? And here is the limitation of *The Adventures of Augie March*: they are equally the artistic adventures of Saul Bellow superimposed upon the life of a puppet protagonist. Following the shorter, less encumbered *Dangling Man* (1944) and *The Victim* (1947), this book is a *Statement Novel*: the Artist has arrived. It is a work not about progress (as with the traditional *Bildungsroman*) or teleology but about the "internally done" work of processing. While Augie does manage to fuse the picaresque with *Bildung*, the latter palpably weighs down the former (all those heavy verbs in the catalogue cited above). This attempt at fusion finally just emphasizes the tension between these two literary modes. Alter is correct in his assessment that, "Unlike the genuine picaroon, Augie does not seek experience for its own sake but rather as a means for finding him-self. Consequently his journey, particularly in the later chapters of the book, is arduous and painful with few of the picaresque roadside pleasures and not much of the picaresque sense of delight" (124). The lightness of the clas-sical picaresque gives way to prolixity and even sententiousness. The *Bil-dungsroman* is at its core an earnest form because the stakes—an individu-al's process of *becoming*—are so high. From Yiddish culture, Bellow imbibed a lightness, a satiric impulse; the novel is informed by this spirit but not ultimately pervaded by it. Bellow seemed, at least at this relatively early point in his career,[5] to perceive a kind of authorial ponderousness as the price of admission to the American canon.

From *Polit* to *Nimlat*

When the novelist and journalist David Grossman was eight, his father brought him a story by Sholem Aleichem, thus opening a temporally and geographically remote-seeming world that would not only entrance the boy but secure him a radio career. A popular Israeli quiz show aimed at adults solicited participants for an episode devoted to the youngest of the Yiddish *klasikers*, and a ten-year-old Grossman, by now well versed in the fictions of Kasrilevke and environs, sent in a postcard to apply. Although the grownups conspired to keep him from competing and winning the kitty, they did recognize an unusually self-possessed and literate preado-lescent: an ideal candidate for a child radio actor in an era when those were scarce on the Israeli airwaves.[6] He took on an after-school position more remunerative than his father's day job—one that would mature with him into serious daily journalism.

Yesh yeladim zigzag (1994) appeared midway through Grossman's nov-elistic career thus far, following the formally intricate and experimental fic-tions *See Under: Love* (*Ayen erekh: ahava*, 1986)[7] and *The Book of Intimate Grammar* (*Sefer hadikduk hapenimi*, 1991).[8] Indeed, Grossman regarded *Zigzag* as a light project that would help him recover from writing *The Book of Intimate Grammar* and *Sleeping on a Wire*, his wrenching nonfiction study of Palestinian Israelis. With a plot of self-discovery that unfolds just a week before the protagonist's bar mitzvah, *The Zig Zag Kid* has been de-scribed[9] as a coming-of-age novel, a detective story, and a picaresque; it is all of these. This novel also furnishes an ideal study in the afterlife of the *polit*, as it recapitulates and complicates many motifs and preoccupations of this study's earlier chapters. As in Sholem Aleichem's Pale of Settlement, we find ourselves on a train with a swindler, a self-described con man playing a very delicate game on whose object his "mark" can at first only speculate. The boy realizes that he is party to a seduction but must decide at every turn whether to willingly continue. Like Rabon's traumatized soldier, the protagonist, Nonny, is propelled along and kept from rest by the memories and half-memories that haunt his psyche. He too will redeem himself through an act of narration, this time a collaborative one. His seducer and guardian angel both—who turns out to also be his maternal grandfather—indulges a keen sense of styyyle. Benya Krik's red convertible, with its horn blaring the theme from *I Pagliacci*, is transposed to a Bugatti, but the sentiment is the same: "Special car gives style,[10] no?" He pronounced the word "'style' as though tasting something sweet" (73). While allegorizing soul and nation in the manner of the *Bildungsroman*, Grossman nevertheless manages to infuse the book with the sweetness and lightness of the joyful outlaw. In terms of the modern Jewish picaresque, his achievement is to turn the *polit* into the *nimlat*. It is a subtle etymological shift between two roots whose close relationship dates back to biblical Hebrew. But whereas the *palit* (in biblical Hebrew) is the refugee from war or oppression, the *nimlat* is the outlaw or fugitive from justice. A short while into their acquaintance, Nonny and his grandfather hijack the train on which they've met, compelling the engineer at gunpoint to stop and let them off. As the reality of their deed sinks in, the compunctious boy names their status as *nimlatim mehahok*. Betsy Rosenberg translates this phrase, quite felicitously and understandably, with the idiomatic English "fugitives from justice" (74). A more literal rendering, though, would be "fugitives from the law." Nonny and the criminal genius Felix Glick are on the lam from the very idea of The Law instantiated by the boy's detective father; the erosion of the opposition between law and lawlessness, police and outlaw, is one of the book's deep subjects.

Truth be told, it would be unfair caricature to reduce Yakov ("Koby") Feuerberg, Nonny's father, to a mere mouthpiece for law and propriety. When he boards the Haifa-bound train in Jerusalem, Nonny is ostensibly being sent by his father and his not-quite-stepmother, Gabi, to visit his uncle Shilhav, a renowned pedagogue and tiresome lecturer of small children. This Shilhavization (*shilhuv*), as Gabi has cleverly denominated it, is a pre-bar mitzvah rite of passage within the extended family. Part of the book's lightness inheres in important matters left implicit or merely glanced on, such as the divergence between brothers with respect to surnominal nomenclature. The illustrious uncle has Hebraicized his surname to Shilhav (a root meaning to excite, impassion, or inflame—which applies ironically to the pedantic professor). Koby, an erstwhile daredevil, has retained the Yiddish-Germanic name Feuerberg, indicating the volcanic temperament discernible in him and his son alike. The European name hints at something not fully assimilable in Koby and reminds us that he has doubled down on "the law" only as an expedient to purge himself of the irresistible allure of lawlessness represented by his long-gone wife Zohara—Nonny's mother. Koby is deeply decent, the stabilizing prose to Zohara's, Gabi's, and finally Nonny's poetry. Grossman adhered to his usual immersive methods of book research, spending six months with the Jerusalem police (Shainin 138); it is easy to imagine him respecting and enjoying an easy rapport with men like Koby Feuerberg.

Felix Glick's pleonastic name is quite telling too. He has doubled up on joy and happiness—leaving no room for any admixture of guilt or regret. Although "they called Felix Glick world's greatest swindler" (156), his crimes are victimless, like Laz Roitshvantz's, and he allows great wealth to flow through his fingers unimpeded by personal greed. Arguably his most serious crime or sin was that of being a neglectful father, having little to do with Zohara until her eighteenth birthday. But even this failing could be remediated: together, they embarked on an instructive Grand Tour, in which father imparted to daughter his vast store of knowledge about the art of the swindle. And with only the minimum necessary measure of lawlessness, the journey Felix masterminds for Nonny will serve a similarly redemptive function. Even before committing the brazen crime that will kick off their shared odyssey, Felix breaks the laws of Hebrew grammar and usage with impunity, unfurling a rather charming idiolect that constantly highlights his unassimilable foreignness. He uses the wrong prepositions, fails at gender agreement, lops off syllables, resorts to archaisms and elaborate periphrases, and occasionally even generates nonsense incomprehensible to Nonny. His most enduring and delightful solecism is a failure to apprehend the use of the infinitive, producing such brave locutions as, "You must to dare!" These deviations from the norm refresh Modern Hebrew just as Babel's Yiddishisms injected vitality into his Russian.

Laws and Games

Nonny begins to suspect that his scheduled Shilhavization is being derailed when he witnesses a ruse whereby two men, their wrists cuffed together, enter his otherwise empty railway compartment and sit opposite him. One wears a police uniform, the other a cartoonishly striped prisoner's uniform (or costume). When the policeman falls asleep, the prisoner unlocks the cuffs, switches their garb, and then chains himself anew to the other man—but now their roles are reversed. When they exit the car, Nonny notices an envelope, which he opens to find a letter alternating between Gabi's small, round letters and his father's scrawl. After congratulating the bar mitzvah boy, the letter goes on to invite him to play an elaborate game of adventure they have planned. Nonny takes in stride the invitation to play and is surprised only by the intricacy of the "operation," as Nonny imagines Gabi must have billed the proposed caper to his father. Nonny's childhood with Koby, measured out by a shadow police career with regular "promotions," has prepared him to view not only crime-fighting but life itself as a game. Games are subject to rules, of course, just as life imposes laws. Nonny's sense of security resides in his adherence to the rules, and the worst mistakes of his life have occurred through his knowingly contravening them. Although the book's Jewish context is subtle and the bar mitzvah signifies more as a developmental marker than as a religious ritual, Nonny is able to appreciate the special irony of setting off on a criminal jag at just that moment:

> A little outlaw. A little law unto himself.
> Just thinking of it gives me the chills.
> At the end of the week was my bar mitzvah. (176)

In a more traditional setting, the bar mitzvah would inaugurate the child into majority and therefore culpability for his actions under Jewish law. Even transposed to a secular milieu, there remains a preoccupation with the claims of the law upon the individual. It should also be noted that Hebrew has a rich vocabulary for law itself, but the term used here is *hok*, a word counterposed in rabbinic literature to *mishpat*. While *mishpat* is legislated according to human reason and is therefore potentially universal, *hok* is the particularistic law of divine fiat, unsusceptible to modulation or moderation. It is The Law, in its most pure and implacable—moderns might venture "Kafkaesque"—form. Although it might seem far-fetched to retrieve these antiquarian and antiquated residual meanings, there is good reason to think in theological/cosmological terms about a story of crime and crime-fighting. Detective fiction is the last gasp of a religious worldview giving way to a thoroughly secular one. It posits a deeply ordered, rational universe susceptible to God-like observation and detection, even if that function has now been vouchsafed to a mortal detective. Crime represents a rent in the weave that finally emphasizes the prevailing regularity in the warp and weft all around it.

The adventure with Felix is designed to acquaint Nonny with the life story and legacy of his departed mother, Zohara, a larger-than-life figure who "was a law unto herself" (220) and who could not ultimately have sustained a contented domesticity with Nonny's earnest and stolid father. The dichotomies between the boy's progenitors are figured as bourgeois versus bohemian, real-life versus cinematic, and poetry versus prose, but most of all as law versus outlaw: "I was the son of a policeman and a criminal" (228), he admits ruefully. Nonny struggles throughout the novel to make sense of his hereditary place in "the everlasting war between law and crime" (178). Striking out on grand adventures—operating a hijacked locomotive, as well as a car and a bulldozer, dining at the best restaurant in the country, Nonny reflects, "I was both the greatest and the most despicable kid in the whole world" (146). His self-concept balances on a knife's edge: "A master of crime is Nonny Feuerberg, soon to be the best detective in the whole wide world!" He acknowledges the proximity of crime and law, assuming that he will eventually have to pass decisively from one realm into the other. The law/outlaw framework suggests a sharp binary, but Felix and Lola's (his grandmother's) role in Nonny's psychic life is to call into question the necessity of self-divagation. His adventure begins with the switcheroo between cop and prisoner on the train but ends with Felix affirming his synthetic identity: "You are kid like nobody else. You are like crook and you are also good. Big jumble!" (304). The Hebrew word translated as "jumble" is *salat*, itself a calque from "salad"—a harmonious admixture of ingredients, each of which retains its distinctive flavor. The language of laws and rules turns out to be suppler than first imagined, stretching to accommodate the "'Law of . . . of our adventure. It is special law!'" (139). Special cars, special laws: Grossman alchemizes irregularity into specialness as deftly as Sholem Aleichem transmuted exile into diaspora.

Nonny is finally able to harmonize and contain this "big jumble" because of the common denominator between the warring factions of his lineage: delight in the ludic aspects of both criminality and law enforcement. Although in Koby's nomenclature, seasoned criminals and the men who foil them are both referred to as "professionals," there is nevertheless a pervasive sense of play. Early on in his adventure, he cannot help guiltily admiring Felix's insouciance and daring, "As if it was all a game to him and the only law was his law" (51). It eventually emerges that his parents—who met when his father apprehended his mother at a prank-cum-jewelry heist and then promptly fell in love with his captive—would never have met but for their shared sense of gamesmanship: "'Zohara is running! Running and laughing! Because she wants to play her recorder there, yes? Because for her is one big game, yes?'" (251). Nonny is able to persist in the spree with his grandfather because he imagines it all to be arranged by his father and Gabi, even after Felix admits, "'nothing in this entire game is legit. The only question is: Do you still want to play?'" (109). Like a Sholem Aleichem story on speed, the game requires mobility and dissembling: "'Because we must to keep changing everything, cars, Purim[11] costumes, cover stories. Otherwise police will catch up with Felix, and then no more game!'" (108). Yet this call to deceive and dissemble uncovers for Nonny the acting talent that his actress grandmother, Lola Ciperola (neé Katz), has bequeathed to him and that Gabi has quietly nurtured and reinforced.

A Worthy Dulcinea

David Grossman is a genius of indirection, and his most breathtaking maneuver in this novel is to deflect attention away from Gabi, the police department secretary who has assisted Koby and mothered Nonny since Zohara's mysterious disappearance about twelve years prior to the action. Gabi, who wears black because it is slimming and who sardonically rues the world's lack of "inner beauty contests," has long been in love with Koby, to say nothing of her feelings for the baby whose pacifier used to get lost in his father's holster. Until the clarifying ordeal of Nonny's escapade, the hard-boiled detective cannot bring himself to move on from his marriage to the cinematic Zohara and settle into the mundane domesticity that beckons with Gabi and that she has all but provided anyway by ironing shirts and doing other housework—before retreating to her own apartment each night. When Felix asks Nonny who will be the Dulcinea to inspire him on their shared quest, he names Gabi without hesitation; not only does he champion her troth, but he is terrified that she has arranged this outing for him in order to enforce her ultimatum and finally break up with his diffident father while the boy is otherwise occupied.

Koby attributes his delays to not being ready or able (*mesugal*) to move on with his life, but it is impossible to overlook the implicit contrast between Zohara's beauty and excitement, her stormy but thrilling temperament, and Gabi's more quotidian if loving and dependable existence. But one thing that Nonny already knows—and that his adventures with Felix throw into ever-greater relief—is that there are realms in which Gabi is truly extraordinary. One of these is her linguistic creativity, whereby "She had her own special terminology for everything" (7).[12] The list of her neologisms is long and rich: the verbal noun *shilhuv* (an invention Nonny extends by saying, *kevar shulhavti*, "I already underwent Shilhavization"), as well as the acronyms SOS (Sweaty Ornery Slob; *na'amum: nirgan atzbani meyuza umedublal*), IBS (International Brat Scale; *mamshuk: maasei meshuvah vekundes*), YUMTUM scale (*telekutzel: taanug lekarbayim vetsoholah lemeayim*) (94). These linguistic acrobatics are the mirror image of Felix's outrageous malapropisms, inspiring admiration for her facility and good humor.

Felix fortifies Nonny by admiring not only his father's detective skill but also Gabi's cleverness and subtlety. Before Nonny or the reader can, Felix grasps the scale and audacity of the plot that Gabi has set in motion:

> "She is a very special person," said Felix wistfully, running his finger over the black ring on his right hand. "She is more clever than Felix, more than your Mr. Father, too, I think. Real smart apple!"
>
> "Do you mean it? You really think she's special?" Living with Gabi for so long, an seeing the way Dad treated her, sometimes made me forget how smart and special she truly was.
>
> Felix thought awhile and selected his words with care: "I think, if I understand her plan right—I say, Bravo, Miss Gabi! You are real smart apple!" (136)

Gabi turns out to be the grand architect of the plot and true heroine of the book. By cultivating in Nonny an appreciation for the acting of Lola Ciperola (claiming it, all the while, as her own fan obsession), she has prepared the boy to know and love his grandmother. Every month over the course of years, she has taken him to tour the chocolate factory where his parents had met and then to wait outside Lola's house in Tel Aviv, in the hope of a chance encounter, and then to the beach, which Gabi tolerated for the deep satisfaction it afforded Nonny. More than anyone, she has labored to keep Zohara's memory alive for the boy—or to instill the knowledge that would allow for the retrieval of that memory at the right time, under the right circumstances. And then she orchestrates those circumstances! "'I think,' said Felix, 'that Miss Gabi finds very nice, smart way to tell you about

Zohara'" (222). The way that she finds is the essence of picaresque poetics: metonymy. To please his Dulcinea, Nonny has only to follow the metonymic chain that leads to Felix's golden ear of wheat and Lola's purple scarf. These details enable him to solve for himself the mystery of their relation to each other, to Zohara, and ultimately, to him:

> Felix was her father. Lola was her mother.
> The golden ear of wheat and the purple scarf.
> The parents of my mother, Zohara. (245)

Gabi's possible involvement—about which the novel remains coy—marks a new direction for the picaresque: Nonny's adventure is orchestrated, and loving parents are just out of view. Motl was a child-*pícaro* traveling with his loving family, but this is something else again. Grossman's version of *Bildung* is a happy convergence whereby what's best for Nonny (learning about his lineage) also brings about Gabi's happiness, which in turn consolidates the boy's. Felix and his grandson hope equally to unlock for Nonny his past and to secure his future by freeing Koby to marry Gabi. Ultimately, Nonny chooses indeterminacy: "maybe Gabi had played a slightly larger role in my kidnapping than I first supposed." From the narrative vantage point of middle age, he reflects, "I never did find out the answer to my question, and consequently deposited it in the bureau of questions I delight in musing about without ever wanting to know the answer, because while it's true that knowledge is power, mystery has its own special sweetness" (309).

Koby, the novel makes clear, is surely not in on the ruse. He repeats his personal history by apprehending Felix Glick for a second time at the novel's end, but after a tense scene in which the young Mount Feuerberg very nearly explodes, another win-win solution is found. The compromise allows Felix to escape a massive manhunt, and it involves the grandfather literally binding father and son to one another (304). Sitting in a basement bank vault, their extremities tied together, Nonny finally makes his saturnine father laugh for the "first, last, and only" time. This is Bakhtin's purifying, liberating laughter. It is also the distinctively picaresque laughter that Robert Alter describes: "a courageous affirmation, almost a form of devotion. It is his refusal to take himself or life too seriously, his refusal to be choked by rancor, his refusal to become anything less than the observer, the appreciator, the enjoyer, anything less than the man who is capable of the miracle of daily rebirth" (132). Through the completion of his picaresque journey, Nonny has succeeded at awakening in his father something of his dormant boldness and joy.

Zig Zag Nation

The *Zig Zag Kid*'s Israeli[13] and Jewish[14] framing remains in the background; if anything, Nonny's family dynamics run against the current of history. Zohara was coming to terms with a very personal volatility during an over-whelmingly political era: "All this occurred in the stormy days before Israel became a state and the Jews were trying to oust the British and teenagers like Zohara were joining the underground, performing heroic deeds, tough-ing out beatings, arrest, and jail" (222). But even though his mother was not one of those heroic teenagers, there is a discernible soul-nation allegory whereby Nonny Feuerberg undergoes a process of education and integra-tion. The *Bildungsroman* safeguards the past, retrieving bits of it for the purpose of integration and repair. One of Felix's most magical gifts to Nonny is the restoration of the Humber Pullman, the car on which father and son lavished much care but which Koby had to sacrifice in payment of a debt incurred by Nonny at the nadir of his young life. The car is restored, Nonny is allowed to drive it, but just as important, he is able to turn the wheel back over to Felix and snuggle with his grandmother in the back seat *while the adult drives*. "I felt wonderful," Nonny muses at that moment. "As if I had fixed whatever it was that had gone wrong in my life. As if I had mastered something inside me" (273). The repair consists not only of the restored car but of being able to trust the adults in his life to make things work well enough so that he can be a child again.

On the cusp of symbolic adulthood, Nonny secures for himself the abil-ity to mature at his own pace as the object of adult solicitude. If the adven-ture with Felix is a "rite of passage," then Nonny passes not into manhood but into a safe adolescence. Contrast this with the unseasonable youths who populate the *Bildungsromane* of nearly a century earlier: "Moretti argues that World War I finally shattered an already dying genre by destroying the fabric of intergenerational exchange and evacuating the residual heroic ele-ments from the European concept of the rite of passage" (Esty 20).[15] In this novel, Grossman reweaves that fabric, restoring the parent-child relation-ship as a trustworthy dynamic of care. Nonny's treasured bar mitzvah "gifts" include not only parents but grandparents! He can step back—zig zag back, in fact—from the frightening adult world of "professional" criminals and law enforcers to be a kid again. Esty observes that "What Moretti's model leaves unexplored is the crucial symbolic function of nationhood, which gives a finished form to modern societies in the same way that adulthood gives a finished form to the modern subject" (Esty 4). But not all nations are the same or have similar horizons. The particular soul-nation allegory that Grossman traces is suited to Israel's unique circumstances. The *Bildungsroman* does not come to full fruition for the Jews of Europe because Yiddishland does not mature as a conventional nation, certainly not in any time frame synchronized with the rest of Europe. The Jewish state emerges as the rest of the (developed) world is moving beyond national-historical time, beyond the age of nations and into an age of global empire. Zionism is belated and partial as a national container. *The Zig Zag Kid* gives voice to this belatedness. It is *Bildung* for an era of skepticism and postmodernity, a return to linear narration when the linear figures as a zigzag rather than a straight line.

To illustrate this point, it is worth examining the narrative architectonics whereby Grossman constructs the heart of Nonny's story—his backstory. Koby, Nonny, and Gabi form a triad: they are three people who know each other implausibly well and are capable of thinking as one. Felix and Lola can and do bring him to the relevant sites, but Nonny must narrate portions of his own prehistory: his parents' first meeting and subsequent romance, the early days of their marriage, and his own infancy. "'Oh dear,'" Lola says in acknowledging the difficulty of the feat, "'It must be very hard for you to tell this story, and to hear it, too'" (259). Only his peculiar mental melding with his family members enables Nonny to fill in these lacunae. With his grandparents present and his nuclear family physically absent but mentally present, Nonny is able to engage in what can only be called collaborative narration (253–60), an unusual if not singular aspect of this novel as it builds toward its climax. The same sort of intuition allows Nonny to read the letter on the train and feel "sure she used the word 'operation.' She knew that would get him" (24). The individual, Grossman implies, is no longer the sole unit of interest for the picaresque, or even for the *Bildungsroman*; the family matters. Thus, family traits and knowledge can be distributed among three people (with another dead and two more as grandparents, all orbiting the nucleus) who, together, make a coherent whole. We might even think in terms of a picaresque *function*, having to do with delinquency or lawlessness, questioning authority and received notions, and celebrating the carnivalesque. Not everything falls on Nonny: he can let Felix drive, let adults accompany him through his trials.

This narrative communitarianism, dissolving the borders of the self, might be the only allegory that meets the exigencies of this particular nation: a small country whose relations with its geopolitical neighbors are fraught. But the danger of communitarianism is conformity, which Grossman resists by privileging the unassimilable element: the *zigzag* kid[16] who won't fit in any of the square or round boxes—receptacles, containers—waiting to receive him at school or other institutions. Here is where *Bildung* most desperately needs the picaresque, for the *polit* represents above all that which will not be assimilated or contained. The root P.L.T. carries into Modern Hebrew; in the simplest verb form, it means to blurt out, to over-spill, to discharge or divulge. The word is used a couple of times with reference to Nonny (*polit* that he is) to describe an impulsive speech act. He can't quite rationally justify continuing his adventure with Felix, but nevertheless, he *blurts* out, "so we'll go on" (72) ("*az kvar namshikh,' palateti*"). A fanciful translation, very much to the point of this study, might read, "So we'll go on, I *polit*-ed."

The Adventures of Augie March couldn't end, but *The Zig Zag Kid* ends very satisfyingly, with the repurposing of a storybook convention. In Hebrew "*sof*" means "The End." Gabi, with Lola's purple scarf and Felix's golden ear of wheat before her, with Koby's delicate diamond engagement ring rammed onto her pinkie finger, writes in the air to Nonny from behind her fiancé's back: *sof-sof*. It not only doubles the ending but means "at last." Grossman's vision is not a utopian one. The narratively fortified family doesn't promise perfection (witness the too-small engagement ring), just an enhanced ability to bear up under life's challenges and hardships. Life might never get better than this intimate moment, witnessed by strangers in a restaurant just a couple of days before the bar mitzvah of this latter-day *polit*—but at *very* long last, a *sof-sof* that was a tumultuous century in the making, life might just be good enough.

NOTES

Introduction

The opening epigraphs come from Chandler, *Romances of Roguery*, 59–60; Bakhtin, "Forms of Time and of the Chronotope in the Novel," 61; Bauman, *Theory, Culture & Society* 28 (2011): 133.

1. This resonant if baleful phrase opens Anita Brookner's first novel, *A Start in Life*, and also provides the title for a popular undergraduate course on the novel offered by Judith Ryan at Harvard University.

2. Miguel de Cervantes, *Don Quixote de la Mancha*, trans. Tobias Smollett (New York: Noonday, 1986).

3. It is natural to read the Quixote as an idiosyncratic madman, according to the novel's plain sense. However, David Quint offers a highly nuanced analysis of the text's interpolated novellae and generally polyphonic nature, suggesting that the *hidalgo* provides a lens onto renaissance Spanish society during its transition from feudalism to early modernity. In this account, the deep substructure of novel is cultural, reaching beyond the protagonists. See *Cervantes's Novel of Modern Times: A New Reading of Don Quijote* (Princeton: Princeton University Press, 2003).

4. As Todd Hasak-Lowy writes in his valuable study of this novella in relation to the realist tradition, "Benjamin the Third's belief in the ontological primacy of texts over proximate reality distinguishes him in no way from his community" (17). See chapter 1 of Hasak-Lowy's *Here and Now: History, Nationalism, and Realism in Modern Hebrew Fiction* (Syracuse: Syracuse University Press, 2008), 1–33. See also Leah Garrett's "The Jewish *Don Quixote*," *Cervantes: Bulletin of the Cervantes Society of America* 17.2 (1997): 94–105, as well as the treatment of this material in her book *Journeys beyond the Pale: Yiddish Travel Writing in the Modern World* (Madison: University of Wisconsin Press, 2003), 38–56.

5. Abramovitsh had in fact already demonstrated this mastery with the 1869 publication of his breakthrough novel *Fishke der krumer* (*Fishke the Lame*).

6. In this respect, Abramovitsh is heir to a comic-pedagogic tradition that seeks to laugh readers out of their vices, as practiced by Cervantes (especially in the *Novelas Ejemplares*), Fielding, and Swift.

7. See Dan Miron, "Passivity and Narration: The Spell of Isaac Bashevis Singer," *Judaism* 41.1 (1992): 6–17. A later version of the essay also appears in Miron's collection *The Image of the Shtetl* (Syracuse: Syracuse University Press, 2000), 335–51.

8. As Ruth R. Wisse describes in her now-classic study *The Schlemiel as Modern Hero* (Chicago: University of Chicago Press, 1971).

9. The root .ט.ל.פ derives from the older .ט.ל.מ. See Wilhelm Gesenius, *Hebräisches und chaldäisches Handwörterbuch über das Alte Testament*, accessed at http://books.goo gle.co.il/books?id=OdCgLyh_oT0C&printsec=frontcover&source=gbs_ge_summa ry_r&cad=0#v=onepage&q&f=false, p. 354, where he glosses p.l.t. as "Fluechtling, durch die Flucht entkommen."

10. The Hispanist Américo Castro speculated that the author of *Lazarillo de Tormes*, commonly hailed as the first picaresque novella, was a crypto-Jew. See Robert Alter's note 21 on p. 74 in *Rogue's Progress*. For an account of the historical connection between the *pícaro* and the *converso*, see Yael Halevi-Wise's essay "The Life and Times of the Picaro-Converso from Spain to Latin America" in her edited volume *Sephardism* (Stanford: Stanford University Press, 2012). See also the thorough and nuanced treatment in Yirmiyahu Yovel's book *The Other Within: The Marranos: Split Identity and Emerging Modernity* (Princeton: Princeton University Press, 2009). For the purposes of our study, the genealogical connection between the (sometimes converso) *pícaro* and the *polit* remains a loose one. My aim is not to connect the diachronic dots of the Jewish *pícaro's* development throughout modernity but rather to focus on what the analytic of the *polit* can contribute to the study of Yiddish literature and other contemporaneous Jewish literatures of Central and Eastern Europe.

11. This figure has received thorough treatment in Ruth Wisse's *The Schlemiel as Modern Hero*, as well as in Sanford Pinsker's *The Schlemiel as Metaphor* (Carbondale: Southern Illinois University Press, 1971).

12. Gangsters and other kinds of Jewish criminals have been analyzed in several recent studies, including Rachel Rubin's *Jewish Gangsters of Modern Literature* (Chicago: University of Illinois Press, 2000) and Jarrod Tanny's *City of Rogues and Schnorrers: Russia's Jews and the Myth of Old Odessa* (Bloomington: Indiana University Press, 2011).

13. Peter Brooks discusses the "horizontal" definition of "plot" in the sense of plotting coordinates on a graph, map, or other representation of one's location in space. See *Reading for the Plot: Design and Intention in Narrative* (New York: Knopf, 1984), 12.

14. *The Image of the Shtetl and Other Studies of Modern Jewish Literary Imagination* (Syracuse: Syracuse University Press, 2000).

15. The significance of such symbolic places is elaborated more fully in Marc Caplan's insightful study of Rabinovitsh's Kasrilevke stories. See his "Neither Here nor There: The Critique of Ideological Progress in Sholem Aleichem's Kasrilevke Stories" in *Modern Jewish Literatures: Intersections and Boundaries*, ed. Sheila E. Jelen, Michael P. Kramer, and L. Scott Lerner (Philadelphia: University of Pennsylvania Press, 2011), 127–46. Caplan reminds us of I.L. Peretz's declaration, "We Jews live without geography!" (128).

16. This is not to imply that "nature" was unimportant to Abramovitsh. Indeed, he

perpetually critiques traditional Jewish culture as being alienated from salutary nature. However, Miron's point stands insofar as his attachment to the natural world was abstract and nonspecific.

17. Stephen Jay Gould, *Time's Arrow, Time's Cycle: Myth and Metaphor in the Discovery of Geological Time* (Cambridge: Harvard University Press, 1987).

18. See, for instance, Doris Sommer's *Foundational Fictions: The National Romances of Latin America* (Berkeley: University of California Press, 1991) for an account of the Latin American dime novel romance as a disseminator of nationalist ideology.

19. What is discussed here as cyclical and linear time may be related—though not precisely correlated—to the concepts of "open" and "closed" time, which in turn corresponds to narrative functions of classification and transformation, as discussed by Mikhail Krutikov in *Yiddish Fiction and the Crisis of Modernity, 1905–1914* (Stanford: Stanford University Press, 2001). See especially 2–4.

20. See Yohanan Petrovsky-Shtern, *Jews in the Russian Army, 1827–1917: Drafted Into Modernity* (Cambridge: Cambridge University Press, 2009).

21. See Miron's *A Traveler Disguised* for a thorough account of the workings of the Mendele persona, especially chapters 5–7.

22. In *Unseasonable Youth: Modernism, Colonialism, and the Fiction of Development* (New York: Oxford University Press, 2012).

23. In *Chronoschisms* (Cambridge: Cambridge University Press, 1997), 52.

24. See Tzvetan Todorov, *Mikhail Bakhtin* (Manchester: Manchester University Press, 1984), 83, 91 for a discussion of Bakhtin's novelistic genre theory. Also see Nele Bemong and Pieter Borghart's introductory essay "Bakhtin's Theory of the Literary Chronotope: Reflections, Applications, Perspectives" in their edited volume of the same name (Gent, Belgium: Academia Press, 2010), 8 for a discussion of the significance of the chronotope for genre theory. See also Michael Holquist's discussion of the chronotope in his *Dialogism* (New York: Routledge, 1990), 106–11. Caryl Emerson and Gary Saul Morson offer an extremely thorough treatment of the concept in their *Mikhail Bakhtin: Creation of a Prosaics* (Stanford: Stanford University Press, 1990), 366–432.

25. See Thomas O. Beebee, *The Ideology of Genre: A Comparative Study of Generic Instability* (University Park: Pennsylvania State University Press, 1994). Beebee argues that literary genres can both reveal and reinforce cultural ideologies: "Genre gives us not understanding in the abstract and passive sense but use in the pragmatic and active sense" (14). See also Bart Keunen, "Bakhtin, Genre Formation, and the Cognitive Turn: Chronotopes as Memory Schemata" *CLCWeb: Comparative Literature and Culture* 2.2 (2000): http://docs.lib.purdue.edu/clcweb/vol2/iss2/2: "we need to learn from Bakhtin that motivic chronotopes (action schemata) are linked to generic structures. The latter are in Bakhtin's perspective the bearer of a world model. If genological analysis is neglected, schema theory becomes a kind of 'history of ideas' approach that links motifs with information from the 'cultural context.'" See also Michael Sinding, building on the work of George Lakoff on framing and genre as it applies to politics: his recent project "Framing the World: Genre as Worldview" is a study of how metaphor and narrative interact in structuring moral and political worldviews, particularly during the forma-

tion of modern liberalism and conservatism in the eighteenth-century debate over the French Revolution. A digital summary may be accessed at http://www.networkinstitute. org/wp-content/uploads/2013/02/Framing-the-World-Genre-as-Worldview.pdf.   See also Tzvetan Todorov, "The Origin of Genres" in *Modern Genre Theory*, ed. David Duff (London: Longman, 2000), 193–209 and at greater length, *The Fantastic: A Structural Approach to a Literary Genre* (Ithaca: Cornell University Press, 1975). See also Gérard Genette, "Three Basic Ways of Imagining Life and the Universe," in *The Architext: An Introduction* (Berkeley: University of California Press, 1992). For a review of approaches to genre, see *Genre: An Introduction to History, Theory, Research, and Pedagogy* by Anis S. Bawarshi and Mary Jo Reiff (West Lafayette: The Parlor Press and WAC Clearinghouse http://wac.colostate.edu, 2010).

26. M.M. Bakhtin's "Forms of Time and of the Chronotope in the Novel" (abbreviated FTC) in *The Dialogic Imagination*, ed. Michael Holquist, trans. Caryl Emerson and Michael Holquist (Austin: University of Texas Press, 1981), 84–258.

27. See Bemong and Borghart: "a *definitive* definition of the concept is never offered" (5) and J. Ladin, "Fleshing Out the Chronotope" in *Critical Essays on Mikhail Bakhtin*, ed. Caryl Emerson (New York: Hall, 1999), 212–36. See p. 213.

28. Bemong and Borghart discern and painstakingly catalogue five levels of abstraction within the critical engagement of the chronotope concept (6–7).

29. See "Reading, Walking, Mourning: W.G. Sebald's Peripatetic Fictions" in *Journal of Narrative Theory* 34.3 (2004): 304–34.

30. See this chapter in Giancarlo Maiorino's excellent collection *The Picaresque: Tradition and Displacement* (Minneapolis: University of Minnesota Press, 1996), especially pp. 276–78 for a review of picaresque criticism since the 1960s. A version of the same essay, entitled "The Picaresque Novel: A Protean Form," appeared in a symposium on "The Picaresque Tradition" in *College Literature* 6.3 (1979): 182–204.

31. Mancing drily notes—and resists—the critical tendency to define the picaresque out of its very existence: "At times it seems as though the elimination of one or several works from the generally accepted canon of picaresque novels were an end in itself" (*College Literature* 182).

32. See Ulrich Wicks, "The Nature of Picaresque Narrative: A Modal Approach," *PMLA* 89.2 (Mar. 1974): 240–49.

33. See J. A. G. Ardila, "Introduction: Transnational Picaresque," *Philological Quarterly* 89.1 (Winter 2010); Here Ardila introduces a special issue devoted to the transnational picaresque that revisits the authorship and poetics of *Lazarillo* and encompasses colonial and Russian picaresque traditions.

34. See "Toward a Definition of the Picaresque" in Guillén's *Literature as System: Essays Toward the Theory of Literary History* (Princeton: Princeton University Press, 1971), 71–106.

35. While Wicks first adumbrates the "modal approach," Marcia A. Morris expands significantly upon modal versus generic approaches to the picaresque. See her study *The Literature of Roguery in Seventeenth- and Eighteenth-Century Russia* (Evanston: Northwestern University Press, 2000), 4.

36. Paul West, *The Modern Novel* (London: Hutchinson, 1965), 140. I first became aware of this passage through Gordana Yovanovich's *Play and the Picaresque: Lazarillo de Tormes, Libro de Manuel, and Match Ball* (Toronto: University of Toronto Press, 1999), 43.

37. For example, see S. Ortiz Taylor's article "Episodic Structure and the Picaresque Novel" in *Journal of Narrative Theory* 7.3 (1977): 218–25, where she proposes the bead necklace as an analogy to the structure of the picaresque: smaller, nonuniform beads (episodes) strung together to constitute a larger circle (the whole plot) (218). It is worth noting that the eminent Yiddish critic Meir Viner also proposed a bead necklace image in discussing the structure of *Motl peysi dem khazns*. See Miron's *The Image of the Shtetl*, 201.

38. A number of Spanish scholars have recently attempted to lay to rest the long-assumed anonymity of the novella. See Mercedes Agulló y Cobo, who makes a strong case for its being the work of Diego Hurtado de Mendoza in her study *A vueltas con el autor del Lazarillo* (Madrid: Calambur, 2010). However, this thesis was strenuously rejected by some, including Rosa Navarro Durán. For a summary of the controversy, see Joseph V. Ricapito, "Further Comments on Alfonso de Valdés as Author of Lazarillo de Tormes," *Philological Quarterly* 89.1 (Winter 2010): 95–107.

39. Dates of publication are slightly less certain; printings seem to have appeared within a year of each other in Alcalá, Spain (1554) and Antwerp (1555; the Low Countries were then under the Spanish Crown).

40. While completing the revisions to this manuscript, I was pleasantly startled to come across a recent, parallel study of the picaresque in modernist German literature, whose author stakes a similar claim about the resurgence of the picaresque as a response to the predicaments of modernity. See Bernhard F. Malkmus's study *The German Picaro and Modernity: Between Underdog and Shape-Shifter* (New York: Continuum, 2011).

41. Except for the antisentimentalism, these traits diverge dramatically from the four features that Halevi-Wise identifies with the *pícaro-converso*: lineage, delinquency, anti-idealism, and conversion.

42. See Robert S. Stone, "Pito Pérez: Mexican Middleman" in *Mexican Studies/Estudios Mexicanos* 21.2 (2005): 369–402.

43. See James Mandrell, "Questions of Genre and Gender: Contemporary American Versions of the Feminine Picaresque" in *Novel* 20.2 (1987): 149–70.

44. See his brief study *The Picaresque* (London: Methuen, 1977).

45. See Gillian Beer, *Darwin's Plots: Evolutionary Narrative in Darwin, George Eliot, and Nineteenth-Century Fiction* (New York: Cambridge University Press, 2004), where she links *Bildung* to ideals of growth and transformation: "Evolutionary theory brings together two imaginative elements implicit in much nineteenth-century thinking and creativity. One was the fascination with growth expressed also in *Natürphilosophie* and in *Bildungsroman*. The other was the concept of transformation" (97).

46. A partial inventory of these optics might include but would certainly not be limited to the following: nationalism from within (Ian Watt); nationalism from without (Pascale Casanova); gender (Nancy Armstrong); Marxism (Georg Lukacs); historical

198 NOTES TO PAGES 20–21

materialism (Richard McKeon). Plus, Benedict Anderson, Homi Bhabha, Timothy Brennan, and Franco Moretti.

47. Pericles Lewis braids together the intertwining strands of political history, intellectual history, and literary experimentation in *Modernism, Nationalism, and the Novel* (Cambridge: Cambridge University Press, 2000). See especially the section on "The Modernist Novel and the Crisis of Liberal Nationalism," 3–12. Jed Esty emphasizes the shift from nation to colonial empire as having "unsettled the progressive and stabilizing discourse of national culture by breaking up cherished continuities between a people and its language, territory, and polity" (6). Mark Anderson traces the nineteenth-century novel of property giving way to the modernist travel narrative. In representational terms, the age of modernism saw a collapse of biographical plot structures that aim at unification and totality, a flattening and undoing of realist possibilities.

48. "Moretti proposes a more Darwinian thesis, according to which modernism had to abandon the bildungsroman and seek new formal possibilities for the novel. For him, the genre no longer presides over the symbolic adjustment of protagonists to their place in bourgeois society, nor does it sustain the master allegory of modernization that was so successfully inscribed in the nineteenth-century bildungsroman. . . . Moretti argues that World War I finally shattered an already dying genre by destroying the fabric of intergenerational exchange and evacuating the residual heroic elements from the European concept of the rite of passage" (Esty 20).

49. *Modernism: 1890–1930*, ed. Malcolm Bradbury and Jim McFarlane (London: Penguin, 1976). This source was called to my attention by Allison Schachter's discussion of it in *Diasporic Modernisms: Hebrew and Yiddish Literature in the Twentieth Century* (New York: Oxford University Press, 2011).

50. "[T]here will be a new form, and . . . this form will be of such a type that it admits the chaos and does not try to say that the chaos is really something else. . . . To find a form that accommodates the mess, that is the task of the artist now" (Samuel Beckett, in an interview with Tom Driver, "Beckett by the Madeleine," in *Columbia University Forum* (Summer 1961): 23.

51. See Italo Calvino's essay on "Lightness" from *Six Memos for the Next Millennium* (Cambridge: Harvard University Press, 1988), where he opposes the picaresque to the weight of the world: "I tried to find some harmony between the adventurous, picaresque inner rhythm that prompted me to write and the frantic spectacle of the world, sometimes dramatic and sometimes grotesque. Soon I became aware that between the facts of life that should have been my raw materials and the quick light touch I wanted for my writing, there was a gulf that cost me increasing effort to cross. Maybe I was only then becoming aware of the weight, the inertia, the opacity of the world" (4).

52. Timothy Brennan, "The National Longing for Form" in *Nation and Narration*, ed. Homi K. Bhabha (London: Routledge, 1990), 44–70.

53. See Gillian Beer's discussion of recapitulation as a quintessential Victorian image in *Darwin's Plots*, 99.

54. Esty offers an elegant gloss and elaboration of this idea: "This idea of a homeland . . . becomes increasingly nationalized in nineteenth-century literature, first in Brit-

ish and French, then in U.S. and Russian realism. By this I mean that the *kairos* of national-historical time becomes the semivisible guarantor that the *chronos* of modernity can be made meaningful in the bildungsroman's grammar of plot" (Esty 47).

55. See Olga Litvak's *Haskalah: The Romantic Movement in Judaism* (New Brunswick: Rutgers University Press, 2012).

56. See Miron's "Passivity and Narration: The Spell of Isaac Bashevis Singer" in *Judaism: A Quarterly Journal of Jewish Life and Thought* 41.1 (1992): 6–17. See also the slightly altered version in Miron's collection *The Image of the Shtetl*, 335–51.

57. As described by Doris Sommer in *Foundational Fictions*.

58. Quotations in this paragraph are drawn from Miron's remarks at an invited seminar at the University of Florida, Center for Jewish Studies, Gainesville, October 18, 2008.

59. Anita Norich, *The Homeless Imagination in the Fiction of Israel Joshua Singer* (Bloomington: Indiana University Press, 1991).

60. John Ardila reminds us that the "classical" *pícaro* grows and becomes educated. His reading of Lazarillo is more teleological and sequentially driven than my own: "They are also novelistic in as much as they have, in Northrop Frye's terms, a *hence* structure, where one episode is the logical result of the previous one. This is particularly noticeable in Lazarillo, whose eponymous protagonist learns from his previous experiences in order to develop psychologically and survive in a ferocious society" (Ardila 4).

61. From Russell Reising's aptly titled study *Loose Ends: Closure and Crisis in the American Social Text* (Durham: Duke University Press, 1996): "The arbitrariness and abruptness of Huck's decision *not* to struggle to right the wrongs he has experienced suggests Mark Twain's cynicism, perhaps, but it could equally suggest his honesty. *Adventures of Huckleberry Finn* stops without in any way ameliorating the moral, economic, cultural, juridical, racial and political evils it has so pointedly represented; no changes of heart, of law, of ethics intervene into the sickness of the novel's world" (2).

62. See Krutikov's chapter on "The Economic Crisis," especially pp. 12–16.

63. See Miron's study *A Traveler Disguised: The Rise of Modern Yiddish Fiction in the Nineteenth Century* (Syracuse: Syracuse University Press, 1996), chapter 2.

64. Stella Bolaki, *Unsettling the Bildungsroman: Reading Contemporary Ethnic American Women's Fiction* (New York: Rodopi, 2011).

65. Piret Peiker, "Post-communist Literatures: A Postcolonial Perspective," originally in Estonian in *Vikerkaar* 10–11 (2005). Translated and republished in English in Eurozine. www.eurozine.com/articles/2006-03-28-peiker-en.html.

66. For a differently angled consideration that engages postcolonial discourse, see Allison Schachter's *Diasporic Modernisms*.

67. See Caplan's *How Strange the Change: Language, Temporality, and Narrative Form in Peripheral Modernisms* (Stanford: Stanford University Press, 2011).

68. For example, see Geraldine Heng's *Empire of Magic: Medieval Romance and the Politics of Cultural Fantasy* (New York: Columbia University Press, 2003) and Jeffrey Jerome Cohen's *The Postcolonial Middle Ages* (New York: Palgrave Macmillan, 2001).

69. This limited scope and fragmentary style is typical of much Yiddish literature.

Sholem Aleichem and Y.L. Peretz, both enshrined as "classic" authors, confined their attempts at full-scale novels to a fraction of their total output.

70. Roman Jakobson, in his essay "Two Aspects of Language and Two Types of Aphasic Disturbances," argues for an encompassing opposition between metaphor (the logic of substitution) and metonymy (the logic of sequencing and contiguity) in denominating and organizing experience. The lyric poem is a prototypical instance of the former, while picaresque fiction—with its emphasis on contingency, contiguity, and sequences of events—furnishes an extreme example of the latter. The implications of Jakobson's thesis for literary analysis are elaborated by David Lodge in "The Language of Modernist Fiction: Metaphor and Metonymy" in *Modernism: A Guide to European Literature 1890–1930*, ed. Malcolm Bradbury and James McFarlane (New York: Penguin, 1991), 481–96 and in Barbara Johnson, *A World of Difference* (Baltimore: Johns Hopkins University Press, 1987), ch. 14, 155–58.

71. See "The Fragmentation of Narrative Perspective in Y.L. Peretz's *Bilder fun a Provints-Rayze*," *Jewish Social Studies: History, Culture, Society* 14.1 (2007): 63–88.

Chapter 1

1. The phrase is borrowed from Roger Ebert's review of David Mamet's film *House of Games. Roger Ebert's Four Star Reviews—1967–2007* (Kansas City: Andrews McMeel, 2007).

2. One of the distinguishing features of Yiddish literature is the temporal compression under which it developed. See David G. Roskies, "The Achievement of American Yiddish Modernism" in *Go and Study: Essays and Studies in Honor of Alfred Jospe*, ed. Raphael Jospe and Samuel Z. Fishman (Washington, DC: B'nai Brith Hillel Foundations, 1980), 353–68. "It was, for lack of a better term, the European Connection, when a hundred years of cultural development were compressed into ten" (354).

3. Compare Rabinovitsh, for instance, with his contemporary Joseph Conrad, who also paired the mimesis of orality with nonlinear narration.

4. See his essay "The Future of Literature," published in *Forverts* March 17, 1972, in which he argues that new literary fashions have displaced authors' concern about the most important aspect of a novel: "At least the pulp novel tells a story, even if it's second-rate, unconvincing, and glued together with saliva; ultimately the reader wants to be told a story. The plot is finally the most important thing. In the chaos of Fashion, and in an effort to save the world while standing on one foot, modern literature has forgotten the very most important thing: the plot" [my translation]. I am grateful to Dr. David Stromberg of the Hebrew University of Jerusalem for directing my attention to this essay, as well as to two others that Bashevis published later that year in *Forverts* (July 1 and 7, respectively), in which he writes further about the future of literature in general and Yiddish literature more specifically.

5. See Dan Miron, "Passivity and Narration" in *The Image of the Shtetl*, 340.

6. "The Pleasure of Disregarding Red Lights: A Reading of Sholem Aleichem's Monologue 'A Nisref'" in *Arguing the Modern Jewish Canon* (Cambridge: Harvard University Press, 2008), 201–31.

7. Most Yiddish literature, as Miron points out, grows out of Enlightenment striving. While Allison Schachter mentions "the fractured social conditions of diasporic culture that Jewish authors sought to overcome" (12), I would urge that Rabinovitsh and Bashevis belong together because they fundamentally acceded to the fracturing and did not seek to overcome it.

8. This is not a complete departure from Iberian antecedents, where the theme of *desengaño* pervaded the work of such Golden Age authors as Cervantes, Calderon de la Barca, Quevedo, and María de Zayas.

9. See Victor Ehrlich's brief but important article, "A Note on the Monologue as a Literary Form: Sholem Aleichem's *Monologn*—A Test Case," in *For Max Weinreich on His Seventieth Birthday*, 44–50. See also Ken Frieden's discussion of *skaz* and fn. 2 on p. 184 of *Classic Yiddish Fiction*.

10. James Wesley Childers, *Tales from Spanish Picaresque Novels: A Motif Index* (Albany: SUNY Press, 1977), 146–82.

11. See Ross Chambers, *Story and Situation: Narrative Seduction and the Power of Fiction* (Minneapolis: University of Minnesota Press, 1984) and *Room for Maneuver: Reading (the) Oppositional (in) Narrative* (Chicago: University of Chicago Press, 1991).

12. For a parallel treatment of another aspect of Rabinovitsh's rejection of positivist values, see Marc Caplan's essay about how the Kasrilevke stories expose the author's gnawing sense that progress is impossible: "Neither Here nor There: The Critique of Ideological Progress in Sholem Aleichem's Kasrilevke Stories," in *Modern Jewish Literatures: Intersections and Boundaries,* ed. Sheila E. Jelen, Michael P. Kramer, and L. Scott Lerner (Philadelphia: University Press of Pennsylvania, 2011), 127–46.

13. Much of Rabinovitsh's narrative framing, especially in the *Railroad Stories*, underscores the arbitrary nature of these chance encounters and the correspondingly arbitrary nature of authorial control. The most extreme example of the author conspicuously asserting his power is the story "Baranovitsh Station," with its abrupt ending governed by the exigencies of train travel. The centrality of that ending is of course reflected in the story's title.

14. Although Rabinovitsh takes pains to show that stasis is no guarantee of moral rectitude or "traditional" values, as the raconteur in the monologue "Chabne" attests.

15. Philip Fisher elaborates this theory of games in relation to literary texts in *The Vehement Passions* (Princeton: Princeton University Press, 2002), 130–31.

16. See Peter L. Bernstein, *Against the Gods: The Remarkable Story of Risk* (New York: Wiley and Sons, 1996), especially chapter 14 on game theory.

17. See Jacques Ehrmann, "Homo Ludens Revisited," trans. Cathy Lewis and Phil Lewis in *Yale French Studies* no. 41, Game, Play, Literature (1968): 31–57.

18. Ehrmann cites Roger Caillois's definition of play, which stipulates, among several other characteristics, that it be "unproductive: it creates neither goods nor wealth nor new elements of any kind; and, except for redistribution of property within the circle of players, it results in a situation identical to that with which it began" (Ehrmann 35).

19. A gamble might be Rabinovitsh's most optimistic economic motif. A darker vi-

sion prevails in "Benny's Luck," in which the deck of life, and the dreidel, is stacked with "a gimel on every side!"

20. See Jonathan Karp, "Economic History and Jewish Modernity: Ideological Versus Structural Change," *Jahrbuch des Simon-Dubnow Instituts* 6 (2007): 249–67. Mikhail Krutikov approaches productivization as part of a shifting economic structure through the work of Jacob Lestschinsky, who saw the turn to productive labor as a needed abandonment of the "broker's legacy." See *Yiddish Fiction and the Crisis of Modernity, 1905–1914*, 14–16.

21. See Janet E. Mullin, "'We Had Carding': Hospitable Card Play and Polite Domestic Sociability Among the Middling Sort in Eighteenth-Century England," *Journal of Social History* (Summer 2009): 989–1008.

22. The *Mahari Bruna* emphasizes that this form of levity is only suitable to days when the supplicatory prayer *tahanun* is not recited; correspondingly, the *Noheg Ketson Yosef* restricts card playing for stakes to Hanukkah and Purim. Another source posited card play as a pastime for children, in order to keep them awake until the lighting of the Hanukkah lamp (which does not address the obviously widespread custom of gambling among adults).

23. See "*Literarisher pinkes*," *Bikher velt* 1.4–5 (1922): 465.

24. This aspect of the story illustrates Krutikov's observation that "A society in a state of transition is characterized by the simultaneous presence of different economic modes competing for hegemony" (13).

25. "*A zeks un zektsik*" is also structured with a series of prefatory anecdotes, followed by the recounting of one main swindle. That story inserts this structural apparatus into a frame of ultimate significance.

26. A partial catalogue of this motif, which occurs mostly in the first half of the story, would include the following passages: "Nowadays a game of cards is an everyday affair" (372) "*haynt zenen kortn a vokhediker gang*"; "*hayntlike tsaytn*" (Y 201); "There was a time, if you know what I mean" (372) "*amol, oyb ir hot in dem a gefil . . .*" (Y 201); "Riva-Leah, the gabai's wife, of blessed memory (she has gone to her rest these many years)" (372); "I merely wanted to show you what a forbidden thing cards used to be and how carefully we had to hide our knowledge of them" (374).

27. Yet one of the most ironic aspects of Rabinovitsh's enduring legacy is that this mordant anti-nostalgist gave rise to an entire industry of nostalgia of the most unreconstructed, restorative sort through the predations of *Fiddler on the Roof*. Perhaps the built-in irony of an anti-nostalgic project is that it must risk trafficking in nostalgia to get its point across. For more on the *Fiddler* industry, see Alisa Solomon, *Wonder of Wonders: A Cultural History of* Fiddler on the Roof (New York: Henry Holt, 2013). For an account of "restorative" versus reflective nostalgia, see Svetlana Boym, *The Future of Nostalgia* (New York: Basic, 2001), xviii, 41–56.

28. Dan Miron refers to these lines as "refrains" and claims that "the oft-repeated formulaic sentence, plays a very important structural and musical role" in Sholem Aleichem's monologues and other stories (219). See "The Pleasure of Disregarding Red

Lights" in *Arguing the Modern Jewish Canon: Essays on Literature and Culture in Honor of Ruth R. Wisse*, ed. Justin D. Cammy et al. (Cambridge: Harvard University Press, 2008), 201–31.

29. I am indebted to David Roskies, during a conversation on November 23, 2012, for this application of the centrifugal/centripetal distinction so central to Mikhail Bakhtin's thought.

30. See Murav, *Music from a Speeding Train: Jewish Literature in Post-Revolution Russia* (Stanford: Stanford University Press, 2011), especially pp. 100, 209, and 272.

31. See Ezrahi 11 regarding the train as interior Jewish space.

32. See Daniel Brower, *The Russian City Between Tradition and Modernity, 1850–1900* (Berkeley: University of California Press, 1990). See "Railway Journey and Urban Travelers," 42–53.

33. See Walter Friedman, *Birth of a Salesman*. See "The Traveling Salesman," 56–87 and especially 57.

34. See Roy Church, "Salesmen and the Transformation of Selling in Britain and the US," *Economic History Review* 61.3 (2008): 695–725, cited by French and Popp.

35. Michael French and Andrew Popp, "'Ambassadors of Commerce': The Commercial Traveler in British Culture, 1800–1939," *Business History Review* 82 (Winter 2008): 789–814.

36. See Dan Miron's essay "Journey to the Twilight Zone," in *The Image of the Shtetl.* It was translated from the original Hebrew "*Masa be'ezor hadimdumim,*" which appeared as the afterword to Miron's Hebrew translation of the *Railroad Stories*, published in 1989. The circumstances of composition are detailed on pp. 256–64.

37. *Classic Yiddish Fiction: Abramovitsh, Sholem Aleichem, and Peretz*, by Ken Frieden (Albany: SUNY Press, 1995).

38. Joan Didion famously prefaced *Slouching Toward Bethlehem*, a collection of nonfiction reportage, with the admonition, "Writers are always selling somebody out." See Ken Frieden's formulation of a similar idea in his discussion of "A Game of Sixty-Six" in *Classic Yiddish Fiction*, 196–97.

39. As Dan Miron explains, Rabinovitsh solicited as a commodity material about railway travel, but he scrupled that it had to be unembellished by the source's own literary pretenses, like raw cotton or metal (261).

40. This need for other Jews does nothing to inhibit an amiable scorn for them when they are present: "God forgive me for speaking frankly, but we Jews are a revolting people. It's practically impossible to play a game of sixty-six with a crowd of Jews around. Before you know it, they're standing all over you and telling you what card to play and whether to trump or not. You can't get rid of them, they stick to you like flies!" (210).

41. See Ross Chambers, *Loiterature*, especially pp. 54–55 on wasting time as a bourgeois privilege.

42. From Norbert Guterman's English translation of the tale in the Library of America Edition, ed. Ilan Stavans, 60–68.

43. See Khone Shmeruk, "The Use of Monologue as a Narrative Technique in the

Stories of Isaac Bashevis Singer," which serves as an introduction to *Der shpigl un andere dertseylungen*, ed. Khone Shmeruk (Jerusalem: Magnes [in conjunction with the Yiddish Department of the Hebrew University], 1975), xix–xx.

44. See "Seductions and Disputations: Pseudo-dialogues in the Fiction of Isaac Bashevis Singer" in *Beyond the Modern Jewish Canon: Arguing Jewish Literature and Culture, A Festschrift in Honor of Ruth R. Wisse* (Cambridge: Harvard University Press, 2008), especially pp. 299–306.

45. The phrase is drawn from Dorothy Holland, William Lachicotte, Jr., Debra Skinner, Carole Cain, *Identity and Agency in Cultural Worlds* (Cambridge: Harvard University Press, 1998).

46. Published in *Svive* 1.2 (1943).

47. This seminal essay, in which Bashevis Singer argues that concern to employ an authentic Yiddish vocabulary must constrain the subject matter of Yiddish prose to Old World themes, is available in English translation in *Prooftexts* 9.1 (1989): 5–12.

48. See David G. Roskies, "*Di shprakh fun derekh-haSaM: Vi der sotn redt af yidish,*" in *Hahut shel hen: shai leHava Turnianski* [*A Touch of Grace: Studies in Ashkenazi Culture, Women's History, and the Languages of the Jews Presented to Chava Turniansky*], ed. Israel Bartal, Galit Hasan-Rokem, et al. (Jerusalem: Zalman Shazar Center for Jewish History and the Center for Research on Polish Jewry, The Hebrew University, 2012), 69–85.

49. As Ken Frieden writes about the series, "Temptation is at the center of Singer's stories that purport to be 'Memoirs of the Evil Inclination.' A demon tests a man or a woman, who either withstands or succumbs to the test. But Singer's demons discover that the very possibility of temptation, as understood by traditional Jewish sources, has been undermined by changes in the modern world" (264). Frieden's account partakes of an interior, psychological view of good and evil whereby the internal quality is revealed by testing. Yet Bashevis Singer's demonic tales are less tests than pitched battles, which the *yeytser-hore* is favored to win. See Frieden, "I.B. Singer's Monologues of Demons," *Prooftexts* 5 (1985): 263–68.

50. J.L. Austin, *How to Do Things With Words* (Cambridge: Harvard University Press, 1975).

51. For clear, concentrated formulations regarding the codification of the laws of speech, see Maimonides's Mishne Torah, *De'ot*, chapter 6 and his commentary on *Avot* 1:16.

52. B. Arakhin 15b.

53. Translated by Martha Glicklich and Cecil Hemley and cited from *The Collected Stories of Isaac Bashevis Singer* (New York: Farrar, Straus, Giroux, 1999). Also in connection with the theme of Bashevian passivity, see Avraham Nowersztern's essay "History, Messianism, and Apocalypse in Bashevis's Work" in *The Hidden Isaac Bashevis Singer*, ed. Seth L. Wolitz (Austin: University of Texas Press, 2001), 28–61.

54. Ken Frieden has understood the scene this way, writing, "The dialogues between the Rabbi and the demon ... are like internal debates held by the Rabbi with himself. Once again, this emphasizes the psychological significance of traditional Jewish spirits"

(267). Once again, our reading must emphasize the figural significance of these spirits, and the conversational, outward-looking dimension of these interactions.

55. See my "Seductions and Disputations" for a fuller discussion of the Bashevian critique of available language, especially pp. 315–18.

56. See Roskies, *Bridge*, 300 and his fn. 55 and 56.

57. See Gershom Scholem, "Shabbetai Zevi" in *Encyclopedia Judaica*.

58. Angela S. Moger, "The Obscure Object of Narrative" in *Yale French Studies* 63 (1983): 129–38.

59. The Yiddish couplet bears recording:

> On a yidish os
> Iz a shed a yid—oys

Chapter 2

1. See Viner's article "On Sholem Aleichem's Humor," *Prooftexts* 6.1, Special Issue on Sholem Aleichem: The Critical Tradition (1986): 41–54.

2. The Art of Fiction No. 42, *The Paris Review*, interviewed by Harold Flender.

3. These two linear views, as well as their subversion in children's science fiction, are articulated in Susan Honeyman's article "Mutiny by Mutation: Uses of Neoteny in Science Fiction," *Children's Literature in Education* 35.4 (2004): 347–66. Within the realm of Yiddish fiction, Marc Caplan points out that Y.L. Peretz conceives of time's directionality as (negative) entropy rather than (positive) progress: "Rather than bringing the shtetl forward 'into the twentieth century,' the journey brings the narrator backward, away from the linear conception of time on which modernity is premised, into a social space in which time only registers in the accretion of decline and decay" (76) in "The Fragmentation of Narrative Perspective in Y.L. Peretz's *Bilder fun a Provints-Rayze,*" *Jewish Social Studies: History, Culture, Society* 14.1 (2007): 63–88.

4. See Gillian Beer, *Darwin's Plots: Evolutionary Narrative in Darwin, George Eliot, and Nineteenth-Century Fiction* (New York: Cambridge University Press, 2004) and Peter Brooks, *Reading for the Plot: Design and Intention in Narrative* (New York: Knopf, 1984).

5. The concept of arrested development is at the center of Rebecca Elise Rainof's dissertation "Purgatory and the Fictions of Maturity, from Newman to Woolf" (Princeton, 2008), where she discerns in the English novel from *Little Dorrit* to *Ulysses* a counter-tradition to the *Bildungsroman* in novels that envision cases of "adult-onset 'arrested development,'" and as a result, face the challenge of accommodating the prolonged inactivity of their protagonists in novels that demand progression (6).

6. See especially Stephen Jay Gould, *The Mismeasure of Man, Revised and Expanded* (New York: W.W. Norton, 2006); Ashley Montagu, *Growing Young* (Westport: Greenwood Publishing Group, 1989); John R. Morss, *Growing Critical: Alternatives to Developmental Psychology* (London: Routledge, 1996); and Weston La Barre, *Shadow of Childhood: Neoteny and the Biology of Religion* (Norman: University of Oklahoma Press, 1991).

7. Honeyman 357.

8. Baal Makhshoves, in commenting on the novel, laments a Jewish (and Christian) failure to give childhood its due dignity, arguing that children assume significance in traditional Jewish society only when they begin to mimic adult behaviors and that the Jewish child "is caged in by thousands of pedagogical rules that transform his childhood into a trying and gloomy period of life" (*Prooftexts*, Special Issue on Sholem Aleichem: The Critical Tradition [January 1986], p. 13).

9. Naomi Sokoloff, *Imagining the Child in Modern Jewish Fiction* (Baltimore: Johns Hopkins University Press, 1992).

10. On the distinction between *golus* and Diaspora, see Ezrahi 128.

11. See Ruth Wisse, "The Classic of Disinheritance" in *New Essays on* Call It Sleep, ed. Hana Wirth-Nesher (Cambridge: Cambridge University Press, 1996), 61–74. Wisse discusses "childhood as the archetypal immigration" (61).

12. "Demonstrating the flux of changing circumstances and the breakdown of previous meanings, Mottel shows adults are childlike in the unpreparedness and vulnerability, even as childish resilience and disregard for tragedy come to signify an all-important vitality" (Sokoloff 62).

13. See Ezrahi 123, Miron 249.

14. Such forward movement was encapsulated in the self-serious name *Forverts*, the organ aimed at acculturating an immigrant readership. Thanks to my colleague Professor Peter Höyng for making this point.

15. The same question of how to end is foregrounded by Avraham Nowersztern in his masterful study of Menakhem-Mendl, "Sholem Aleykhem's Menakhem-Mendl: Its Textual History and Its Structure," *Tarbiz* 54.1 (1985): 105–46.

16. See Dan Miron's discussion of the shift from Motl as musician to Motl as visual artist in *Image of the Shtetl* 182–85.

17. The phrase comes from Erik's entry *Kasrilevke* in *Farmest: Literarish-kinstlerisher, un kritish-bibliografisher zhurnal* 5–6 (May-June 1935), 153. Translations from this article and a longer treatment of Erik appear in Marc Caplan's article "Neither Here nor There: The Critique of Ideological Progress in Sholem Aleichem's Kasrilevke Stories" in *Modern Jewish Literatures: Intersections and Boundaries,* ed. Sheila E. Jelen, Michael P. Kramer, and L. Scott Lerner (Philadelphia: University Press of Pennsylvania, 2011), 130–31.

18. See Henri Bergson, *Laughter: An Essay on the Meaning of the Comic* (New York: Macmillan, 1914), 73.

19. See "On Sholem Aleichem's Humor," 44–45.

20. For more on the Russian Bildungsroman, see Lina Steiner's *For Humanity's Sake: The Bildungsroman in Russian Culture* (Toronto: University of Toronto Press, 2011).

21. Nowersztern makes the same point in his thorough analysis of the novel, cited above.

22. Max Viner promulgates the foremost of these Marxist readings.

23. See *The Further Adventures of Menachem-Mendl: New York-Warsaw-Vienna-Yehupetz,* trans. Aliza Shevrin (Syracuse: Syracuse University Press, 2001).

24. The novel's publication history is curious and indicative of the shifting demographics of Bashevis Singer's readership. Serialized in *The Forward*, the novel has never been published as a book in the original Yiddish. However, an excellent English translation by Joseph Sherman was published in 1998, after the author's death. *Shadows on the Hudson*, trans. Joseph Sherman (New York: Plume, 1999). All citations of the novel are from this edition.

25. Secondary literature on the novel is growing but remains sparse and tends to focus on the post-Holocaust setting and the themes to which the survivor experience gives rise. See Lilian R. Furst, "'A Bizarre Double Game': Isaac Bashevis Singer, *Shadows on the Hudson* (1998)" in *Random Destinations: Escaping the Holocaust and Starting Life Anew* (New York: Palgrave Macmillan, 2005), 119–34; Peter C. Herman, "*Shadows on the Hudson*: Isaac Bashevis and the Problem of Post-Holocaust Judaism," *Studies in American Jewish Literature* 24 (2005): 158–79. Several of the essays in Hugh Denman's *Isaac Bashevis Singer: His Work and His World* (Leiden, Netherlands: Brill, 2002) either mention *Shadows* directly or bear on it indirectly or partially. See especially Joseph Sherman's contribution, "Translating '*Shotns Baym Hodson*' [*Shadows on the Hudson*]: Directly Encountering Isaac Bashevis Singer's Authorial Dualism," 49–80.

26. Menakhem-Mendl blithely ignores the needs of his wife and children but does nothing to actively betray them. The ideals of family life remain intact, if the actuality is deferred.

27. See John Guzlowski, "Isaac Singer and the Threat of America" in *Shofar: An Interdisciplinary Journal of Jewish Studies* 20.1 (2001): 21–35 for an account of changing perspectives on Jewish assimilation and acculturation in Bashevis's various novels set in the United States.

28. Eric S. Rabkin: "Infant Joys: The Pleasures of Disempowerment in Fantasy and Science Fiction," in *Nursery Realms: Children in the Worlds of Science Fiction, Fantasy, and Horror,* ed. Gary Westfahl and George Slusser (Athens: University of Georgia Press, 1999): 3–19. Quoted by Honeyman 354.

29. Of Grein: "But he still looked boyishly young: tall, slim, with a head of golden hair that covered the beginnings of a bald patch, a high forehead, a cleft chin. . . . Margolin used to say that he looked like a yeshiva boy from Scandinavia" (14).

Waiting for Anna to emerge from the motel bathroom: "How utterly childish everyone is who seems to be an adult!" (48).

Waking with Anna in hotel for the first time: "He felt like a child who wakes and does not know whether he is lying lengthwise or crosswise in his bed" (54); "A boyish irresponsibility possessed Grein" (68); "Driving slowly on with hands stiff from the cold, Grein was possessed by the joy and obstinacy of a schoolboy" (198).

When it snows during her father's party, Anna runs to the window "With childlike excitement," (17); "embraced him like a little girl" (55); "She now smiled in exactly the way she had in those days: childishly, eagerly, even a little foolishly, with that girlish admiration of another that a man can never really comprehend" (119).

Even apart from the affair between Anna and Grein, metaphors of juvenility are employed to express both the joyful abandon and the susceptibility to irrational fear that mark childhood. "Afterward they walked about with their arms twined around each other, Esther going backward and Grein pushing her forward as children at play sometimes do" (218).

"Like a schoolboy, he was filled with the dread of seeing a corpse, and with shame before Yasha Kotik" (297).

"Since he had seen Luria's corpse, . . . he had developed a schoolboy's fear of the dark" (315).

"'He hid from your father in the bathroom,' said Kotik with schoolboy mischievousness, wagging a finger" (303).

"God was beginning to show his might. All through his life, Kotik had been secretly afraid of Him and His vengeance. He had been aware of how God lowered at him from heaven and postponed, deferred, held back the day of retribution. A schoolboy explanation hovered on his tongue: God is slow to anger and full of loving-kindness" (505).

30. All references to this novel are cited from *Enemies, A Love Story* (New York: FSG, 1972). The Yiddish original, *Soynim, di geshikhte fun a libe*, appeared serially in *Forverts* in 1966.

31. For a fuller consideration of this passage and of *Enemies*, see Janet Hadda's *Passionate Women, Passive Men: Suicide in Yiddish Literature* (Albany: SUNY Press, 1988), 177–96.

32. As Joseph Sherman points out, the Yiddish original features the word "*shpin*," or spider, rather than a cockroach. "A cockroach connotes dirt; Boris hates Kotik because, like a spider, Kotik is poisonous" (79).

33. Furst draws our attention to the contrast in furnishings, p. 122.

34. This novel also thrusts us back to the literal meaning of *polit* as escapee. As Furst writes of the characters collectively, "the long narrative uncovers the pervasive disorientation these escapees suffer as a result not just of their physical relocation but also of their existential dislocation" (127).

35. Herman makes the excellent point that "Even the rabbis who discounted the importance of interior (and anterior) conviction assumed that the deed not only precedes thought, but will ultimately shape thought, that is to say, if one *acts* like a person of faith, and one will ultimately *become* a person of faith" (170).

36. Furst also points out the framing function of the novel's three gatherings at Boris Makaver's home (131).

37. Here is a partial catalogue of the phrase's occurrences in the novel:

-Jacob Anfang's impotence: "Madame, for me it is too late—both spiritually and physically" (233).
-Anna regarding the dead Luria: "'But now it's too late! Too late!'" (304).
-After Grein announces to a convalescing Leah that he is returning to her: "What difference did it make to her now? her eyes seemed to say. It's too late, too late" (381).
-He could almost hear Satan arguing with him: "'It's too late, in any event. Since you cannot repair anything, everything must remain as it is'" (419).

-Grein to Margolin: "Everything that generations of Jews built up at the risk of their lives I destroyed in a few years. You're right—it's already too late. Only now can I see how much I've ruined" (446).

-"Only here had the Master of the Universe blessed him with another union and perhaps with a son to recite Kaddish over him. But who could know whether it was not too late?" (489).

38. Sir Walter Scott's historical novels, Bakhtin maintains, imported adventuristic time from Greek romances into later European fiction. See FTC 95–96.

39. Attributing the observation to Sigmund Freud, Stephen Jay Gould writes, "The most important scientific revolutions all include, as their only common feature, the dethronement of human arrogance from one pedestal after another of previous convictions about our centrality in the cosmos." *Dinosaur in a Haystack: Reflections in Natural History* (New York: Random House, 1995), 164–65.

40. Peter Herman probes the theological implications of the novel's atomic motif, pp. 162–63.

41. Although it is beyond the purview of this discussion, Kotik's character offers a fascinating entry point for a discussion of language and speech within the novel. His silver tongued facility in several languages is at once his greatest strength and liability. See Sherman's treatment of Kotik as a speaker on p. 72 of "Translating 'Shotns baym hodson'" and my dissertation, "Power in the Tongue: The Ethics of Speech and Dialogue in Modernist Fiction." Furst also takes up the question of the characters' multilingualism as a token of their dislocation (129–30).

42. This palpable disapproval may have partaken of some ambivalence on Isaac Bashevis Singer's part about his own authorial persona as a *komedyant*. For more on this view of him, see Irving Saposnik's "A Tale of an Umbrella" in Denman's collection, especially p. 100.

43. *The Penitent* (New York: Farrar, Straus, Giroux, 1983), 44. Yiddish original: *Der bal-tshuve* (Tel Aviv: Peretz, 1974). In the Yiddish version: "*Zey bavundern kolerley rotskhim, zoynes, falshe neviyim, komedyantn*" (Y 47).

44. *The Magician of Lublin*, trans. Elaine Gottlieb and Joseph Singer (New York: Penguin, 1960). Yiddish edition: *Der kuntsnmakher fun Lublin* (Tel-Aviv: Y.L. Perets, 1979).

Chapter 3

1. "Where Do We Go From Here? This Is The Real Dope," http://www.gjenvick.com/Military/WorldWarOne/Brochures/1919WhereDoWeGoFromHereTheRealDope.html#ixzz1YhuLUwzE.

2. The language of game or sport in relation to the war was hardly unique to Meloney. As British prime minister (1916–22) Lloyd George told an interviewer, "The British soldier is a good sportsman. He enlisted in this war in a sporting spirit—in the best sense of that term. He went in to see fair play to a small nation trampled upon by a bully. He is fighting for fair play. He has fought as a good sportsman. By the thousands he has

died a goods sportsman. He has never asked anything more than a sporting chance. He has not always had that. When he couldn't get it, he didn't quit. He played the game." Interview with Roy Howard of the United Press of America (28 September 1916), quoted in *The Times* (29 September 1916), 7.

3. See Adam R. Seipp, *The Ordeal of Peace: Demobilization and the Urban Experience in Britain and Germany, 1917–1921* (Burlington: Ashgate, 2009), 4–5.

4. Frederic Logan Paxson, in his 1941 classic *The Great Demobilization and Other Essays* (Madison: University of Wisconsin Press, 1941), highlights the suddenness of the reversal wrought by demobilization: "There was no plan for the demobilization of the armed forces; and none would have been accepted by the men, anxious to be released, or by their people, anxious to have them back" (11–12).

5. See Peter Gatrell's review in *Kritika* (6.3: 557–66) of four books about World War I POWs. As Gatrell notes, "The hard-pressed Habsburg authorities understandably came under pressure to repatriate POWs without excessive delay. . . . Officials were convinced that POWs who had witnessed the Bolshevik revolution would import the new 'bacillus' to the homeland. . . . General Max Ronge, the head of the Intelligence Bureau for the Austrian General Staff, took charge of the arrangements for identifying Bolshevik sympathizers among the returning prisoners. He spoke of the need for a 'moral and sanitary quarantine'" (565). When we recall how recently the germ theory of disease had been corroborated, as well as the devastating effects of the Spanish flu of 1918, the imagery of contagion is hardly surprising.

6. Russia's withdrawal from the Great War so jeopardized Allied interests that the Allied forces mounted an expedition to protect those interests in shipping, railroads, and other critical transportation and natural resources. See Robert L. Willett, *Russian Sideshow: America's Undeclared War, 1918–1920* (Washington, DC: Brassey's, 2003).

7. Josef Haller's Army, or the Blue Legion, fought with France but often killed Jews whose professed neutrality they doubted. See Feigue Cieplinski, "Poles and Jews: The Quest for Self-Determination 1919–1934," *Binghamton Journal of History* (Fall 2002), accessed at http://www2.binghamton.edu/history/resources/journal-of-history/poles-and-jews.html. See also Mark Levene, *War, Jews and the New Europe: The Diplomacy of Lucien Wolf, 1914–1919* (Oxford: Littman Library, 2009); Carole Fink, *Defending the Rights of Others: The Great Powers, the Jews, and International Minority Protection, 1878–1938* (Cambridge: Cambridge University Press, 2006), 227; and Pavel Korzec, "Polish-Jewish Relations During World War I" in *Hostages of Modernization: Studies on Modern Antisemitism, 1870–1933/39*, Vol. 2, ed. Herbert Strauss (Berlin: Walter de Gruyter, 1993), 1034–35.

8. The Polish Legions fought for the Austro-Hungarian Empire. Little information is available in English about the demobilization of this unit, but presumably it was marked by the same haphazard quality as the Austro-Hungarian army itself. See R. F. Leslie, *The History of Poland Since 1863* (Cambridge: Cambridge University Press, 1983), 98.

9. Not only demobilized soldiers satisfy the conditions of the picaresque but also soldiers enmeshed in the gears of a bureaucratized war machine. Jaroslav Hašek's

Schwejk from the First World War and Joseph Heller's Yossarian from the Second come to mind as characters that are technically still mobilized but inert and lacking agency. Their drama has less to do with warfare per se than with the bureaucracy that has become necessary to support it.

10. Some older picaresque works drew their energy or comic force from precisely this tension, including *Simplicissimus*, *The Luck of Barry Lyndon*, and *Kim*.

11. As is well documented in a great swath of modernist fiction, from Hemingway and Fitzgerald to Remarque and Joseph Roth, and a great deal of verse as well ("Dulce et decorum est . . .").

12. For Russian Jewry especially, conscription was an animating fear that drove not only many literary plots (including the *Kitser masoes* of this book's introduction) but much real-life immigration as well. See Olga Litvak's *Conscription and the Search for Modern Russian Jewry* (Bloomington: Indiana University Press, 2006).

13. J. M. Coetzee, "Emperor of Nostalgia" (a review of the *Collected Stories of Joseph Roth*) in *New York Review of Books* 49.3 (February 28, 2002). Coetzee continues: "Some began to look to Palestine as a national home; others turned to the supranational creed of communism."

14. See Francisco J. Romero Salvadó, *Spain 1914–1918: Between War and Revolution* (London: Routledge, 2002), ix.

15. *The Good Soldier Schwejk* by Jaroslav Hašek; *The Case of Sergeant Grischa* (1927) by Arnold Zweig; and *Through the Wheat* (1923) by Thomas Alexander Boyd, as a few examples.

16. See Wolitz's "On Israel Rabon's Di gas" in *Khulyot Journal of Yiddish Research* 7 (2002). Accessed electronically at http://yiddish.haifa.ac.il/khulyot/khulyot7.html.

17. The English translation, by the author's son Joseph Singer, condenses the 346-page Yiddish novel into 267 pages in English. Such a severe abridgement will inevitably leave out some rich details of the original, but to the translator's credit, he judiciously preserves almost all essential content with respect to plot and often reaches a reasonable approximation of the author's tone.

18. This is clearly the case with Gabriel Dan, who is returning home to Vienna. Part of the mystique in which Rabon shrouds his protagonist (no name, no hometown) is the omission of any identifying information about his combat unit. Most Galician Jews who fought in the war fought on the side of the Austro-Hungarian Empire, in whose domain their natal territory fell at the outset of the war.

19. These three novels might be compared quite fruitfully to Avigdor Hameiri's Hebrew novel *Hashigaon hagadol* (*The Great Madness*), which is set in Budapest and Galicia during the Great War. However, that novel tells the story—in refreshingly vivid and compelling terms—of an urban Jewish cosmopolite's transformation into a patriotic Habsburg soldier. At its core, Hameiri's great work is a novel of mobilization rather than demobilization, a distinction that will gather force from the argument below.

20. See Phelan's *Living to Tell About It: A Rhetoric and Ethics of Character Narration* (Ithaca: Cornell University Press, 2005).

21. Jon Hughes, *Facing Modernity: Fragmentation, Culture and Identity in Joseph*

Roth's Writing in the 1920's, MHRA Texts and Dissertations Volume 67, Bithell Series of Dissertations (London: Maney/MHRA, 2006).

22. *The Ordeal of Peace*, cited above. More broadly and quite convincingly, Seipp's book places the Great War in the larger context of European urbanization. "Trends that were evident in the prewar urban landscape," he argues, "did not vanish into the maw of the war. Instead, they were temporarily halted, diverted, or mobilized into the national war effort and emerged after the war" (25).

23. In Ivan Berend's *Decades of Crisis: Central and Eastern Europe Before World War II* (Berkeley: University of California Press, 1998).

24. The most recent comprehensive treatment is Olga Litvak's *Haskalah: The Romantic Movement in Judaism* (New Brunswick: Rutgers University Press, 2012), a work of revisionist historiography that underscores the romantic over the enlightenment aspects of the movement. See also Shmuel Feiner's *The Jewish Enlightenment*, trans. Chaya Naor (Philadelphia: University of Pennsylvania Press, 2004); Feiner's *Haskalah and History: The Emergence of a Modern Jewish Historical Consciousness* (London: Littman Library, 2004); and Moshe (Murray Jay) Rosman's *How Jewish Is Jewish History?* (London: Littman Library, 2008). Many more geographically focused histories engage the essential nature of Haskalah/Haskole. See especially Jay Harris's *Nachman Krochmal: Guiding the Perplexed of the Modern Age* (New York: NYU Press, 1991); Israel Bartal's *The Jews of Eastern Europe, 1772–1881*, trans. Chaya Naor (Philadelphia: University of Pennsylvania Press, 2002; 2005); Michael Stanislawski's *Tsar Nicholas I and the Jews* (Philadelphia: Jewish Publication Society of America, 1983); and Steven Zipperstein's *The Jews of Odessa: A Cultural History, 1794–1881* (Stanford: Stanford University Press, 1986).

25. See Feiner's *Jewish Enlightenment*, where he describes the maskilic Dorshe Leshon Ever society, who "used rhetoric intended to mobilize, propagandize, and galvanize ('rise up!' 'revive!' 'build!' 'awaken!')," p. 207. See also Feiner's "The Invention of the Modern Age: A Chapter in the Rhetoric and Self-Image of the Haskalah," *Dappim: Research in Literature* 11 (1998): 9–29.

26. See Feiner's *The Jewish Enlightenment* (Philadelphia: University of Pennsylvania Press, 2004): "The early Haskalah was rooted in the Jews' feelings of inferiority and affront because of their backwardness in relation to their contemporaries in acquisition of knowledge, rational shaping of life, and expansion of their intellectual horizon. Over time, new motives were added, such as the desire to regenerate the Jews and the belief that it was possible to reshape the society and culture and heal all its ills" (370). Also, in Feiner's *Haskalah and History*: "Judged on the basis of their acculturation, openness to European society, and adoption of new lifestyles, the maskilim were not the first modern Jews in Europe. They were, however, unquestionably the first who were conscious of being modern Jews, and the first to advocate a modernist, transformational ideology" (v).

27. See Miron's *Bodedim bemo'adam: lediyokana shel harepublika ha'ivrit bitehilat hamea ha'esrim* [*When Loners Come Together: A Portrait of the Hebrew Literary Republic at the Turn of the Twentieth Century*] (Tel Aviv: Am Oved, 1987), especially 62–64.

28. For a careful consideration of the transformations in Jewish reading practices

during this period and the emergence of a reading public for literature, see Amos Bitzan's dissertation "The Problem of Pleasure: Disciplining the German-Jewish Reading Revolution, 1770–1870" at UC Berkeley, 2011.

29. Shmuel Ettinger enumerates these trends: "from Wissenschaft des Judentums, to neo-Orthodoxy in Germany, to social and intellectual radicalism and the flowering of the socialist movement among Jews in Eastern Europe, and just so to the nationalist movement which, in many respects, represents a direct continuation of the Haskalah movement." Cited in Litvak (75), who in turn cites it from Mordechai Zalkin, "Between the Humanists and Nationalists: Developments in the Study of the Jewish Enlightenment in the State of Israel" [Heb.], *Zion* 74 (2009): 177. Original: Shmuel Ettinger, "*Yehudim betsavat hahaskalah*" (1980).

30. See Feiner, *Haskalah and History*, 344–48.

31. To this point, Litvak cites Eli Lederhendler: "In Lederhendler's reading, Eastern European Jewish intellectuals were no prototypical Jewish liberals, content to live and let live and inclined to respect individual rights at the expense of collective responsibilities. Their tendency toward social authoritarianism, their fierce combativeness, their commitment to Jewish 'reconstruction,' and their idealism anticipated and informed the political style of Eastern European Jewish populism that appeared under various party standards at the turn of the twentieth century" (58). See Lederhendler's *The Road to Modern Jewish Politics: Political Tradition and Political Reconstruction in the Jewish Community of Tsarist Russia* (Oxford: Oxford University Press, 1989).

32. Berdyczewski, '*Al devar hahasidut*', 264; id., '*Olam ha'atsilut*', 8–9.

33. See Dan Miron, "Passivity and Narration: The Spell of Isaac Bashevis Singer" in *Judaism* 41.1 (1992): 6–17, from which the citation is drawn. A later version of the essay also appears in *Image of the Shtetl*, chapter 8, 335–51.

34. Upward social mobility was on the agenda, as was lateral movement from *shtetl* to city, or in some variations, to productive farm.

35. Atomic movement figures as a trope for modernity in many literary works of the first half of the twentieth century. The motif develops in parallel with the shift from Niels Bohr's model of the atom to that suggested by quantum theory.

36. In the original Yiddish (pp. 333–34), this characterization stretches over five paragraphs, but the translation in this case captures the essentials.

37. In the Yiddish, he is called *der firkantiker parshoyn* ("square character").

38. The juxtaposition of Benjamin Lerner with Rabon's and Roth's protagonists in this chapter encapsulates what Jed Esty refers to as "the rewriting of the nineteenth-century realist 'action hero' into the passive subject of naturalist and modernist fiction" (109).

39. I scruple to note that Lerner is never technically demobilized but rather deserts the Russian Imperial Army.

40. Marc Caplan points out that such an unreconstructedly maskilic character was a jarring anachronism in 1927, akin to placing an unreconstructed hippie in a novel set in 2015. Singer, who had Zola, Gorky, and Mann as his models, was revisiting the Haskalah as a failed project (personal communication March 2013).

41. Indeed Singer, a student of painting in young adulthood, did sit out the Great War in an artists' atelier. For his biography, see Anita Norich's *The Homeless Imagination in the Fiction of Israel Joshua Singer* (Bloomington: Indiana University Press, 1991). For a brief treatment of *Steel and Iron* specifically, see pp. 21–22.

42. Paula E. Hyman, "Gender, Antisemitism, and Jewish Identity in the Fin de Siecle" in *Mediating Modernity: Challenges and Trends in the Jewish Encounter with the Modern World*, ed. Lauren B. Strauss and Michael Brenner (Detroit: Wayne State University Press, 2008).

43. The text describes her being pinned down for the exam—mandated as retribution for her refusing the advances of the German estate manager appointed after Lvovich's departure—like a butterfly, the examiners ogling her genitalia, and then her fainting. The chapter ends, no further mention is made of her character, and the narrative picks up with Benjamin's escape from prison. The omission of what happens after she faints may or may not be a bit of decorous Victorianism eliding rape.

44. Miss Malgosha's character is used to lampoon the way that extreme Jewish self-hatred bends into anti-Semitism. When Gnendl reveals that she has left home to evade a repugnant suitor, Miss Malgosha exclaims, "'I knew you were of noble blood! . . . You always were so idealistic . . . so—un-Jewish"—this despite the speaker's own Hasidic origins.

45. Here is an instance of Anita Norich's argument, discussed in the introduction, that Yiddish modernism is more inflected than its Western European counterpart by the vicissitudes of history.

46. A more contemporary translation would acknowledge that the plain sense has less to do with manhood per se than with personhood or even leadership, but this more archaic and literal translation complements the discussion of Benjamin Lerner's maskilic masculinity.

47. When I.J. Singer turned his gaze on Łodz, publishing his masterful multigenerational saga *Di brider ashkenazi* (*The Brothers Ashkenazi*, 1936), it would be to fulfill some of the ambitions of plenitude announced in his first, more limited novel. His tale of twin brothers, divergent from birth, would chronicle how the city became the industrial behemoth so inhospitable to the returning soldiers limned by Roth and Rabon. It was novel of progress turned awry by history, but a nineteenth-century style novel of progress nonetheless.

Chapter 4

1. It occurs eight times in his masterful study *Unseasonable Youth*.

2. Although at the end of *Unseasonable Youth*, Esty cautions against applying the judgment of "belatedness" even to non-European fictions written after 1945. "When we use a genre like the bildungsroman to track formal variation across time and space . . . we do not need to present the later, so-called peripheral texts as belated echoes of an original European or Western problematic" (208).

3. J.M. Coetzee, "Emperor of Nostalgia" (a review of the *Collected Stories of Joseph Roth*) in *New York Review of Books*, February 28, 2002.

4. Franz Kafka, *Amerika: The Man Who Disappeared*, trans. Michael Hofman (New York: Schocken, 1996).

5. See Mark M. Anderson on the stranded object in Kafka in *Kafka's Clothes: Ornament and Aestheticism in the Habsburg Fin de Siècle* (New York: Oxford University Press, 1992). The novel is about mobilization, transfer, and *Verkehr* ("traffic")—commercial, sexual, spatial, material.

6. This section heading owes a debt to Cindy Gabrielle's "The Poetics of Dissolution: The Representation of Maori Culture in Janet Frame's Fiction," *Journal of Postcolonial Writing* 46.2 (2010): 209–20. In the abstract to her article, Gabrielle notes, "Self dissolution shall emerge in this reading as the key to a utopian state consisting of the total permeability between the self and the remainder of the world." Roth's Gabriel Dan toys with a similar idea.

7. Bettina Matthias clearly thinks it is the latter: "What seems like a saving gesture turns out to be a measure to ensure that these people will stay on their upper floor until the day they die" (130). See her *The Hotel as Setting in Early 20th-Century German and Austrian Literature* (Rochester, NY: Camden House, 2006).

8. See Chone Shmeruk, "Yisroel Rabon and His Book *Di gas* ("The Street")," in *Di gas* by Yisroel Rabon (Jerusalem, 1986), xxxviii (v-l). A slightly altered essay by Shmeruk was also published as "Yisroel Rabon and His Novel *Di gas*" in *Polin* 6 (1991): 231–52. Shmeruk catalogs some of the many parallels with Roth's *Hotel Savoy* but writes, "It is doubtful if Rabon knew of Roth's book before he wrote *Di gas*" (fn. 42 on xxix). However, the uncanny commonalities extend throughout the book, including such obvious matters of place and character as the following: Circus Vangoli and the Varietes; Doli the clown and Santschin the clown; Jason the wrestler and Zwonimir as beefy hedonists to whom each narrator becomes, at least fleetingly, a sidekick; an atmosphere of roiling labor militancy ("To Director Zavadsky's" in Roth is echoed by "To Neuner's, to Neuner's!" in *Hotel Savoy*); an indeterminate, anticlimactic ending with the protagonist moving on to some new place with a chance or casual acquaintance.

9. For instance, consider the keen observing eye at work in a passage like the following description of Uncle Phoebus Bohlaug's son-in-law as "well set up, good-humored, reddish blond man with a bull neck, who spooned away bravely at his soup, left a clean plate and never opened his mouth while the conversation rolled over him" (22).

10. All citations of *Hotel Savoy* are from John Hoare's translation (New York: Overlook Press, 2003).

11. See Richard Sennett, *The Fall of Public Man* (New York: W.W. Norton, 1974), 39.

12. The novella calls to mind a set of images for modernity partaking of both Marshall Berman's economic analysis (*All That Is Solid Melts into Air*) and Zygmunt Bauman's sociological one (*Liquid Modernity*).

13. See Marc Augé's *Non-Places: Introduction to an Anthropology of Supermodernity* (New York: Verso, 1995).

14. The bibliography on Rabon is painfully short, given his talents. Brukhe Lang (Beatrice Lang Caplan), "Yisroel Rabon: Shtrikhn tsu a literarisher biografye" (M.A. thesis, Columbia University, 1996) includes an annotated bibliography of Rabon's works

and of secondary sources, and an appendix of Rabon's short stories, poetry, and essays collected from periodicals; Chone Shmeruk, "Yisroel Rabon and His Book *Di gas* ("The Street")," in *Di gas* by Yisroel Rabon (Jerusalem: Sifrut Yidish, 1986), v–l; the article also appears in Hebrew in the same volume; Itzhak Yanasowicz (Yitskhok Yanasovitsh), *Łodzsher yorn: Mentshn, svives, gesheenishn* (Tel Aviv: Perets Farlag, 1987). See also Ephraim Sicher, "On Both Sides of the Front: Isaac Babel and Israel Rabon in the Polish-Soviet War" in *Shvut* 3 (1996): 147–58. And finally Seth Wolitz's article "On Israel Rabon's *Di gas*," *Khulyot Journal of Yiddish Research* 7 (2002). Accessed electronically at http://yiddish.haifa.ac.il/khulyot/khulyot7.html.

15. Not only does Chone Shmeruk read the novel in this way, as we shall chronicle amply below, but Seth Wolitz gestures at a similarly Hobbesian view of the text. He upends the declaration of a kindly Łodz matron who helps the narrator, who dismisses his gratitude by saying, "We do not live among wolves." Wolitz adds, darkly, "Perhaps the novel's aim is precisely to show that we do indeed live among wolves" (222, my trans.).

16. Shmeruk, as cited above.

17. Shmeruk writes, in his essay introducing *Di gas*, "Despite all the differences in nature and style between the digressive stories appearing in *Di gas*, most have one goal: again and again they demonstrate alienation in various forms and possibilities, as a parallel to the basic situation which concerns the writer in this novel" (xxxii).

18. Details of Rabon's biography are culled from Leonard Wolf's afterword in his English translation of the novella, *The Street: A Novel* (New York: Shocken, 1985) as well as the entry for Rabon in YIVO's digitized encyclopedia of Eastern European Jewish life, http://www.yivoencyclopedia.org/article.aspx/Rabon_Yisroel.

19. From Shmeruk's introduction: "The temporal boundaries of the narrative present in this novel are from the ninth week of his stay in Łodz, when his money runs out, until he leaves for the city of Katowice. The period under discussion lasted probably four to five months, almost certainly from September to January. According to certain indications in the story, we can place these months at the end of 1922 or 1923 and the beginning of 1923 or 1924" (xxiv–xxv). We can date the narrated events given Fabianik's age of nine, with corroboration from the Jew from Komarno, who counts eight years between his escape at the beginning of World War I and the telling of his story.

20. The type is by no means restricted to interwar or Yiddish literature. See Rachel Harris's discussion of Ya'akov Shabtai's novel *Past Continuous* (1977) in her "Decay and Death: Urban Topoi in Literary Depictions of Tel Aviv," *Israel Studies* 14.3 (2009): 75–93 (see especially pp. 88–89).

21. Once again, Shmeruk does not seem to acknowledge their textual function as storytellers, seeing them instead as reinforcing the fact of the protagonist's alienation: "If we look closely at many of the characters who populate *Di gas*, we find that the only justification for their appearance in the novel is again and again to present situations of alienation in different ways" (xxxiii).

22. Chiming with Shmeruk's reading of him, Y.Y. Trunk called Rabon "the most asocial writer in Polish Yiddish literature," a writer who does not believe in any form of community. "Community is [for him merely] 'bringing together people—animals under

one dark fate'" (98, quoted in *Leksikon fun der nayer yidisher literatur*, Vol. 8 (New York: Alveltlekher yidisher kultur-kongres, 1981), 283.

23. Chone Shmeruk, "Yisroel Rabon and His Novel *Di gas*" in *Polin* 6 (1991).

24. See Raymond Williams, *The Country and the City* (New York: Oxford University Press, 1975).

25. See Moretti, *Signs Taken for Wonders: On the Sociology of Literary Forms* (New York: Verso, 2005), 117.

26. See Hana Wirth-Nesher, *City Codes: Reading the Modern Urban Novel* (New York: Cambridge University Press, 1996), 17. Wirth-Nesher elegantly summarizes the existing literature theorizing the city and the urban chronotope (pp. 18–21).

27. Whereas Spengler rued the new anonymity, Georg Simmel saw in the metropolis potential for the enhancement of individual freedom and intensification of intellectual life. Wirth-Nesher points out that this probably owes to his outsider perspective as a Jew in a German city.

28. See Wolitz 221, where he recalls the cozy associations of the phrase "*af der yidisher gas*" ("on the Jewish street") for *shtetl* Jewry and thus points up Rabon's irony in deploying the "di gas" to capture the harsher urban reality.

29. See Marc Caplan's article on Kasrilevke regarding the question of Jewish urban space: "Neither Here nor There: The Critique of Ideological Progress in Sholem Aleichem's Kasrilevke Stories" in *Modern Jewish Literatures: Intersections and Boundaries*, ed. Sheila E. Jelen, Michael P. Kramer, and L. Scott Lerner (Philadelphia: University Press of Pennsylvania, 2011). See also Murray Baumgarten's *City Scriptures: Modern Jewish Writing* (Cambridge: Harvard University Press, 1982), which investigates the mythos entwining the passage from *shtetl* to city with the passage from traditional religion to freethinking.

30. See Chana Kronfeld on peripheral modernisms: *On the Margins of Modernism: Decentering Literary Dynamics* (Berkeley: University of California Press, 1996). See Deleuze and Guattari on major and minor literary traditions in *Kafka: Toward a Minor Literature* (Minneapolis: University of Minnesota Press, 1986). Rabon's Yiddish novella—or any Yiddish literature—would not technically satisfy Deleuze and Guattari's definition of a "minor literature," which they scruple to say "doesn't come from a minor language; it is rather that which a minority constructs within a major language" (16). Nevertheless, much of their characterization of the "minor literature" may be applied constructively to Yiddish texts.

31. Once again, Shmeruk reads the scene differently, of a piece with the alienation theme: "His fantastic adventures, his many identity changes and wanderings are only expressions of his inability to belong to and become part of society. This is also true of his friends in the circus, for even though they are together, they are unable to form one consolidated group. This manifests itself in the description of the separate groups in the circus wagon car as its leaves Łodz, which demonstrates the remoteness that exists between these people who wander together" (xxxii).

32. See Peter N. Dunn, *Spanish Picaresque Fiction: A New Literary History* (Ithaca: Cornell University Press, 1993).

33. Shmeruk, in keeping with his darker reading, interprets the same episode in a different light and hears the old men's speech not as *daytshmerish* but as actual German: "Another revelation of alienation is described at the end of the third chapter, in a meeting between two asthma sufferers, in the early morning after a sleepless night. They discuss their suffering and their inability to live with their sickness. They are also without hope, though this time the reason is a chronic disease. In order to add a dimension of strangeness to these characters, their discussion is in German."

34. Of the narrator's childhood memory of begging with his mother, Shmeruk notes: "For the narrator this was his first traumatic meeting with the big city, a meeting that, already in his childhood, determined for him its alienating character" (xxxi). Interestingly, Rabon first published the begging episode independently of the rest of the book with an omniscient narrator telling the story of a boy named Leybl (xxxi).

35. For an account of "hard" reality, see Philip Fisher, *Hard Facts: Setting and Form in the American Novel* (New York: Oxford University Press, 1986).

36. The essay is cited from its publication in *The Blackwell City Reader, Second Edition*, ed. Gary Bridge and Sophie Watson (Malden: Blackwell, 2010), 103–10.

37. This history is drawn from Delphine Bechtel's article "Urbanization, Capitalism, and Cosmopolitanism: Four Novels and a Film on Jews in the Polish City of Łódz," *Prooftexts* 26 (2006): 79–106, and Leonard Wolf's afterword to his translation of Rabon's novella, and the entry on Łodz in the YIVO Encyclopedia of Jews in Eastern Europe (www.yivoencyclopedia.org).

38. See Winston Chu, *The German Minority in Interwar Poland* (Cambridge: Cambridge University Press, 2013), who writes, "To contemporary observers, Łódz captured the fears of an onrushing capitalist modernity, including increasing individualism and the loss of one's cultural and national roots" (117). I am grateful to my colleague Astrid Eckert for calling my attention to Chu's work.

39. Shmeruk and Bechtel cite different sources for their population figures, but the two sources agree. Shmeruk cites *Pinkas Hakehillot, Encyclopaedia of Jewish Communities, Poland*, Vol. I, *The Communities of Lodz and its Regions* (Hebrew) (Jerusalem, 1976), 17. The reference appears in Shmeruk's fn. 53 on p. xxxvii. Bechtel cites a Polish source: Wiesław Puś, *Żydzi w Łodzi w latach zaborow 1793–1914* (Łódź: Wydawnictwo Uniwersytetu łódzkiego, 2001), 26–27. See also Małgorzata Laurentowicz-Granas and Joanna Manžett-Kubiak, *Pałace 'ziemi obiecm canej'* (Łodt: Zora, 1997), 7–8; on Jewish architects, see also Stanisław Łukawski, *Łodzka Secessia* (Łodt: Zora, 1997) and Jerzy Malenczyk, *A Guide of Jewish Łodz* (Warsaw: Our Roots, 1994).

40. See "The Work of Art in the Age of Mechanical Reproduction," in *Illuminations: Essays and Reflections* (New York: Shocken, 1969), 217–51.

41. This passage, with its emphasis on the Hebraic characters in which Yiddish is written, illustrates Wolitz's point that the novella is crafted in part as a warning about the dangers of linguistic assimilation (229). Wolitz and Shmeruk both pay careful attention to the language question as it is dealt with in Rabon's fiction, and both single out the frustrated, underappreciated poet Vogelnest as Rabon's cautionary study in the pitfalls of linguistic assimilation. Shmeruk writes, "Rabon gives powerful expression to his sta-

tus and problem as a Polish writer of Jewish origin when he brings this character to the empty circus in the middle of the night in order to read his poetry" (xlii). As with Henry Roth's *Call It Sleep*, this book belongs to a class of fictions written in one language but understood to represent conversations that take place in another. Shmeruk notes this phenomenon and, predictably, fits it into the theme of alienation that he considers ubiquitous in the novella:

> The linguistic situation that is understood from Rabon's book sharpens the nature of its characters in a very concrete way, including that of the narrator himself who, despite his "writing" in Yiddish, belongs to that thin layer of Jews in Poland who adopted the Polish language of the environment for themselves. It is difficult to free oneself from the feeling that with all the advantages this adaptation could bring, it is understood from *Di gas* that the linguistic problem as an existential problem becomes an additional and difficult part of the basic situation of alienation. (Shmeruk xlii)

42. It will come as no surprise by now that Shmeruk sees in the beggars' house more evidence for his emphasis on alienation: "And the entire gallery of strange characters who populate the Łodz shelter for beggars (Chapter 27)—are they not all, each in his own way, another living example of the basic situation of alienation, which at times acquires a grotesque nature, and with which the reader with growing amazement becomes acquainted in his reading of Rabon's novel?" (xxxiv).

43. Shmeruk notes that Rabon's poetry and his earlier memoir *Balut* are both saturated with grotesque elements. In her introduction to *Satan in Goray*, Ruth Wisse argues that his extreme demonological and sexual imagery furnishes Isaac Bashevis Singer with a vivid vocabulary for considering moral problems. Rabon's grotesquerie might serve an analogous function, or it might have done so in his earliest fiction. Perhaps Rabon's work, like Isaac Bashevis Singer's, would have modulated over the course of a long career from grotesque, outrageous imagery to a more muted realism only punctuated by brief incursions of the grotesque. Since his career was cut short, we are regrettably unable to know what further inflection a "late" Rabon might have undergone.

44. "The novel ends in this enigmatic way, the hero descending again in a protective hole, just as he had hid himself in a cellar behind the scene of a circus or in the belly of a dead horse on the front. More than requiring a national or cultural identity, he is in need of a primeval return to the motherly womb, to a safe and protective haven that will salvage him from a hostile world" (Bechtel 99).

45. Esty sees the turn from the marriage plot as a function of "broken *Bildung*": "What is most radical about Wells's broken *Bildung* is perhaps this deromanticization and decentering of the marriage plot, something otherwise associated with the queer modernisms (and narrative innovations) of Wilde, Woolf, Forster, and Stein" (Esty 120).

46. See *Story and Situation: Narrative Seduction and the Power of Fiction* (Minneapolis: University of Minnesota Press, 1984).

Chapter 5

1. This title was both too resonant and too fitting not to borrow from Ruth Wisse's survey course "The Yiddish Novel Under Tsars and Stripes."

2. Once again, see Jed Esty's study *Unseasonable Youth* for an account of the warping of the *Bildungsroman* and its temporality in colonial contact zones.

3. A brief survey of studies of the picaresque indicates this tendency: *The Rogue's Progress*, Alexander Parker's *Literature and the Delinquent*, etc.

4. Criminality is forcefully present in some Yiddish fiction, notably in the work of I.M. Weissenberg, Sholem Asch, Joseph Opatoshu, and Oyzer Warshavsky. However, in Warshavsky's novel *Di shmuglars* (*The Smugglers*), for example, the shtetl-dwellers who smuggle to survive are portrayed as underdogs and victims, far more subject to German power than as wielding power themselves.

5. See *Encyclopedia of Modern Jewish Culture*, Vol. 2, edited by Glenda Abramson, 338. Also see Efraim Sicher, *Jews in Russian Literature After the October Revolution: Writers and Artists between Hope and Apostasy* (Cambridge: Cambridge University Press, 1995), 204. In his biography of Ehrenburg, cited below, Joshua Rubenstein notes that *Laz Roitshvantz* was Ehrenburg's first novel to be refused for publication outright (100).

6. See Joshua Rubenstein, *Tangled Loyalties: The Life and Times of Ilya Ehrenburg*, 97.

7. Ehrenburg's original *Burnaya zhizn lazika roitshvantsa* was rendered twice into English. All citations here are from Alec Brown's translation, *The Stormy Life of Laz Roitshvantz* (London: Elek Books, 1965).

8. Published in Berlin in 1921 (and translated into English, French, Yiddish, Czech, Spanish by 1930), *Julio Jurenito* was an earlier picaresque novel that touched, among the many subjects that received ironic treatment, on the likely fate of European Jewry. The characters are various international stereotypes, and the menacingly exact German is the eerily prescient portrait of a proto-Nazi. A Russian Jewish character named "Ilya Ehrenburg" represents the author's ethnicity, but the book is not saturated with the Jewish texts and folkloric material that permeate *Laz Roitshvantz*.

9. Perhaps the extent of this long suffering even suggests an identification with the myth of the Eternal Jew, the figure who mocked Jesus and was thus condemned to wander the earth without respite. However, it would be too pat to assume a complete identification on Laz's part. His nomadic distress is inflected by his Jewishness but not caused by it. For a brief treatment of the archetype of the Eternal Jew, see Erik Butler's *Metamorphoses of the Vampire in Literature and Film: Cultural Transformations in Europe, 1732–1933* (Rochester: Camden, 2010), 142–43.

10. Excerpted here from Benjamin Pinkus, *The Soviet Government and the Jews, 1948–1967: A Documented Study* (New York: Cambridge University Press, 1984), 44.

11. See Warshawsky's *Smugglers: A Novel in Three Parts*, trans. Golda Werman (New York: Gefen, 2008). A similar spirit animates Joseph Opatoshu's criminal novel *Untervelt*.

12. This is bracingly evident in Peretz's short story collection *Khsidish* (Vilna [Vilnius]: B. Kletskin, 1915). See Marc Caplan's "The Fragmentation of Narrative Perspective in Y.L. Peretz's *Bilder fun a Provints-Rayze*," *Jewish Social Studies: History, Culture, Society* n.s. 14.1 (2007): 63–88.

13. An-sky's most famous literary production was the play *The Dybbuk*, but his ethnographic expedition has fired the scholarly imagination as notably as his *belles lettres*. Here is a partial bibliography of primary and secondary texts. S. An-ski, *The Dybbuk and the Yiddish Imagination: A Haunted Reader*, ed. and trans. Joachim Neugroschel (Syracuse: Syracuse University Press, 2000); S. An-ski, *The Dybbuk and Other Writings*, ed. David G. Roskies, trans. Golda Werman (New Haven: Yale University Press, 2002); S. An-ski, *The Enemy at His Pleasure: A Journey through the Jewish Pale of Settlement during World War I*, ed. and trans. Joachim Neugroschel (New York: Henry Holt, 2003); Rivkah Gonen, ed., *Back to the Shtetl: An-sky and the Jewish Ethnographic Expedition, 1912–1914* (Jerusalem: Israel Museum, 1994), in Hebrew and English; David G. Roskies, "S. Ansky and the Paradigm of Return," in *The Uses of Tradition: Jewish Continuity in the Modern Era*, ed. Jack Wertheimer (New York and Cambridge: Harvard University Press, 1992), 243–60; Gabriella Safran and Steven Zipperstein, eds., *The Worlds of S. An-sky: A Russian Jewish Intellectual at the Turn of the Century* (Palo Alto: Stanford University Press, 2005). Most recently, see Gabriella Safran's biography *Wandering Soul: The Dybbuk's Creator* (Cambridge: Harvard University Press, 2011) and Nathaniel Deutsch's study *The Jewish Dark Continent: Life and Death in the Russian Pale of Settlement* (Cambridge: Harvard University Press, 2011).

14. See (and hear) the explanation of the cholera wedding here: http://www.museu moffamilyhistory.com/ce/kirshenblatt/kirshenblatt-black-wedding-wav.htm.

15. See Michael Stern, "Tevye's Art of Quotation" in *Prooftexts* 6.1, Special Issue on Sholem Aleichem: The Critical Tradition (1986): 79–96.

16. An important difference, though, is that while Tevye's stories are embedded in the domestic developmental project of raising and marrying off children, Laz's stories *are* the constitutive events. Whereas Tevye's quotations and perorations could be stripped away and there would still be a story there (albeit an impoverished one), in Laz's case, the collection of anecdotes *is* the novel.

17. Bakhtin, FTC 159.

18. Gary Saul Morson and Caryl Emerson, *Mikhail Bakhtin: Creation of a Prosaics* (Stanford: Stanford University Press, 1990).

19. Ironically, when impersonating an Östjüdisch wonder-rabbi to the rapidly assimilating Jews of Frankfurt, Laz does not see fit to embellish his speech with any sustained Jewish narratives, although there are small nuggets and halachic factoids sprinkled throughout and marshaled, always, to Laz's own material and usually gastronomic benefit. He cites the rabbinic idea of there being 613 limbs and organs "little thing-ums" (158) and speciously comforts mourners with his wholly invented knowledge of a Jewess in Mainz "whose confinement was badly held up merely because the Almighty had not got a free soul to hand" (160). He passes off dirt from a local park as his own precious trove of Holy Land earth. He liberally hands out a series of manufactured lenien-

cies regarding mourning practices, kashrut and Sabbath observance and the requirement to fast on Yom Kippur. Some are quite creative: he advises a restaurateur that since he can't fry the cutlets in butter, it would be better to serve pork instead. By serving "the other white meat," there's not a chance of boiling a kid in its mother's milk!

20. In *The Novelness of Bakhtin: Perspectives and Possibilities*, ed. Jørgen Bruhn and Jan Lundquist (Gylling, Denmark: Museum Tusculanum Press, 2001).

21. "True to Ehrenburg's conception of the Jew who is an alien everywhere, Roitshvanets negates the Zionist claim to 'normalize' the status of the Jews by returning them to their ancestral homeland" (Sicher 202).

22. Speculation as to Ehrenburg's "supposed treachery" relies mostly on the fact that he outlived Stalin and thus survived numerous purges. This longevity suggests a certain level of cooperation with the regime. Rubenstein's biography is sympathetic and seeks to clear Ehrenburg's name. One of the few specific accusations against Ehrenburg, available to the English-language reader at least, is lodged by Nathalie Babel, in the afterword to Peter Constantine's translation of her father's complete works. Ehrenburg lied to Evgenia Borisovna (Nathalie's mother) about the date of Babel's death and asked her to sign a document falsely attesting to their divorce, an event which had never occurred. Rubenstein addresses these accusations, explaining that the document probably would have secured widow's benefits for Babel's second wife, Antonina Pirozhkova, noting also that Ehrenburg led the charge for Babel's rehabilitation under the thaw and authored the introduction to a new volume of Babel's works released with official sanction at that time.

23. As Mikhail Krutikov reminds me, the Soviet system did not become monoglossic all at once: "At that early stage, the Soviet system was not stable and monoglossic yet—it is quite fluid, and Lazik's speech can be seen as a response to its solidification" (personal communication, June 2014). As the New Economic Program winds down, the society grows "increasingly intolerant to all kinds of marginality," including the alterity that Laz represents.

24. It will be useful to bear this in mind as the discussion below turns to Babel and *Verkehr*.

25. See Richard Bradford, *Stylistics* (New York: Routledge, 1997).

26. See Sicher 200 and Krutikov's *Yiddish Fiction and the Crisis of Modernity: 1905–1914*, 205–206 for treatments of this motif, as well as M.Y. Berdichevsky's promulgation of it through his story *"Dos fayfele" Musterverk* Vol. 87, 113.

27. An insightful study of both authors' work, set in the context of Soviet-born writers who have departed Russia and found other literary and linguistic homes, is available in Adrian Wanner's *Out of Russia: Fictions of a New Translingual Diaspora* (Evanston: Northwestern University Press, 2011). Another study of German literature, which devotes a chapter to "The Picaresque as a Means to Reckon with the GDR," is Jill Twark's *Humor, Satire, and Identity: Eastern German Literature in the 1990s* (Berlin: Walter de Gruyter, 2007).

28. See "The Urban Literary Café and the Geography of Hebrew and Yiddish Modernism in Europe" in *Forms of Sociality*, 433–58.

29. Frozen confections come in two varieties: (1) quiescent (frozen in a restful, un-stirred state, as are popsicles and ices) and (2) agitated before freezing, like ice cream, in a process known, poetically enough for our peripatetic *polit*, as *overrunning* (!).

30. Although he might have intended to do so. One of the notorious facts of Babel's arrest and subsequent execution is that he was denied access to any of his manuscripts-in-progress. They were confiscated by the NKVD and have never surfaced. His common-law second wife, Antonina Pirozhkova, recalls in her memoir, "He told me, 'I'm writing a novella in which the main character is a former Odessa gangster like Benia Krik. His name is Kolya Topuz and so far, at least, that's also the name of the novella. I want to show how this sort of man adapts to Soviet reality. Kolya Topuz works on a collective farm during collectivization, and then he goes to work in a Donbass coal mine. But since he has the mentality of a gangster, he's constantly breaking out of the limits of normal life, which leads to numerous funny situations.' Babel spent a great deal of time writing, and he finished many works. Only his arrest prevented his new works from coming out" (107). See A.N. Pirozhkova, *At His Side: The Last Years of Isaac Babel* (South Royalton: Steerforth Press, 1998).

31. As articulated by Mark M. Anderson in *Kafka's Clothes: Ornament and Aestheticism in the Habsburg Fin de Siècle* (New York: Oxford University Press, 1992).

32. For portraits of Odessa, see Steven J. Zipperstein's *The Jews of Odessa: A Cultural History, 1794–1881* (Stanford: Stanford University Press, 1986) and Jarrod Tanny's *City of Rogues and Schnorrers: Russia's Jews and the Myth of Old Odessa* (Bloomington: Indiana University Press, 2011).

33. See Pinsker 440–44 for a thorough account of their participation in—and retreat from—the city's café culture. He mentions such luminaries as Bialik, Ahad-Ha'am, Simon Dubnov, and S.Y. Abramovitsh.

34. Robert Alter notes Babel's "hyper-lucid and somewhat unconventional perception" (144) in "Babel, Flaubert, and the Rapture of Perception" in *The Enigma of Isaac Babel: Biography, History, Context*, ed. Gregory Freidin (Stanford: Stanford University Press, 2009).

35. See Zsuzsa Hetenyi, *In a Maelstrom: The History of Russian-Jewish Prose (1860–1940)*, trans. János Boris (Budapest, Hungary: Central European University Press, 2008).

36. Hetenyi criticizes both the Constantine translation, edited by Nathalie Babel, and the McDuff translations for including among the Odessa Stories more than the four short stories Babel had originally united under that banner. See her fn. 35 on p. 184 of *In a Maelstrom*. She notes the switch from first-person to third-person narration in "Froim Grach," speculating that the narrator's retreat is no accident. For more specific information about the sequence of publication, see Isaak Babel', *Sochineniia* (Moscow: Khudozhestvennaia literatura, 1990), Vol. I, 443–44.

37. "Froim Grach," for example, was written in 1933 but published only after Babel's posthumous rehabilitation.

38. In "The Fragmentation of Narrative Perspective in Y.L. Peretz's *Bilder fun a Provints-Rayze*," *Jewish Social Studies: History, Culture, Society* 14.1 (2007): 63–88.

39. Nor did he confine himself to the visual sense, writing in "Berestechko": "Beres-

techko stinks inviolably to this day. The smell of rotten herring emanates from everyone. The shtetl reeks in expectation of a new era" (272).

40. *The Composite Novel: The Short Story Cycle in Transition* by Maggie Dunn and Ann Morris (New York: Twayne, 1995).

41. See Mary M. Stolberg, *Fighting Organized Crime: Politics, Justice, and the Legacy of Thomas E. Dewey* (Boston: Northeastern University Press, 1995), 165, for a discussion of how mobsters in New York in the 1920s and 1930s controlled the trucking industry and thus in turn other industries, such as the garment industry. Truckers were susceptible to mafia coercion and control because they operated independently and couldn't organize as easily as factory or shop workers. Although the milieu is different, many of the same conditions seem to obtain.

42. See Gabriella Safran, "Isaak Babel's El'ia Isaakovich as a New Jewish Type," *Slavic Review: American Quarterly of Russian, Eurasian and East European Studies* 61.2 (2002): 253-72. "Other scholars have already begun the project of setting Babel's stories within the tradition of Russian narratives about prostitution. Specifically, Aleksandr Zholkovskii and Mikhail Iampol'skii analyze Babel's fascination with exchange—of money, the body, or words—and his resulting obsession with prostitutes" (259). A.K. Zholkovskii and M.B. Iampol'skii, Babel/Babel (Moscow, 1994), 12-13, 317-68.

43. ". . . a red automobile with a music box for a horn playing the first march from the opera *I Pagliacci* on Seredinskaya Square. In broad daylight the car raced over to the little house in which Aunt Pesya lived. Its wheels thundered, it spat smoke, gleamed brassily, reeked of gasoline, and honked arias on its horn" (151). Rubin cites the Pagliacci horn as an instance of *ostranenie* (defamiliarization or estrangement). "Babel relies upon *ostranenie* to make topical points about the status of Jews, and the Jewish writer, in Russia. . . . Babel uses the textual instability he models upon the commotion of Odessa to recreate in the reader a sense of anxiety and paradox that mirrors the position of the Jews in Imperial Russia" (22).

44. It is interesting to note, however, especially in light of Laz Roitshvantz's desacralized Palestine, that Jerusalem figures as just one more international exporter of luxury goods. Mark how different these oranges are from the totemic Holy Land date that helps to launch Benjamin III on his quest.

45. It was widely practiced in Europe at that time for mostly observant Jews to drink wine of non-Jewish origin; the scruple for kosher wine was maintained by relatively few.

46. This prohibition is *yayin nesekh*, Shulchan Aruch Yoreh Deah 123:1. However, there is a secondary prohibition of *yeynam stam* or *yeynam mishum bnotam*. The rabbis were fully aware of the sensual implications of food.

47. This phrasing recalls other peculiarly emotional food descriptions that verge on synesthesia, delivered in passing, such as "his meatball, which smelled of happy childhood" (162).

48. Cited from Rubin 34, where she in turn quotes Shklovskii's original text, *Isaac Babel* 12-14.

49. A paradigmatic case is Henry Roth's *Call It Sleep*. For a thorough treatment of the problematics of representing Yiddish in another language (in Roth's case, English), see

Hannah Wirth-Nesher's *Call It English: The Languages of Jewish American Literature* (Princeton: Princeton University Press, 2006).

50. In his essay "Odessa," describing the European, sunny, life-affirming ethos of his hometown, Babel recurs to the French: "So I am biased, I admit it. Maybe I'm even extremely biased, but *parole d'honneur*, there is something to this place! And this something can be sensed by a person with mettle who agrees that life is sad, monotonous—this is all very true—but still, *quand meme et malgre tout*, it is exceedingly, exceedingly interesting" (77).

51. Here I refer to the fact that Babel wrote in Russian; however, as Mikhail Krutikov reminds me, the Odessan dialect itself mixes Russian, Ukrainian and Yiddish without treating Russian as *the* privileged language (personal communication June 2014).

52. This is not entirely dissimilar to Tevye's grudging acceptance of the check with which son-in-law Pedohtsur wishes to ship him off to the Land of Israel.

53. A writer of screenplays, Babel might also be grouped among other authors of the 1920s who kept the cinema always in mind, most famously F. Scott Fitzgerald. This constant awareness resulted in a profusion of physical details about clothing and scenery, as well as short scenes that could be transposed to the cinematic vocabulary of takes.

54. Consider in this light the emphasis on Basya Grach's trousseau, p. 163.

55. Zudechkis is by no means the only dilatory narrator, just the one who manifests the most self-awareness about the practice of digression. The unidentified narrator of "The King" pauses his account of Dvoira Krik's wedding long enough to relate the contrastive tale of Benya's marriage to Zilya Eichbaum: "You should know the story of Sender Eichbaum, because it's a story definitely worth knowing.... And now, having told the story of Sender Eichbaum, we can return to the marriage of Dvoira Krik, the King's sister" (135, 136).

56. See his *Loiterature* (Lincoln: University of Nebraska Press, 1999).

57. That holds, of course, as long as any given specimen of Jewish manhood had better luck than Babel's and wasn't executed by the state.

Epilogue

1. Sidra deKoven Ezrahi articulates the difference in *Booking Passage: Exile and Homecoming in the Modern Jewish Imagination* (Los Angeles: University of California Press, 2000), 105, 116.

2. Yiddish poetry is a different story, of course; poems fit inside a suitcase better than novels.

3. See the final chapter of Robert Alter's *The Rogue's Progress*, as well as "Saul Bellow's *The Adventures of Augie March* and Its Picaresque Antecedents" by Philip O. Gericke, *Pacific Coast Philology* 25.1/2 (1990): 77–83 and "From *Lazarillo* to *Augie March*: A Study into Some Picaresque Attitudes" by Anna Katona, *Angol Filológiai Tanulmányok / Hungarian Studies in English* 4 (1969): 87–103.

4. *Augie March* has never been made into a film and probably won't be. It has been said that this novel could have been two hundred pages shorter or longer with no dis-

cernible effect on its shape or rhythm. As an indication of its bloat, consider how similar is the sentiment expressed some sixty pages hence: "And since I never have had any place of rest, it should follow that I have trouble being still, and furthermore my hope is based upon getting to be still so that the axial lines can be found. When striving stops, the truth comes as a gift—bounty, harmony, love, and so forth" (514).

5. Eventually, Bellow will work out an internal balance between compression and dilation, of which *Herzog* is the chief exemplar. The letters and embedded recollections render that novel discursively picaresque without the need for much in the way of picaresque event.

6. Grossman recounts this story in an interview with Jonathan Shainin, *Paris Review, The Art of Fiction* 194 (September 1, 2007): 125–59.

7. New York: Farrar, Straus, and Giroux, 1989, trans. Betsy Rosenberg.

8. New York: Farrar, Straus, and Giroux, 1994, trans. Betsy Rosenberg.

9. Although there are English-language studies of *See Under: Love, The Book of Intimate Grammar*, and *Be My Knife*, most of the secondary literature on *The Zig Zag Kid* is in Hebrew. Here is a sampling:

> Rivka Kashtan, "Ma sheme'ahore ha kelasteron: masa ishi beikvot 'Yesh yeladim zigzag'" [Behind the police sketch: a personal journey in the footsteps of The Zigzag Kid] *Iton 77: Yarhon le-sifrut ule-tarbut* 199, 16–19;
>
> Uriel Zohar, "*Meahore mishak hamasekhot: al David Grossman: Yesh yeladim zigzag*" [Behind the game of masks: on David Grossman's *Zigzag Kid*] ibid., 20–23;
>
> Bayta Gur, "*Lo levad bezigzagiuto: Yesh yeladim zigzag, me'et David Grossman*" [Not alone in his zigzags: *The Zigzag Kid* by David Grossman] in *Yarhon le-sifrut ule-tarbut* (Jerusalem: Keter, 2008), 350–54;
>
> Efrat Stein, "*Oy. The Oyness of Life: ledarko shel Grossman beyetzirat tahdishim meta-leshoniyim*" [Oy, the oyness of life: toward an understanding of Grossman's meta-linguistic neologisms] in *Haivrit safa haya* 4 (2006): 453–68.

10. As an added gloss to Hebrew equivalent, *signon*, the original text uses the English word "style," spelling it out phonetically as *stayl*.

11. Purim, with its customary dress-up, is the novel's recurring shorthand for the carnivalesque. There are references to "Purim costumes" (92), 102–103. "'Grown men in costume! Would you believe it? On the regular Haifa run?'" (102); "'Like princess in fairy tale . . . with clothes like nobody else . . . her dresses, her hats . . . like Purim all year long'" (234).

12. The Hebrew reads, "*lekhol davar yesh la hagdara pratit*"—a private definition.

13. References to Israeli history and culture include the following: "if I started brooding about it I would end up feeling sorry for myself, and if there's one thing that dad can't stand, it's self-pity, and a lot of his friends were killed in war, but he tried not to dwell on them, because that's the way it is, you get no insurance in this life, and not everyone makes it to the end, and those who do must never look back" (90); "someone hurrying by with a suspicious package in his hand"—a term suggestive of the potentially

explosive materials that many objects in Israel are presumed to contain until safely defused (175); and a mention of Golda Meir (213).

14. References to Jewish religious culture include the following: "like a precious *etrog* packed in wadding" (113); "rigged up banderillas out of broken rakes decorated with crepe paper from the sukkah" (141); Felix served lavish feasts on Friday nights with challah baked by Abdullah and non-kosher sausage and shrimp (153–54); "'Who am I, prophet Elijah?'" (189).

15. See Moretti, *Modern Epic: The World-System from Goethe to Garcia-Marquez*, trans. Quentin Hoare (London: Verso, 1996), 195.

16. The novel's title phrase comes from Gabi defending Nonny to his teacher, Mrs. Marcus. "'Not all children fit neatly into the square framework the school provides, you see. Some kids are round, some are shaped like a figure eight, some like a triangle, and some'—her voice dropped dramatically as she raised her hand high in the style of that famous actress Lola Ciperola playing Nora in *A Doll's House*—'like a zigzag!'" (88).

SELECTED BIBLIOGRAPHY

Primary Sources

Abramovitsh, S. Y. *Kitser masoes fun binyomin hashlishi* [Brief Travels of Benjamin the Third]. In *Geklibene Verk*, vol. 2 [Selected Works]. New York: YKUF.

Abramovitsh, S. Y. *Tales of Mendele the Book Peddler: Fishke the Lame and Benjamin the Third*. Trans. Ted Gorelick and Hillel Halkin. New York: Schocken, 1996.

Babel, Isaac. *The Complete Works of Isaac Babel*. Trans. Peter Constantine. New York: W.W. Norton, 2005.

Babel, Isaac. *Konarmiia; Odesskie rasskazy; P'esy*. Chicago: Russian Language Specialties, 1965.

Bellow, Saul. *The Adventures of Augie March*. New York: Penguin, 1996.

Ehrenburg, Ilya. *Burnaya zhizn Lazika Roytshvantsa* [The Stormy Life of Lasik Roitschwantz]. Munchen: W. Fink, 1974.

Ehrenburg, Ilya. *The Stormy Life of Laz Roitschvantz*. Trans. Alec Brown. London: Elek Books, 1965.

Grossman, David. *The Zig Zag Kid*. Trans. Betsy Rosenberg. New York: Picador, 1993.

Grossman, David. *Yesh yeladim zig zag*. Tel Aviv: Hakibbutz hame'uhad, 1994.

Rabinovitsh, Sholem. *The Further Adventures of Menachem-Mendl: New York-Warsaw-Vienna-Yehupetz*. Trans. Aliza Shevrin. Syracuse: Syracuse University Press, 2001.

Rabinovitsh, Sholem. *Ayznban geshikhtes: ksovim fun a komivoyazsher* [Railroad stories: Tales of a commerical traveler]. In *Ale verk fun sholem-aleykhem*, vol. 26. New York, 1927.

Rabinovitsh, Sholem. *Tevye the Dairyman and The Railroad Stories*. Trans. Hillel Halkin. New York: Schocken, 1987.

Rabinovitsh, Sholem. "Cnards." In *Favorite Tales of Sholem Aleichem*. Trans. Frances and Julius Butwin. New York: Random House, 1990.

Rabinovitsh, Sholem. "Knortn." In *Ale verk fun sholem-aleykhem*, vol. 17. New York, 1927.

Rabinovitsh, Sholem. *The Letters of Menakhem-Mendl*, and *Sheyne-Sheyndl and Motl, the Cantor's Son*. Trans. Hillel Halkin. New Haven: Yale University Press, 2002.

Rabinovitsh, Sholem. *Menakhem-mendl.* In *Ale verk fun sholem-aleykhem*, vol. 2. New York, 1927.

Rabinovitsh, Sholem. *Motl, peysi dem khazns* (Motl, peysi the cantor's). In *Ale verk fun sholem-aleykhem*, vols. 13–14. New York, 1927.

Rabon, Israel. *The Street: a novel.* Trans. Leonard Wolf. New York: Schocken, 1985.

Rabon, Israel. *Di gas.* Jerusalem: Magnes, 1986.

Roth, Joseph. *Hotel Savoy.* München: Der Hör Verlag, 1994.

Roth, Joseph. *Hotel Savoy* (English). Trans. John Hoare. New York: Overlook Press, 2003.

Singer, Isaac Bashevis. *Collected Stories,* 3 Vols. Ed. Ilan Stavans. New York: Library of America, 2015.

Singer, Isaac Bashevis. *The Collected Stories of Isaac Bashevis Singer.* New York: Farrar, Straus, Giroux, 1999.

Singer, Isaac Bashevis. *Der shpigl un andere dertseylungen.* Ed. Khone Shmeruk. Jerusalem: Magnes, 1975.

Singer, Isaac Bashevis. *Enemies, A Love Story.* New York: FSG, 1972.

Singer, Isaac Bashevis. *The Penitent.*

Singer, Isaac Bashevis. *The Magician of Lublin.* Trans. Elaine Gottlieb and Joseph Singer. New York: Penguin, 1960. Yiddish edition: *Der kuntsnmakher fun Lublin.* Tel-Aviv: Y.L. Perets, 1979.

Singer, Isaac Bashevis. *Shadows on the Hudson.* Trans. Joseph Sherman. New York: Plume, 1999.

Singer, Isaac Bashevis. *Shotns bam hodson. Der Forverts.* Published serially, 1957–58.

Singer, Isaac Bashevis. *Soynim, di geshikhte fun a libe. Der Forverts.* Published serially, 1966.

Singer, Israel Joshua. *Shtol un ayzn.* Vilna: B. Kletskin, 1928.

Singer, Israel Joshua. *Steel and Iron.* Trans. Joseph Singer. New York, Funk and Wagnalls, 1969.

Secondary Sources

Agulló y Cobo, Mercedes. *A vueltas con el autor del Lazarillo.* Madrid: Calambur, 2010.

Alter, Robert. "Babel, Flaubert, and the Rapture of Perception." In *The Enigma of Isaac Babel: Biography, History, Context.* Ed. Gregory Freidin. Stanford: Stanford University Press, 2009.

Alter, Robert. *The Rogue's Progress: Studies in the Picaresque Novel.* Cambridge: Harvard University Press, 1965.

Anderson, Mark M. *Kafka's Clothes: Ornament and Aestheticism in the Habsburg Fin de Siècle.* New York: Oxford University Press, 1992.

An-ski, S. *The Dybbuk and Other Writings.* Ed. David G. Roskies. Trans. Golda Werman. New Haven: Yale University Press, 2002.

An-ski, S. *The Enemy at His Pleasure: A Journey through the Jewish Pale of Settlement during World War I*. Ed. and trans. Joachim Neugroschel. New York: Metropolitan Books, 2003.

Ardila, John. "Introduction: Transnational Picaresque." *Philological Quarterly* 89, no. 4 (2010): 1–11.

Augé, Marc. *Non-Places: Introduction to an Anthropology of Supermodernity*. New York: Verso, 1995.

Austin, J. L. *How to Do Things with Words*. Cambridge: Harvard University Press, 1975.

Bakhtin, M. M. *The Dialogic Imagination*. Ed. Michael Holquist. Trans. Caryl Emerson and Michael Holquist. Austin: University of Texas Press, 1981.

Bartal, Israel. *The Jews of Eastern Europe, 1772–1881*. Trans. Chaya Naor. Philadelphia: University of Pennsylvania Press, 2005.

Bauman, Zygmunt. *Liquid Modernity*. Cambridge: Polity Press, 2000.

Baumgarten, Murray. *City Scriptures: Modern Jewish Writing*. Cambridge: Harvard University Press, 1982.

Bawarshi, Anis S., and Mary Jo Reiff. *Genre: An Introduction to History, Theory, Research, and Pedagogy*. West Lafayette, IN: Parlor Press and WAC Clearinghouse, 2010. http://wac.colostate.edu/.

Bechtel, Delphine. "Urbanization, Capitalism, and Cosmopolitanism: Four Novels and a Film on Jews in the Polish City of Łódz." *Prooftexts* 26 (2006): 79–106.

Benjamin, Walter. "The Work of Art in the Age of Mechanical Reproduction." In *Illuminations: Essays and Reflections*, 217–51. New York: Schocken, 1969.

Beckett, Samuel. "Beckett by the Madeleine." In *Columbia University Forum* (Summer 1961).

Beebee, Thomas O. *The Ideology of Genre: A Comparative Study of Generic Instability*. University Park: Pennsylvania State University Press, 1994.

Beer, Gillian. *Darwin's Plots: Evolutionary Narrative in Darwin, George Eliot, and Nineteenth-Century Fiction*. New York: Cambridge University Press, 2004.

Bemong, Nele, and Pieter Borghart. *Bakhtin's Theory of the Literary Chronotope: Reflections, Applications, Perspectives*. Ghent, Belgium: Academia Press, 2010.

Berend, Ivan. *Decades of Crisis: Central and Eastern Europe Before World War II*. Berkeley: University of California Press, 1998.

Bergson, Henri. *Laughter: An Essay on the Meaning of the Comic*. New York: MacMillan, 1914.

Berman, Marshall. *All That Is Solid Melts into Air: The Experience of Modernity*. New York: Penguin Books, 1988.

Bernstein, Peter L. *Against the Gods: The Remarkable Story of Risk*. New York: Wiley and Sons, 1996.

Bhabha, Homi. *Nation and Narration*. New York: Routledge, 1990.

Bitzan, Amos. "The Problem of Pleasure: Disciplining the German-Jewish Reading Revolution, 1770–1870." Dissertation, UC Berkeley, 2011.

Bolaki, Stella. *Unsettling the Bildungsroman: Reading Contemporary Ethnic American Women's Fiction*. New York: Rodopi, 2011.

Bradbury, Malcolm, and Jim McFarlane. *Modernism: 1890–1930.* London: Penguin, 1976.

Bradford, Richard. *Stylistics.* New York: Routledge, 1997.

Brookner, Anita. *A Start in Life.* New York: HarperCollins, 1982.

Brooks, Peter. *Reading for the Plot: Design and Intention in Narrative.* New York: Knopf, 1984.

Brower, Daniel. *The Russian City between Tradition and Modernity, 1850–1900.* Berkeley: University of California Press, 1990.

Bruhn, Jørgen, and Jan Lundquist, eds. *The Novelness of Bakhtin: Perspectives and Possibilities* Gylling, Denmark: Museum Tusculanum Press, 2001.

Butler, Erik. *Metamorphoses of the Vampire in Literature and Film: Cultural Transformations in Europe, 1732–1933.* Rochester, NY: Camden, 2010.

Calvino, Italo. *Six Memos for the Next Millennium.* Cambridge, MA: Harvard University Press, 1988.

Caplan, Marc. "The Fragmentation of Narrative Perspective in Y. L. Peretz's *Bilder fun a Provints-Rayze*." *Jewish Social Studies: History, Culture, Society* 14, no. 1 (Fall 2007): 63–88.

Caplan, Marc. *How Strange the Change: Language, Temporality, and Narrative Form in Peripheral Modernisms.* Stanford: Stanford University Press, 2011.

Caplan, Marc. "Neither Here nor There: The Critique of Ideological Progress in Sholem Aleichem's Kasrilevke Stories." In *Modern Jewish Literatures: Intersections and Boundaries*, 127–46. Ed. Sheila E. Jelen, Michael P. Kramer, and L. Scott Lerner. Philadelphia: University of Pennsylvania Press, 2011.

Cervantes, Miguel de. *Don Quixote de la Mancha.* Trans. Tobias Smollett. New York: Noonday, 1986.

Coetzee, J. M. "Emperor of Nostalgia." *New York Review of Books*, February 28, 2002.

Cohen, Jeffrey Jerome. *The Postcolonial Middle Ages.* New York: Palgrave Macmillan, 2001.

Chu, Winston. *The German Minority in Interwar Poland.* Cambridge: Cambridge University Press, 2013.

Church, Roy. "Salesmen and the Transformation of Selling in Britain and the US." *Economic History Review* 61, no. 3 (2008): 695–725.

Chambers, Ross. *Loiterature.* Lincoln: University of Nebraska Press, 1999.

Chambers, Ross. *Story and Situation: Narrative Seduction and the Power of Fiction.* Minneapolis: University of Minnesota Press, 1984.

Cieplinski, Feigue. "Poles and Jews: The Quest for Self-Determination, 1919–1934." *Binghamton Journal of History* (Fall 2002), http://www2.binghamton.edu/history/resources/journal-of-history/poles-and-jews.html.

Deleuze, Gilles, and Pierre-Félix Guattari. *Kafka: Toward a Minor Literature.* Minneapolis: University of Minnesota Press, 1986.

Deutsch, Nathaniel. *The Jewish Dark Continent: Life and Death in the Russian Pale of Settlement.* Cambridge: Harvard University Press, 2011.

Denman, Hugh. *Isaac Bashevis Singer: His Work and His World.* Leiden: Brill, 2002.

Dunn, Peter N. *Spanish Picaresque Fiction: A New Literary History*. Ithaca: Cornell University Press, 1993.

Dunn, Maggie, and Ann Morris. *The Composite Novel: The Short Story Cycle in Transition*. New York: Twayne, 1995.

Ebert, Roger. "Review of David Mamet's *House of Games*." In *Roger Ebert's Four Star Reviews—1967-2007*. Kansas City, MO: Andrews McMeel, 2007.

Ehrlich, Victor. "A Note on the Monologue as a Literary Form: Sholem Aleichem's *Monologn*—A Test Case." In *For Max Weinreich on his Seventieth Birthday*, 44–50.

Ehrmann, Jacques. "Homo Ludens Revisited." Trans. Cathy Lewis and Phil Lewis. *Yale French Studies* 41, Special Issue, *Game, Play, Literature* (1968): 31–57.

Emerson, Caryl. *Critical Essays on Mikhail Bakhtin*. New York: G. K. Hall, 1999.

Emerson, Caryl, and Gary Saul Morson. *Mikhail Bakhtin: Creation of a Prosaics*. Stanford: Stanford University Press, 1990.

Esty, Jed. *Unseasonable Youth: Modernism, Colonialism, and the Fiction of Development*. New York: Oxford University Press, 2012.

Ezrahi, Sidra deKoven. *Booking Passage: Exile and Homecoming in the Modern Jewish Imagination*. Los Angeles: University of California Press, 2000.

Feiner, Shmuel. *The Jewish Enlightenment*. Trans. Chaya Naor. Philadelphia: University of Pennsylvania Press, 2004.

Feiner, Shmuel. *Haskalah and History: The Emergence of a Modern Jewish Historical Consciousness*. London: Littman Library, 2004.

Feiner, Shmuel. "The Invention of the Modern Age: A Chapter in the Rhetoric and Self-Image of the Haskalah." *Dappim: Research in Literature* 11 (1998): 9–29.

Fink, Carole. *Defending the Rights of Others: The Great Powers, the Jews, and International Minority Protection, 1878–1938*. Cambridge: Cambridge University Press, 2006.

Fisher, Philip. *Hard Facts: Setting and Form in the American Novel*. New York: Oxford University Press, 1986.

Fisher, Philip. *The Vehement Passions*. Princeton: Princeton University Press, 2002.

French, Michael, and Andrew Popp. "'Ambassadors of Commerce': The Commercial Traveler in British Culture, 1800–1939." *Business History Review* 82 (Winter 2008): 789–814.

Frieden, Ken. *Classic Yiddish Fiction: Abramovitsh, Sholem Aleichem, and Peretz*. Albany: SUNY Press, 1995.

Frieden, Ken. "I. B. Singer's Monologues of Demons." *Prooftexts* 5 (1985): 263–68.

Friedman, Walter. *Birth of a Salesman: The Transformation of Selling in America*. Cambridge: Harvard University Press, 2004.

Furst, Lilian. *Random Destinations: Escaping the Holocaust and Starting Life Anew*. New York: Palgrave MacMillan, 2005.

Gabrielle, Cindy. "The Poetics of Dissolution: The Representation of Maori Culture in Janet Frame's Fiction." *Journal of Postcolonial Writing* 46, no. 2 (May 2010): 209–20.

Garrett, Leah. "The Jewish *Don Quixote*." *Cervantes: Bulletin of the Cervantes Society of America* 17, no. 2 (1997): 94–105.

Gatrell, Peter. "Prisoners of War on the Eastern Front during World War I." *Kritika* 6, no. 3 (2005): 557–66.

Genette, Gérard. *The Architext: An Introduction.* Berkeley: University of California Press, 1992.

Gericke, Philip O. "Saul Bellow's *The Adventures of Augie March* and Its Picaresque Antecedents." *Pacific Coast Philology* 25, no. 1/2 (Nov. 1990): 77–83.

Gonen, Rivkah, ed. *Back to the Shtetl: An-sky and the Jewish Ethnographic Expedition, 1912–1914.* Jerusalem: Israel Museum, 1994.

Grossman, David. "The Art of Fiction No. 194," interview by Jonathan Shainin. *Paris Review,* No. 182 (Fall 2007): 125–59.

Grossman, David. *The Book of Intimate Grammar.* Trans. Betsy Rosenberg. New York: Farrar, Straus, and Giroux, 1994.

Grossman, David. *See Under: Love.* Trans. Betsy Rosenberg. New York: Farrar, Straus, and Giroux, 1989.

Gould, Stephen Jay. *Dinosaur in a Haystack: Reflections in Natural History.* New York: Random House, 1995.

Gould, Stephen Jay. *The Mismeasure of Man.* New York: W.W. Norton, 2006.

Gould, Stephen Jay. *Time's Arrow, Time's Cycle: Myth and Metaphor in the Discovery of Geological Time.* Cambridge: Harvard University Press, 1987.

Guillén, Claudio. *Literature as System: Essays Toward the Theory of Literary History.* Princeton: Princeton University Press, 1971.

Gur, Bayta. "Lo levad bezigzagiuto: Yesh yeladim zigzag, me'et David Grossman" [Not alone in his zigzags: *The Zigzag Kid* by David Grossman]. In *Yarḥon le-sifrut ule-tarbut. Jerusalem: Keter* (2008): 350–54.

Guzlowski, John. "Isaac Singer and the Threat of America." *Shofar: An Interdisciplinary Journal of Jewish Studies* 20, no. 1 (Fall 2001): 21–35.

Hadda, Janet. *Passionate Women, Passive Men: Suicide in Yiddish Literature.* Albany: SUNY Press, 1988.

Halevi-Wise, Yael. *Sephardism.* Stanford: Stanford University Press, 2012.

Harris, Jay. *Nachman Krochmal: Guiding the Perplexed of the Modern Age.* New York: New York University Press, 1991.

Harris, Rachel. "Decay and Death: Urban Topoi in Literary Depictions of Tel Aviv." *Israel Studies* 14, no. 3 (Fall 2009): 75–93.

Hasak-Lowy, Todd. *Here and Now: History, Nationalism, and Realism in Modern Hebrew Fiction.* Syracuse: Syracuse University Press, 2008.

Heise, Ursula K. *Chronoschisms.* Cambridge: Cambridge University Press, 1997.

Heng, Geraldine. *Empire of Magic: Medieval Romance and the Politics of Cultural Fantasy.* New York: Columbia University Press, 2003.

Herman, Peter C. "*Shadows on the Hudson*: Isaac Bashevis Singer and the Problem of Post-Holocaust Literature." In *ReVisioning American Jewish Literature: Yesterday and Today and Tomorrow,* 158–79. Vol. 24 of Studies in American Jewish Literature. Lincoln: University of Nebraska Press, 2005.

Hetenyi, Zsuzsa. *In a Maelstrom: The History of Russian-Jewish Prose (1860–1940)*. Trans. János Boris. Budapest: Central European University Press, 2008.

Hofmann, Michael. "Translating Joseph Roth." *New York Review of Books,* March 28, 2002.

Holland, Dorothy, William Lachicotte Jr., Debra Skinner, and Carole Cain. *Identity and Agency in Cultural Worlds*. Cambridge: Harvard University Press, 1998.

Holquist, Michael. *Dialogism*. New York: Routledge, 1990.

Honeyman, Susan. "Mutiny by Mutation: Uses of Neoteny in Science Fiction." *Children's Literature in Education* 35, no. 4 (December 2004): 347–66.

Hughes, Jon. *Facing Modernity: Fragmentation, Culture and Identity in Joseph Roth's Writing in the 1920s*. MHRA Texts and Dissertations, vol. 67, Bithell Series of Dissertations. London: Maney/MHRA, 2006.

Hyman, Paula E. "Gender, Antisemitism, and Jewish Identity in the Fin de Siecle." *Mediating Modernity: Challenges and Trends in the Jewish Encounter with the Modern World*. Ed. Lauren B. Strauss and Michael Brenner. Detroit: Wayne State University Press, 2008.

Jakobson, Roman. "Two Aspects of Language and Two Types of Aphasic Disturbances." In *Fundamentals of Language,* ed. R. Jakobson and M. Halle. The Hague: Mouton & Co., 1956.

Johnson, Barbara. *A World of Difference*. Baltimore: Johns Hopkins University Press, 1987.

Karp, Joshua. "Economic History and Jewish Modernity: Ideological Versus Structural Change." *Jahrbuch des Simon-Dubnow-Instituts* 6 (2007): 249–66.

Kashtan, Rivka. "*Ma sheme'ahore ha kelasteron: masa ishi beikvot 'Yesh yeladim zigzag,'*" [Behind the police sketch: a personal journey in the footsteps of *The Zigzag Kid*]. *Iton 77: Yarḥon le-sifrut ule-tarbut* 199:16–19.

Katona, Anna. "From *Lazarillo* to *Augie March*: A Study into Some Picaresque Attitudes." *Angol Filológiai Tanulmányok / Hungarian Studies in English* 4 (1969): 87–103.

Keunen, Bart. "Bakhtin, Genre Formation, and the Cognitive Turn: Chronotopes as Memory Schemata." *CLCWeb: Comparative Literature and Culture* 2.2 (2000): http://docs.lib.purdue.edu/clcweb/vol2/iss2/2.

Korzec, Pavel. "Polish-Jewish Relations during World War I." In *Hostages of Modernization: Studies on Modern Antisemitism, 1870–1933/39,* 2:1034–35. Ed. Herbert Strauss. Berlin: Walter de Gruyter, 1993.

Kronfeld, Chana. *On the Margins of Modernism: Decentering Literary Dynamics*. Berkeley: University of California Press, 1996.

Krutikov, Mikhail. *Yiddish Fiction and the Crisis of Modernity, 1905–1914*. Stanford: Stanford University Press, 2001.

La Barre, Weston. *Shadow of Childhood: Neoteny and the Biology of Religion*. Norman: University of Oklahoma Press, 1991.

Lang, Brukhe (Beatrice Lang Caplan). "*Yisroel Rabon: Shtrikhn tsu a literarisher biografye*." M.A. thesis, Columbia University, 1996.

Lederhendler, Eli. *The Road to Modern Jewish Politics: Political Tradition and Political Reconstruction in the Jewish Community of Tsarist Russia.* Oxford: Oxford University Press, 1989.

Leslie, R. F., ed. *The History of Poland since 1863.* Cambridge: Cambridge University Press, 1980.

Levene, Mark. *War, Jews and the New Europe: The Diplomacy of Lucien Wolf, 1914–1919.* Oxford: Littman Library, 2009.

Lewis, Pericles. *Modernism, Nationalism, and the Novel.* Cambridge: Cambridge University Press, 2000.

Litvak, Olga. *Conscription and the Search for Modern Russian Jewry.* Bloomington: Indiana University Press, 2006.

Litvak, Olga. *Haskalah: The Romantic Movement in Judaism.* New Brunswick: Rutgers University Press, 2012.

Lodge, David. "The Language of Modernist Fiction: Metaphor and Metonymy." In *Modernism: 1890–1930 / A Guide to European Literature,* 481–96. Ed. Malcolm Bradbury and James McFarlane. New York: Penguin, 1991.

Maiorino, Giancarlo, ed. *The Picaresque: Tradition and Displacement.* Minneapolis: University Press of Minnesota, 1996.

Maiorino, Giancarlo. "The Picaresque Novel: A Protean Form." *College Literature* 6, no. 3 (Fall 1979): 182–204.

Mandrell, James. "Questions of Genre and Gender: Contemporary American Versions of the Feminine Picaresque." *Novel* 20, no. 2, Twentieth Anniversary Issue: II (Winter 1987): 149–70.

Matthias, Bettina. *The Hotel as Setting in Early 20th-Century German and Austrian Literature.* Rochester, NY: Camden House, 2006.

McKeon, Michael. *Theory of the Novel: A Historical Approach.* Baltimore: Johns Hopkins University Press, 2000.

Meloney, William Brown. "Where Do We Go From Here? This Is The Real Dope." War camp Community Service, 1919. http://www.gjenvick.com/Military/WorldWarOne/Brochures/1919WhereDoWeGoFromHereTheRealDope.html#ixzz1YhuLUwzE.

Miron, Dan. *A Traveler Disguised: The Rise of Modern Yiddish Fiction in the Nineteenth Century.* Syracuse: Syracuse University Press, 1973.

Miron, Dan. *The Image of the Shtetl and Other Studies of Modern Jewish Literary Imagination.* Syracuse: Syracuse University Press, 2000.

Miron, Dan. "Passivity and Narration: The Spell of Isaac Bashevis Singer." *Judaism* 41, no. 1 (Winter 1992): 6–17.

Miron, Dan. "The Pleasure of Disregarding Red Lights: A Reading of Sholem Aleichem's Monologue 'A Nisref'," 201–31. In *Arguing the Modern Jewish Canon.* Cambridge, MA: Harvard University Press, 2008.

Miron, Dan. *When Loners Come Together: A Portrait of Hebrew Literature at the Turn of the Twentieth Century (Bodedim bemoadam).* Tel Aviv: Am Oved, 1987.

Moger, Angela S. "The Obscure Object of Narrative." *Yale French Studies* 63 (1983): 129–38.

Montagu, Ashley. *Growing Young.* 2nd ed. Westport, CT: Greenwood, 1989.

Moretti, Franco. *Modern Epic: The World-System from Goethe to Garcia-Marquez.* Trans. Quentin Hoare. London: Verso, 1996.

Moretti, Franco. *Signs Taken for Wonders: On the Sociology of Literary Forms.* New York: Verso, 2005.

Moretti, Franco. *The Way of the World: The Bildungsroman in European Culture.* London: Verso, 2000.

Morss, John R. *Growing Critical: Alternatives to Developmental Psychology.* London: Routledge, 1996.

Mullin, Janet E. "'We Had Carding': Hospitable Card Play and Polite Domestic Sociability Among the Middling Sort in Eighteenth-Century England." *Journal of Social History* (Summer 2009): 989–1008.

Murav, Harriet. *Music from a Speeding Train: Jewish Literature in Post-Revolution Russia.* Stanford: Stanford University Press, 2011.

Neugroschel, Joachim, ed and trans. *The Dybbuk and the Yiddish Imagination: A Haunted Reader.* Syracuse: Syracuse University Press, 2000.

Norich, Anita. *The Homeless Imagination in the Fiction of Israel Joshua Singer.* Bloomington: Indiana University Press, 1991.

Nowersztern, Avraham. "History, Messianism, and Apocalypse in Bashevis's Work." In *The Hidden Isaac Bashevis Singer,* 28–61. Ed. Seth L. Wolitz. Austin: University of Texas Press, 2001.

Nowersztern, Avraham. "Sholem Aleykhem's Menakhem-Mendl: Its Textual History and Its Structure." *Tarbiz* 54:1 (1985): 105–46.

Parker, Alexander. *Literature and the Delinquent.* Edinburgh: Edinburgh University Press, 1967.

Paxson, Frederic Logan. *The Great Demobilization and Other Essays.* Madison: University of Wisconsin Press, 1941.

Peiker, Piret. "Post-Communist Literatures: A Postcolonial Perspective." *Vikerkaar* 10–11 (2005). In English: *Eurozine.* www.eurozine.com/articles/2006-03-28-peiker-en.html.

Petrovsky-Shtern, Yohanan. *Jews in the Russian Army, 1827–1917: Drafted Into Modernity.* Cambridge: Cambridge University Press, 2009.

Phelan, James. *Living to Tell About It: A Rhetoric and Ethics of Character Narration.* Ithaca: Cornell University Press, 2005.

Pinsker, Shachar. *Literary Passports: The Making of Modernist Hebrew Fiction.* Stanford: Stanford University Press, 2010.

Pinsker, Shachar. "The Urban Literary Café and the Geography of Hebrew and Yiddish: Modernism in Europe." In *Forms of Sociality: Oxford Handbook of Global Modernisms,* 433–58. Ed. Mark Wollaeger and Matt Eatough. New York: Oxford University Press, 2013.

Pirozhkova, A. N. *At His Side: The Last Years of Isaac Babel.* South Royalton, VT: Steerforth Press, 1998.

Quint, David. *Cervantes's Novel of Modern Times: A New Reading of Don Quijote.* Princeton: Princeton University Press, 2003.

Rainof, Rebecca Elise. *Purgatory and the Fictions of Modernity.* Unpublished diss. Princeton University, 2008.

Reising, Russell. *Loose Ends: Closure and Crisis in the American Social Text.* Durham: Duke University Press, 1997.

Roskies, David G. "The Achievement of American Yiddish Modernism." In *Go and Study: Essays and Studies in Honor of Alfred Jospe*, 353–68. Ed. Raphael Jospe and Samuel Z. Fishman. Washington, DC: B'nai Brith Hillel Foundations, 1980.

Roskies, David G. *A Bridge of Longing: Lost Art of Yiddish Storytelling.* Cambridge: Harvard University Press, 1995.

Roskies, David G. "*Di shprakh fun derekh-hasam: vi der sotn redt af yidish.*" In *Hut shel hesed: lekhoved Chava Turniansky.* Jerusalem: Hebrew University Press, 2012.

Roskies, David G. "S. Ansky and the Paradigm of Return." In *The Uses of Tradition: Jewish Continuity in the Modern Era*, 243–60. Ed. Jack Wertheimer. New York: Jewish Theological Seminary, 1999.

Rosman, Moshe. *How Jewish is Jewish History?* London: Littman Library, 2008.

Rubenstein, Joshua. *Tangled Loyalties: The Life and Times of Ilya Ehrenburg.* Tuscaloosa: University of Alabama Press, 1999.

Rubin, Rachel. *Jewish Gangsters of Modern Literature.* Urbana: University of Illinois Press, 2000.

Safran, Gabriella. "Isaak Babel's El'ia Isaakovich as a New Jewish Type." *Slavic Review: American Quarterly of Russian, Eurasian and East European Studies* 61, no. 2 (Summer 2002): 253–72.

Safran, Gabriella. *Wandering Soul: The Dybbuk's Creator.* Cambridge, MA: Harvard University Press, 2010.

Safran, Gabriella, and Steven Zipperstein, eds. *The Worlds of S. An-sky: A Russian Jewish Intellectual at the Turn of the Century.* Palo Alto: Stanford University Press, 2005.

Salvadó, Francisco J. Romero. *Spain 1914–1918: Between War and Revolution.* London: Routledge, 2002.

Schachter, Alison. *Diasporic Modernisms: Hebrew and Yiddish Literature in the Twentieth Century.* Berkeley: University of California Press, 2011.

Seipp, Adam R. *The Ordeal of Peace: Demobilization and the Urban Experience in Britain and Germany, 1917–1921.* Burlington, VT: Ashgate, 2009.

Shmeruk, Chone. "Yisroel Rabon and His Book *Di gas* ("The Street")." In *Di gas* by Yisroel Rabon. Jerusalem: Sifrut Yidish, 1986.

Sicher, Efraim. *Jews in Russian Literature After the October Revolution: Writers and Artists Between Hope and Apostasy.* Cambridge: Cambridge University Press, 1995.

Sicher, Efraim. "On Both Sides of the Front: Isaac Babel and Israel Rabon in the Polish-Soviet War." *Shvut* 3 [19] (1996): 147–58.

Sinding, Michael. *Framing the World: Genre as Worldview.* Amsterdam: Metaphor Lab. http://www.networkinstitute.org/wp-content/University Pressloads/2013/02/Framing-the-World-Genre-as-Worldview.pdf.

Singer, Isaac Bashevis. "The Art of Fiction No. 42," Interview by Harold Flender. *Paris Review* (Fall 1968).

Singer, Isaac Bashevis. "The Future of Literature." *Forverts,* March 17, 1972.

Singer, Isaac Bashevis. *Prooftexts* 9, no. 1 (January 1989): 5–12.

Singer, I. J. *Di brider ashkenazi* [*The Brothers Ashkenazi*]. 1936.

Sokoloff, Naomi. *Imagining the Child in Modern Jewish Fiction.* Baltimore: Johns Hopkins University Press, 1992.

Solomon, Alisa. *Wonder of Wonders: A Cultural History of* Fiddler on the Roof. New York: Henry Holt, 2013.

Sommer, Doris. *Foundational Fictions: The National Romances of Latin America.* Berkeley: University of California Press, 1991.

Stanislawski, Michael. *Tsar Nicholas I and the Jews.* Philadelphia: Jewish Publication Society of America, 1983.

Stein, Efrat. "*Oy.* The Oyness of Life: *ledarko shel Grossman beyetzirat tahshidim metaleshoniyim*" [Oy, the oyness of life: toward an understanding of Grossman's metalinguistic neologisms]. *Haivrit safa haya,* vol. 4 (2006): 453–68.

Steiner, Lina. *For Humanity's Sake: The Bildungsroman in Russian Culture.* Toronto: University of Toronto Press, 2011.

Stern, Michael. "Tevye's Art of Quotation." *Prooftexts* 6, no. 1, Special Issue on Sholem Aleichem: The Critical Tradition (January 1986): 79–96.

Stolberg, Mary M. *Fighting Organized Crime: Politics, Justice, and the Legacy of Thomas E. Dewey.* Boston: Northeastern University Press, 1995.

Stone, Robert S. "Pito Pérez: Mexican Middleman." *Mexican Studies/Estudios Mexicanos* 21, no. 2 (Summer 2005): 369–402.

Summers-Bremner, E. "Reading, Walking, Mourning: W. G. Sebald's Peripatetic Fictions." *Journal of Narrative Theory* 34, no. 3 (Fall 2004): 304–34.

Tanny, Jarrod. *City of Rogues and Schnorrers: Russia's Jews and the Myth of Old Odessa.* Bloomington: Indiana University Press, 2011.

Taylor, S. Ortiz. "Episodic Structure and the Picaresque Novel." *Journal of Narrative Theory* 7, no. 3 (Fall 1977): 218–25.

Todorov, Tzvetan. *Fantastic: A Structural Approach to a Literary Genre.* Ithaca: Cornell University Press, 1975.

Todorov, Tzvetan. *Mikhail Bakhtin.* Manchester: Manchester University Press, 1984.

Todorov, Tzvetan. "The Origin of Genres." In *Modern Genre Theory.* Ed. David Duff. London: Longman, 2000.

Twark. Jill. *Humor, Satire, and Identity: Eastern German Literature in the 1990s.* Berlin: Walter de Gruyter, 2007.

Viner, Meir. "On Sholem Aleichem's Humor." *Prooftexts* 6, no. 1, Special Issue on Sholem Aleichem: The Critical Tradition (January 1986): 41–54.

Wanner, Adrian. *Out of Russia: Fictions of a New Translingual Diaspora.* Evanston, IL: Northwestern University Press, 2011.

Warshawsky, Oyzer. *Smugglers: A Novel in Three Parts.* Trans. Golda Werman. New York: Gefen, 2008.

West, Paul. *The Modern Novel.* London: Hutchinson, 1965.

Willett, Robert L. *Russian Sideshow: America's Undeclared War, 1918–1920.* Washington, DC: Brassey's, 2003.

Williams, Raymond. *The Country and the City*. New York: Oxford University Press, 1975.

Wirth-Nesher, Hannah. *Call It English:The Languages of Jewish American Literature*. Princeton: Princeton University Press, 2006.

Wirth-Nesher, Hannah. *City Codes: Reading the Modern Urban Novel*. New York: Cambridge University Press, 1996.

Wisse, Ruth R. "The Classic of Disinheritance." In *New Essays on* Call It Sleep, 61–74. Ed. Hana Wirth-Nesher. Cambridge: Cambridge University Press, 1996.

Wisse, Ruth R. *The Schlemiel as Modern Hero*. Chicago: University of Chicago Press, 1971.

Wolitz, Seth. "On Israel Rabon's *Di gas*." In *Khulyot Journal of Yiddish Research* 7 (2002). http://yiddish.haifa.ac.il/khulyot/khulyot7.html.

Yanasowicz, Itzhak (Yitskhok Yanasovitsh). *Łodzsher yorn: Mentshn, svives, gesheenishn*. Tel Aviv: Perets Farlag, 1987.

Yovanovich, Gordana. *Play and the Picaresque: Lazarillo de Tormes, Libro de Manuel, and Match Ball*. Buffalo: University of Toronto Press, 1999.

Zipperstein, Steven. *The Jews of Odessa: A Cultural History, 1794–1881*. Stanford: Stanford University Press, 1986.

Zohar, Uriel. "*Meahore mishak hamasekhot: al David Grossman: Yesh yeladim zigzag*'" [Behind the game of masks: On David Grossman's *Zigzag Kid*]. 20–23.

INDEX